Pathways after Empire

The New International Relations of Europe

Series Editor: Ronald H. Linden

Pathways after Empire

*National Identity and
Foreign Economic Policy in the
Post-Soviet World*

Andrei P. Tsygankov

ROWMAN & LITTLEFIELD PUBLISHERS, INC.
Lanham • Boulder • New York • Oxford

ROWMAN & LITTLEFIELD PUBLISHERS, INC.

Published in the United States of America
by Rowman & Littlefield Publishers, Inc.
4720 Boston Way, Lanham, Maryland 20706
www.rowmanlittlefield.com

12 Hid's Copse Road, Cumnor Hill, Oxford OX2 9JJ, England

British Library Cataloguing in Publication Information Available

Library of Congress Cataloging-in-Publication Data Available

ISBN 0-7425-1672-5 (cloth : alk. paper)
ISBN 0-7425-1673-3 (paper : alk. paper)

Printed in the United States of America

♾™ The paper used in this publication meets the minimum requirements of American
National Standard for Information Sciences—Permanence of Paper for Printed Library
Materials, ANSI/NISO Z39.48-1992.

The community of political destiny, i.e., above all, of common political struggle of life and death, has given rise to groups with joint memories which often have had a deeper impact than the ties of merely cultural, linguistic, or ethnic community. It is this "community of memories" which, as we shall see, constitutes the ultimately decisive element of national consciousness

Max Weber (1978, 903)

To Julia

Contents

Tables

Figures

Acknowledgments

This book could have not been written without the generous assistance and support of my friends, colleagues, and family. I am indebted to all of them for being available whenever I needed their help and support. Naturally, I alone am responsible for the final product and possible errors it contains.

The book is a revised version of my doctoral dissertation written at the School of International Relations, University of Southern California. John S. Odell, my main dissertation advisor, deserves special credit for shaping my ideas into a viable project. John is everything a graduate student can wish for: an accessible and patient listener, a tough critic, and a resourceful supplier of ways to improve scholarship. I both used and abused these qualities, and have greatly benefited from them. My other dissertation committee members read the entire manuscript and suggested numerous improvements. Andrzej Korbonski provided the region's expertise, Ann Tickner contributed greatly to my understanding of culture and identity issues, and Jeffrey Nugent suggested several ways of making my statistical treatment of the subject more rigorous.

Material support for the researching and writing of the project came from the Institute for the Study of World Politics, the USC Graduate School, and the USC School of International Relations. I also benefited from spending a few weeks at the Hoover Institution, Stanford and would like to express my gratitude to librarian Molly Molloy for her assistance with my research.

Through personal conversations and the reading of various portions of my manuscript, other friends and colleagues contributed valuable comments and ideas for improvement. They are (in alphabetic order) Hayward Alker, Caroline Betts, Coit Blacker, Laurie Brand, Eileen M. Crumm, Karen Dawisha, Paul D'Anieri, Richard Easterlin, Sherman Garnett, Amy Gurowitz, Surupa Gupta,

Mohammed Hafez, Saori Katada, Peter J. Katzenstein, Jeffrey W. Knopf, Timur Kuran, Gail Lapidus, Cecelia Lynch, Daniel Lynch, Andrew Manning, Martha Merritt, Michael McFaul, James McGuire, James Millar, Gunnar Nielsson, Peter Rosendorff, Terry O'Sulliven, Peter Reddaway, Sung Jun Jo, Thomas Schmalberger, and Paul David Steenhausen. Although their suggestions were not always consistent with one another, I appreciate them all. These suggestions caused me to rethink my ideas and ways of defending them, and provided the necessary intellectual context for the emergence of the final product.

I am also indebted to folks in Russia and other former Soviet republics who supported my project and contributed to its progress, either by providing comments or helping me to identify potential interviewees and arrange meetings with them. Dmitri M. Feldman, Boris I. Pruzhinin, Pavel A. Tsygankov, and Andrei V. Zagorski in Russia, Ruslan M. Postolovsky and Sergei V. Sereda in Ukraine, Elena Gapova, Melissa Merrill, and Anton A. Slonimski in Belarus, and Tatyana Muravskaya in Latvia were especially helpful and generous in sharing their time and ideas.

Furthermore, I am grateful to an anonymous reviewer for his or her constructive critique and to my editor Susan McEachern for her encouragements, valuable suggestions, and editorial assistance that helped me, a non-English speaker, to shape my project into a readable manuscript. Also thanks to April Leo for making the process of copy-editing smooth and enjoyable.

My parents Svetlana M. Luchinova and Pavel A. Tsygankov taught me discipline and faith in myself. They never doubted me and were supportive of my research life in the United States. I felt their support constantly, even being five thousand miles away from home. My daughter, in her eagerness to learn, constantly reminded me of my own research responsibilities. Finally, I am grateful to my wife Julia V. Godzikovskaya who shared with me all the ups and downs of graduate school. This book is dedicated to her, as a modest way of expressing my appreciation for her love and support.

Chapter 1
Introduction

The end of the Cold War reinforced the necessity to rethink the historical and cultural bases of world politics. Over the subsequent decade, everyone became increasingly aware of cultural and normative influences in the international arena. Among scholars, the so-called constructivist turn[1] began to document the effects of international norms and identities at least in security and political affairs. This research seriously undermined the view that cultural properties are too elusive to be considered by those committed to standards of rigor and progressive knowledge cumulation.[2] Studies of the world political economy, however, have been much slower in responding to the cultural challenge. A number of subjects, such as economic security, remain almost untouched by this newer angle of vision. Instead the neorealist and neoliberal perspectives remain dominant in international political economy.[3]

In an attempt to move beyond these accounts, this book advances a constructivist analysis of the foreign economic policies of the new states that succeeded the Soviet Union, other than Russia. After 1991 some of them directed their economic activities primarily toward Russia and other former members of the USSR, while others shifted their foreign economic policies sharply away from what used to be the Soviet empire and toward new partners. A central reason for the striking difference in policy outcomes is the substantial variation in the strength of the new nations' national identities. The stronger the identity, the more likely the new state was to shift away from the empire. This study introduces the national identity perspective into international political economy studies, and establishes it for this region with the use of both qualitative and quantitative techniques. If this central idea is valid here, it may be valid in other world regions as well. The book points the way toward further investigations beyond the former Soviet region.[4]

A sophisticated, culture-sensitive understanding of their policies improves upon the still common, simplified perception that all the newly independent states (NIS) will soon become a part of the global "free-market" world, especially those that are strategically located and endowed with plentiful natural resources. Because national identity is involved, the question of "joining" the community of Western developed nations is much more complicated than one might think. Equally, though, we should question expectations that all the former Soviet republics will return to their traditional trading area sooner or later, assuming that only the political ambitions of their leaders are currently driving some away from establishing a customs union on Soviet territory. Some of the NIS, despite being relatively weak as economic entities, are still likely to pursue an aggressive policy of restructuring their trade pattern and thereby "joining" the West.

This national identity perspective is rich with implications for scholarship and government policy, outside as well as inside the former Soviet region. For economic affairs, it points to an overlooked source of national competitiveness and success in adjustment to globalization, as well as a foundation for regional integration. For security affairs, this point of view illuminates postimperial nationalism, the sovereignty dilemmas of weak states, and alliance formation. For comparative politics, the cultural standpoint can add to our understanding of the economic reform process and democratization. For policy, this book points to the importance of recognizing that there is more than one path toward development. It sensitizes us to ways in which culture can be an advantage as well as a constraint.

The Question

Why did the former Soviet republics' responses to the post-1991 environment differ so dramatically? Immediately after the break-up of the USSR, some observers were convinced that the newly independent nations would become, sooner or later, a part of the "free-market" world.[5] Others suggested that the ex-Soviet republics might eventually remain in their traditional areas, and that it was primarily the political ambitions of their leaders that drove them away from establishing some sort of a union on the territory of the former USSR.[6] It soon became evident, however, that the emerging picture did not fit any of these expectations. "Joining" the world community of independent nations has proved to be more difficult than one might think it would be. The prospects for some sort of imperial restoration, too, remain remote, at best. Fortunately or unfortunately, after five years of independence, they pursued fundamentally different patterns of international behavior. At least three distinct patterns of the NIS's foreign economic responses can be identified.[7]

"Loyalists" announced their intentions to remain loyal to their old partners and to establish a regional economic union on the territory of the Soviet Union. They showed little desire to search for new economic partners; instead, they committed themselves to transforming the CIS (Commonwealth of Independent States) into a customs union. Belarus, Kazakhstan, and Kyrgyzstan were among the major "loyalist" NIS.

"Independents" chose to become full-fledged members of the world trading system and to find new, primarily Western economic partners. Despite being closely connected with Russia and other ex-Soviet republics, and even economically dependent on them (oil and gas dependence on Russia is the most obvious aspect), these nations have been much less cooperative with the CIS than the first group. The Baltic republics became the strongest proponents of this type of policy. By 1993-1994, Estonia, Latvia, and Lithuania had signed a number of trade agreements with northern European nations and established the necessary domestic institutions for launching successful market-oriented foreign economic activities.

The third group of nations falls between those poles. Nations that belong to this group pursued a policy, which cannot be identified as staying with the old trading partners, because they made serious efforts to sign new commercial agreements with new partners. However, unlike the Baltic republics, these nations were less committed to following this type of strategy. They also maintained relationships with Russia and the CIS, and while not committing themselves to the CIS as a customs union, they stressed the importance of good relations with Russia and other CIS members. Also unlike the Baltic republics, they were slow and indecisive in establishing domestic economic institutions necessary for shifting their trade pattern toward Western countries. Ukraine, Azerbaijan, Turkmenistan, and some other nations fall in this category.

The question of variation in the economic strategies of the fourteen NIS has not received much attention in the scholarly literature. Economists have been either preoccupied with other foreign trade issues,[8] or dissolved this question into a more general question of economic viability of the NIS.[9] Foreign policy experts, while generally more sensitive to this problem, have failed to analyze it in a systematic way. To date, the best that has been done are small-n comparative studies of some of the NIS's foreign policies mentioning the relevance of the issue of economic restructuring but with no specific focus on it.[10] The first step toward understanding the causes of differences in the NIS's policies is to consider possible general ways of explaining countries' foreign economic policies in a market-oriented international environment.

Insufficient Explanations

Following established International Political Economy (IPE) perspectives, one can imagine at least three different ways of answering this question.[11] This section addresses possible explanations of the observed variation and suggests that none of them is sufficient to account for the newly independent nations' foreign economic policies.

International Market Conditions

The first perspective—from international market conditions—operates on the assumption that market conditions are the strongest stimulus in shaping foreign economic policies. International trade theory assumes, for example, that the point of departure for formulation of foreign trade policy is a country's comparative advantages in resource endowment (natural resources, labor, technology, etc.). If this theory applies,[12] then in a newly independent nation we should see shifts in trade policy and in the direction of trade to the extent that former trade departed from comparative advantage.

This perspective, while being generally applicable to the NIS, misses the fact that they were just emerging out of a command political economy in 1991 and, therefore, lacked the institutions necessary for launching market-oriented trade activities. Conventional trade theory and—more generally—the international market perspective abstracts from national institutions and traditions, and they are not designed primarily to explain government policies in the first place. It is therefore not particularly helpful in clarifying how the new actors of the world economy make their choices and why they choose to direct economic ties toward one country or a set of countries, and not to another. Apart from the idea that each country should have some sort of marketable resource to trade, this perspective does not tell us enough about the variation in their policies of becoming independent actors of the world economy.

International Power Structure

It was in response to the insufficiency of the international market perspective that another perspective—from the international power structure—has emerged. Being driven by different political biases and empirical preferences, it theorizes the influences of international power from the standpoint of the developed and the developing worlds. Neorealists are especially concerned with implications of economic power for national military security and security arrangements; dependency theorists, on the other hand, focus on more equal distribution of economic power and ways of maintaining national autonomy in economic decision making.

Both versions emphasize that the distribution of economic power is of key significance, and no individual nation, whether developed or developing, can afford to
ignore this factor in its foreign economic policy.[13]

The neorealist version makes particularly strong claims arguing that economic
and commercial decisions can be best understood if analyzed as driven by a
nation's power needs.[14] Each nation is expected to use physical resources available, economic and military, for maintaining its security arrangements, particularly
when the efficiency of national security arrangements is questioned. Pursuit of
economic reorientation then can serve as a way to reduce dependence and create a
better security arrangement, rather than as a way to become wealthier. The power
perspective, while it is useful for clarifying the NIS's economic policy motivations, is insufficient for identifying differences across countries' policies. During
1991-1996, at least some of the NIS, such as Ukraine and Belarus, did not experience any direct threats to their security from elsewhere, and yet their foreign economic policies turned out to be quite different. As far as indirect threats go, with
Russia proclaiming the strategy of "reintegrating the Near Abroad" in 1993, the
NIS did face the danger of being pulled back into the Russian "sphere of influence" by means of economic or political coercion,[15] but their reactions to Russian
efforts were far from being homogeneous. Some of the ex-Soviet republics, such
as Ukraine and the Baltics, perceived Russia's newly proclaimed strategy as threatening their security, while some others remained indifferent of Russia's intentions
and were not nearly as worried about their sovereignty and independence.

The dependency perspective also cannot account adequately for the NIS's
varying foreign economic policies. Obviously, during the many decades of empire,
the ex-Soviet republics developed various degrees of economic interdependence
and dependence on the metropole. They became asymmetrically dependent on
Russia's market, fuel, and supplies, as Russia had a more diversified economy and
was richly endowed in natural resources.[16] Yet, such dependence did not prove to
be the only significant factor for understanding the NIS's policies. For example, the
important division among the republics in their endowment in tradable resources,
most notably oil and gas, can be helpful in understanding differences in economic
policy of countries that are drastically different in this respect, but not of those that
are similarly rich or poor with respect to their resources. This division can provide
some insights into why energy-rich Azerbaijan and energy-poor Kyrgyzstan expli-
cate different patterns of behavior, but is of no assistance in understanding policy
variation within the group of energy-poor countries, such as Ukraine and Belarus.

National Political Institutions

The problem with both neorealist and dependency perspectives is their relatively low sensitivity toward domestic perceptions of power resources relevant
for restructuring foreign economic activities. What often matters in foreign pol-

icy decisions is not the international pressure, but the way it is perceived on the national level. As a result, nations that face similar challenges abroad may behave differently. A calculation of power—military or economic—is done by policymakers operating in varying national contexts and, therefore, is incomplete without considering domestic arrangements. One influential way to consider domestic conditions has been to bring the national political institutions perspective into the International Political Economy. What matters in policy formulation, the supporters of this approach claim, is a different composition of social and political institutions as well as an ability of states to overcome the pressures of economic interest groups.[17]

This perspective is an important addition to the previous two perspectives, but it, too, has limitations for explaining the observed variations. Theoretically, the perspective should predict variation in the NIS's foreign economic policies on the basis of variations in their political institutional arrangements. The problem is, however, that having emerged out of the same empire in the 1991, all the newly independent nations inherited domestic institutions that were the product of the same centralized rule and do not vary enough to be able to predict the wide variation in the NIS's foreign economic policies. It is only at later stages that the NIS's political institutions and state structures became relatively more diverse, with more democratic, society-led regimes shaping up in western Eurasia and more authoritarian toward the south of Moscow.[18] Such increasing diversification of the ex-Soviet republics' political regimes is hardly helpful, however, in clarifying their foreign policy choices: for instance, the fact that by 1997, the Baltic nations, Ukraine, and Kyrgyzstan established democratic institutions cannot tell us why these three represented three distinct patterns of economic orientation.[19] Something else must determine the NIS's economic policy formulation, something that has not yet been captured by any of the above-listed perspectives.

The Argument in Brief

In attempting to compensate for the weaknesses of economic and political explanations, I propose to develop a national identity explanation for the former Soviet republics' international economic policies.[20] National identity is a cultural norm that reflects emotional or affective orientations of individuals toward their nation and national political system. It involves symbolic, socially constructed meanings, which is well captured in the Benedict Anderson definition of nation as an "imagined political community."[21]

Rather than looking at national political arrangements, the national identity perspective emphasizes domestic *cultural* institutions thereby highlighting the sources of state structures and identity. It does not treat institutions as endogenous of the state; instead, it sees them as capable of influencing state actions independently.[22] This becomes a major advantage in theorizing about the postimperial nations, or the newly emerged nations, as the NIS are. The NIS are emerging out of an empire and going through the process of nation building. Whereas the NIS do not vary significantly in their political institutions, they are different in their cultural characteristics, such as national memory and cultural perceptions of the empire and the outside world. While sharing the same imperial legacy, the republics differ across various dimensions relevant for understanding their national identities and specifics of their identification vis-à-vis the ex-empire and the ex-metropole. At least three groups of newly independent nations can be identified depending on how strong their national, that is non-imperial, feelings are.

The nations of one group may have had some experience of independent nationhood and, therefore, some sense of national identity before they had been incorporated into the empire. If this independence experience was lengthy enough and the domestic institutions of sovereignty grew relatively strong, these nations also developed a strong connection, both physical and symbolic, with the world of sovereign nations. All this became imprinted in these nations' memories and led to perceiving the metropole as more threatening to their security, while the outside world—as less threatening or even potentially friendly. Assuming the absence of other powerful actors with strong imperial ambitions, the states of this group after the imperial disintegration will be unlikely to make a positive identification with the ex-metropole. Rather, they are likely to relate to various parts of the world of sovereign nations, assuming the growing strength and the only alternative this world represents to the old imperial order in terms of the authority principles.[23] On the other extreme, one can imagine the group of nations that did not have any historical record of independence and had been incorporated into the empire without a well-developed sense of their political identities. This lack of ability to identify themselves with a country or region outside the empire (weak external identification) led them to perceiving the metropole as neutral or potentially friendly and other parts of external environment as threatening to their security.[24] Finally, some nations may fall somewhere in between these two groups, having difficulties establishing their identification with the empire or the world of sovereign nations.[25]

For comparative purposes, it may be useful to conceptualize the effects of national identity on policymakers in terms of degree of national identity strength. Depending on how firmly the national (non-imperial) identity is established and, therefore, how strongly people in the newly independent nations disassociate themselves from the empire and identify with the nation as a non-imperial entity, the policymakers of the newly independent states may view the goals of these nations' survival in a fundamentally different way. A relatively well-developed national identity constitutes a non-imperial reality, thereby exerting a relatively strong regulative effect and providing policymakers with a resource for challenging the institutional legacies of the former empire, and broadening a nation's options in choosing an optimal strategy of international economic adjustment.

The ex-imperial nations, therefore, may vary in their economic policies depending on their abilities to challenge the inherited imperial institutions for the purpose of assuming control over their policies, or, in other words, depending on how strongly they are affected by the national identity norm.

The effect of national identity on policy making is mediated by domestic struggle of culture-based political coalitions. With the decline of an empire, this sense of national difference and national "selfness" gives additional stimulus to a rapid development of nationalist-oriented social movements pursuing goals of nation building. Depending on circumstances, nationalist movements may appeal to the population's linguistic and religious instincts or historical feelings. Nationalists get involved in a political process of competing with empire savers for mobilizing social support. If national identity is strong and a large share of the population has gone through the process of mental disassociation from the empire and identification with the nation, such support turns out to be sufficient. As a result, nationalists replace the old pro-imperial elite as a result of a coup or elections, and set the agenda of economic decision making. If not, decision making is likely to remain under the control of empire savers.

National identity effects on policy making can be operationalized in a number of ways. This study proposes that for the postimperial nations, the factor that is crucial for capturing the level of their national identities development is these nations' historical experience with national independence. Since the Peace of Westphalia, national independence has been a key condition in establishing a modern system of power and authority relationships.[26] Those nations that had enjoyed an experience with independence for a relatively long time (before they were incorporated into the empire) have a relatively better chance of developing and maintaining their non-imperial identity through the time of their colonial existence. For constructing a more inclusive picture, other indicators will be employed as well.

It must be emphasized that by putting forward the national identity perspective, this study does not mean to suggest that other factors are unimportant in the post-Soviet nations' economic behavior. Rather, these factors of market and power nature are insufficient and should be supplemented with national identity considerations. The perspective this study develops merely seeks to point out limitations of conventional approaches and illustrate possible explanatory opportunities of bringing cultural variables into international political economy.

Research Design

This study uses two types of empirical research aimed at generating a new hypothesis for political economy studies and evaluating it at least on a preliminary basis. First will come comparative exploration of a small number of cases or observations. In this phase, I prefer to use comparison across cases as well as detailed case research. The main goal here will be to try to improve the hypothesis by learning more about the process through which national identity conceptions function (or do not function) in politics and policy making on foreign economic issues, and to check for spurious relationships.[27] At the same time, if cases are selected carefully for theoretical reasons, such that they are similar with respect to plausible alternative causes of the main dependent variable, at least those alternatives can be ruled out as threats to the identity interpretation for these cases. Thus, the project will select three republics that vary as to strength of national identity but are relatively similar with respect to other possible influences, in order to isolate the former for particular attention.

Two of the most important rival interpretations are relative security threats and international market conditions. As far as the NIS's economic competitiveness is concerned, the fourteen republics varied in the degree to which they would probably have benefited from abandoning the Soviet trading system and conducting their trade at world prices. According to calculations by Watson, all except Russia and Turkmenistan had enjoyed subsidies under the Soviet system, so that all others were expected to suffer terms-of-trade losses from shifting the same trade to world prices—but in widely varying degrees (see table 1.1). Belarus, Latvia, and Ukraine are adjacent in the center of this spectrum, as roughly equivalent in economic respect and, therefore, represent a reasonable set of cases for comparative examination.[28]

Table 1.1. The Former Soviet Republics: Net Percentage Change in Terms of Trade (rubles to world market prices, in 1990)

Winners	Russia	+35
	Turkmenistan	+33
Losers	Kazakhstan	-2
	Uzbekistan	-8
	Kyrgyzstan	-13
	Ukraine	-15
	Belarus	-20
	Latvia	-25
	Azerbaijan	-26
	Tajikistan	-30
	Estonia	-32
	Armenia	-33
	Lithuania	-35
	Georgia	-45
	Moldova	-53

Source: Watson 1994, 405.

As for the relative security threats, those that had larger military capabilities might have been expected to be less worried about trading with the ex-hegemon than those with weaker military capabilities. All the NIS other than Russia naturally faced a huge disparity in capabilities, but at least in terms of conventional weapons, the weaker republics did not differ dramatically in this respect,[29] and none of the fourteen would stand any chance were it to resist Russia's possible attack. This makes them roughly the same in terms of selection for a qualitative comparison. Ukraine, Belarus, and Latvia then can be selected for our study with the intent to control for power influence on their foreign economic policies.

These three republics amply illustrate the likely range of potential variation in strength of national identity and perception of threat from the ex-metropole. In terms of their experience with national independence, they can be seen as representatives of at least three distinct groups among the fourteen ex-Soviet republics.[30] Baltic republics would exemplify nations with relatively well-developed political identities. Before they had been incorporated into the Soviet empire in 1940, they all enjoyed a quarter-century period of independent nationhood. This period allowed them to develop the sense of awareness of the threat to their identities posed by the Soviet occupation and resist efforts of the Soviet regime to incorporate them culturally. At the other extreme are Belarus, Moldova, and the five Central Asian republics. While different in many dimensions, these nations are similar in having no experience with independent statehood before their incorporation into the Soviet empire. As a result, their sense of being threatened by the ex-metropole continues to be relatively low. Finally, Armenia, Azerbaijan, Georgia, and Ukraine fall somewhere in between those two poles. Compared to Baltic nations, the experience of these nations with national independence was rather short-lived and fragmented, but it proved to be sufficient to develop and retain—even through the period of the Soviet empire—a set of historical myths glorifying the idea of national independence.[31]

For the purpose of this study, it would therefore suffice to select Belarus, Latvia, and Ukraine, as relevant examples from the three identified groups. Latvia, Ukraine, and Belarus amply illustrate the likely range of potential variation in the strength of the effect of national identity. One reasonable proxy for this variable is the number of years of experience as an independent entity the nation has had. Belarus, at one extreme, had had no such experience at all prior to 1991, and Latvia had possessed all the attributes of nationhood during 1921-1940. While Latvia and Belarus may be considered the most "obvious" or the "most likely" cases of the national identity effect, the case of Ukraine is far less obvious and can serve as an additional test of the national identity hypothesis. The Ukraine falls somewhere between Latvia and Belarus in terms of its national identity strength and, therefore, for the national identity hypothesis to be valid, Ukraine should pursue the economic policy falling between those of Latvia and Belarus.[32]

The second phase of the project then attempts a statistical test of the national identity hypothesis, as refined during the first phase. Compensating for the relative shortcomings of small-n analysis, this phase aims at adding rigor to the analysis by employing additional empirical evidence and thereby improving causal inferences of the research. Fourteen of the former Soviet republics during five years of their independence are selected[33] for a quantitative test of the major hypothesis of this project and for assessing relative merits of competing explanations, such as market conditions, relative power, political institutions, and national identities. The evaluation of their relative merits is based on bivariate regressions of various independent variables to the foreign economic policy score. Taken separately, such evaluation, of course, is only tentative and would require further research. However, when complemented with in-depth qualitative investigation, such statistical analysis provides us with extra confidence in evaluating the explanatory potential of the national identity hypothesis.

Organization of the Study

The next chapter develops a national identity explanation for the former Soviet republics' foreign economic policies. It introduces the three main concepts around which this study is organized and establishes a theoretical framework for answering in a preliminary fashion the following set of questions. What is national identity, and what are its basic dimensions? How does the identity get constructed? What are the conditions of its change and stability? How can national identity be compared across cases, and what effects can it possibly have on countries' economic policy making? What is the process through which national identity exerts its effects on policymakers? Finally, how should the answers to these questions be modified for the conditions of postimperial nations, the direct subject of this study?

Chapters 3 through 5 turn to case studies and trace the influences of national identity on Latvia's, Ukraine's, and Belarus's foreign economic policies during 1991-1996. The analysis is focused on how the three behaved vis-à-vis three goals of economic reorientation: minimizing economic ties with old commercial partners; finding potential new partners and establishing necessary domestic institutions for switching trade toward new partners; and signing trade agreements, both bilateral and multilateral, with new partners.

After observing Latvia's, Ukraine's, and Belarus's policies on each of the three stages, chapter 6 extends the analysis beyond the three cases' comparison and explores how the argument made holds against other ex-Soviet republics. The chapter proposes a way of analyzing the fourteen republics' foreign economic orientations and assessing the relative merits of competing explanations. It also suggests a number of cases with deviant behavior, an avenue for further research of the issue, and offers a brief qualitative investigation of two of them.

The final chapter summarizes the overall findings and their implications. It concludes that not only does national identity matter for explaining varieties of the ex-Soviet republics' economic policies, but it seems to be the strongest predictor of their behavior, relative to explanations of economic and political nature. The analysis shows that the ex-Soviet nations' economic considerations turned out to be embedded in varying cultural contexts, and it is only in these cultural contexts that economic interests could be formed and meaningfully function. In addition to summarizing the study's major findings, the chapter addresses alternative explanations and draws the implications of the analysis for theory and policy making.

Notes

1. Most important statements include Wendt 1992; Lapid and Kratochwil 1996; Katzenstein 1996; Finnemore 1996; Duffield 1998; Ruggie 1998; Wendt 1999.

2. For various overviews, see Checkel 1998; Dash 1998; Hopf 1998; Katzenstein et al. 1999; Sterling-Folker 2000.

3. This may be why some scholars went so far as to suggest that the field is stagnating (Jervis 1998, 990). For exceptions investigating various IPE issues from the cultural norms' perspective, see Finnemore 1996; Crane 1999; Williams 1999; Goff 2000; Shulman 2000; Tsygankov 2000a, 2000b.

4. The conceptual universe of cases is potentially rich and includes, in addition to the former USSR, eastern European countries—former members of the Soviet block—and postimperial nations in general.

5. The view was widespread in Ukraine and some other republics during 1990-1991 (see more details in Boffa 1996, 230, 252).

6. Before independence, the NIS were national republics and been forced to trade primarily with one another, rather than with countries outside of the Soviet borders. The share of inter-republican trade comprised up to 85-90 percent of the republics' total trade (Bradshaw 1993, 29). Accordingly, a commonly held expectation was that the former republics would do their best to keep this pattern alive (see, for example, Slay 1991, 2).

7. It is worth emphasizing that this project does not study actual trade flows and trade patterns. Following the research tradition of International Political Economy, it focuses, instead, on the state as a unit of analysis and asks the question about motivations underlying state behavior, not the behavior of private economic actors. Because I study state action, not private activity, the primary focus of my study concerns economic agreements, not patterns of trade or other economic activities. The following chapter returns to this point and specifies the meaning of the term "foreign economic policy" as used in this study.

8. See, WB 1995; Michalopoulos and Tarr 1996.

9. Wyzan 1995.

10. See, for example, Burant 1995; Kulinich 1995; Vares 1995; Kubicek 1997.

11. Chapters 6 and 7 further address the issue of alternative explanations.

12. Each of the IPE perspectives is, of course, based on its own ontological and episte-mological assumptions and worldviews, and some of these assumptions are in conflict and cannot be reconciled (Biersteker 1999). This incommensurability on the level of assump-tions makes a dialogue across paradigms difficult, but not impossible: some room should be granted for juxtaposing and comparing various philosophical beliefs in various empiri-cal situations and with the use of testable propositions.

13. Some major statement representing views from developed and developing worlds, respectively, are Hirschman 1969; Krasner 1978; Gowa 1994 and Wallerstein 1974; Car-doso and Faletto 1979.

14. Holsti 1986; Gowa and Mansfield 1993.

15. Porter and Saivetz 1994; Drezner 1997.

16. Krivogorsky and Eichenseher 1996, 34-35; Shishkov et al 1997, 83-84.

17. Katzenstein 1977; Hall 1986; Mastanduno, Lake and Ikenberry 1989; Keohane and Milner 1996.

18. Gati 1996; Dawisha and Parrott 1997a, 1997b.

19. They each represent the nations with independent, moderate and traditional pro-Russian orientation as it was outlined above in the "Research Question" section.

20. For others more recent efforts to adopt a national identity perspective in interna-tional studies, see especially Lapid and Kratochwil 1996; Katzenstein 1996; Krause and Williams 1997; Prizel 1998.

21. Anderson 1991, 6.

22. Conversely, the state structures approach, as one of its early proponent has recently acknowledged "has typically focused on the variability in the autonomy and the capacity of states, not on their identity" (Katzenstein 1996, 23).

23. Conceptually, this conflict between the two systems of authority relationships was recognized by many scholars of empires, nationalism and state-building (see, for example, Seton-Watson 1977, chaps. 6-8; Doyle 1986; Strange 1996; Dawisha and Parrott 1997; Barkey and von Hagen 1997).

24. This, of course, will be true when holding many other things equal.

25. In his study of economic nationalism, Rawi Abdelal (1999) arrived at a similar line of argument by suggesting that the ex-Soviet republics' politicized identities shaped their economic behavior. Abdelal and I arrived to our conclusions independently, which further validates our studies' results.

26. Other factors, too, can play their role in fostering national identity. For example, ethnicity and religion may under certain conditions reinforce the sense of nation by help-ing it to break with its imperial past. While not excluding these factors from consideration, this study assumes that, at its core, identity and nationalism are modern phenomena that have been established historically, through the process of gradual global expansion of modernity norms. (For the development of linkages between modernity and nationalism, see, Motyl 1992a.) Chapter 2 elaborates on this point.

27. George 1982, 15.

28. This, of course, is only an approximate appraisal. The three are not and cannot be identical: most experts suggest, for example, that Ukraine was somewhat better placed than the other two with regard to their potential for economic restructuring. Yet this is counterbalanced by two circumstances. First, while the three are not economically identi-cal, they are relatively similar and form a group of most economically advanced republics

in the former USSR when compared to most other ex-Soviet republics. Experts' estimations of the NIS's economic viability and potential to integrate their economies into the world economy vary, but they are fairly consistent in terms of suggesting a similarity between Baltics, Ukraine and Belarus (see, for example, Corbet and Gummich 1990; Schroeder 1992; Erikson 1992; Vavilov and Vjugin 1993; Brown and Belkindas 1993; Watson 1994; Krivogorsky and Eichenseher 1997, 35). Second, being economically stronger Ukraine is not the strongest on the national identity dimension (Latvia is), which suggests an additional test for the national identity hypothesis: if the hypothesis has any merit we should not see Ukraine pursuing the most aggressive pattern of economic reorientation.

29. The republics differed in terms of nuclear weapons. Unlike Latvia, Ukraine, and Belarus posessed nuclear arsenals, but by 1994, they transferred those arsenals to Russia.

30. All the former Soviet republics, with the exception of Russia. As the former hegemon, Russia is incompatible with the NIS in its institutions and perceptions of the outside world and, therefore, cannot be analyzed with the use of the tools chosen for the analysis of the rest of the NIS's national identities.

31. In constructing my classification, I found useful typologies of Soviet and post-Soviet nations, offered in the following works: Rakowska-Harmstone 1974; Armstrong 1988; Szporluk 1992; Suny 1993; Dawisha and Parrott 1994; RFE/RL RR, 1993-95; Chinn and Kaiser 1996; Bremmer and Taras 1997; Brzezinski 1997.

32. Unlike Armenia, Georgia, Moldova and Tajikistan, these three have also been relatively peaceful since the Soviet disintegration, which allows us to isolate an additional potentially rival explanation—the republics' participation in military conflicts.

33. As the former hegemon, Russia is incompatible with the NIS in its institutions and perceptions of the outside world and, therefore, will be excluded from the analysis.

Chapter 2
National Identity, Domestic Structures, and Foreign Economic Policy

This chapter develops a national identity explanation for the foreign economic policies of the former Soviet republics.[1] I introduce the three main concepts around which this study is organized and establish a theoretical framework for answering in a preliminary fashion the following set of questions: What is national identity, and what are its basic dimensions? How does the identity get constructed? What are the conditions of its change and stability? How can national identity be compared across cases, and what effects can it possibly have on countries' economic policy making? What is the process through which national identity exerts its effects on policymakers? Finally, how should the answers to these questions be modified for the conditions of postimperial nations, the direct subject of this study?

National Identity

National Identity: Dimensions, Formation, Change

Following recent studies, I will refer to identity as a varying construction of nation and nationhood.[2] National identity is a cultural norm that reflects emotional or affective orientations of individuals toward their nation and national political system. Feelings of attachment, involvement, rejection, and the like are usually referred to as manifestations of identity.[3] National identity should be distinguished from *ethnic* identity. The latter refers to feelings of loyalty and attachment toward an ethnic group and may have nothing to do with institutions of statehood that are normally held responsible for the emergence and maintenance of national identity. Conversely, *national* identity involves the symbolic, socially constructed meanings shared across society as a whole, and not just within ethnic group(s),[4] which are well captured in the Benedict Anderson definition of nation as an "imagined political community."[5] It is, in the words of another prominent theorist, "the community of political destiny, i.e., above all, of common political struggle of life and death" that "has given rise to groups with joint memories which often have had a deeper impact than ties of merely cultural, linguistic, or ethnic community."[6]

Dimensions

National identity is a complex phenomenon, a product of domestic and international history. At least two dimensions of national identity may be introduced as worthy of our attention—unity and distinctness. The unity dimension describes how homogeneous a nation is in sharing various myths and visions about its history, territory, and institutions, as well as in language and religion. It can be seen in both qualitative (various aspects of national unity) and quantitative (overarching degree of strength) terms. National distinctness, on the other hand, describes how similar or different a nation is vis-à-vis other nations/members of international society. A sense of distinctness reflects the external dimension of national identity; in the process of various identification with neighbors and other international actors, a nation identifies itself and learns about various aspects of its uniqueness, specialty, and commonness vis-à-vis the others. The distinctness dimension may then be helpful in understanding the dynamics of threats and alignments in world politics. Both unity and distinctness are integral parts of national identity and refer to societal boundaries in inclusive (creating an overarching collective self-consciousness) and exclusive (separating out those outside the physical or metaphorical boundaries) terms, respectively.[7]

Formation

In contrast to what modernization theorists argued, national identity building is not contingent on the establishment of a Western-like economic and political system; it will go on so long as nations exist facing a variety of challenges from within and abroad.[8] Identity formation is a process that is always open to change and never completed; a national community, in the words of Ernest Renan, is the result of a "plebiscite of everyday life." It has to do with making sense of reality by establishing and reestablishing certain meanings. It is therefore a process of obtaining significance, or *signification,* through which newly emerged and highly contested meanings evolve into meanings that are little contested and institutionalized. The stages of this process and main forces responsible for its development are summarized in figure 2.1.

At stage I, as a result of historical practices,[9] new meanings emerge in a society allowing room for new interpretations of its past and present. Here the newly emerged meanings/interpretations are highly contested and marginal in their influence due to overwhelming power of hegemonic discourse. At stage II, however, the newly emerged meanings receive a chance to increase their influence. Due to conducive institutional arrangements, repetitive historical practices,[10] and activities of political entrepreneurs, the new meanings get spread in a society thereby increasingly obtaining hegemonic status. Finally, at stage III, identity formation reaches the point when the new meanings are sufficiently consolidated and get exploited, both socially and politically, for the purpose of their further consolidation. In the meantime, history does not stop—new meanings emerge challenging the old identity's content and boundaries and encouraging change.[11]

Identity therefore is established through a process of constant competition between old and newly created meanings. It is a relational phenomenon to the extent that it is always constructed via the Self's interaction with its environment. By tipping new meanings, various historical practices play the role of what psychologists refer to as significant Others. The significant Other initiates the process of actor socialization and transfers a socially relevant knowledge and its meaning to the Self, thereby imbuing him or her with the decisive influence.[12]

Nations can relate to their significant Others in various ways. For example, national identity can form through a process of adjustment to various external challenges.[13] Alternatively, national identity formation may be spurred by domestic historical practices. Even when tasks posed by the international system are relatively similar, they are rarely solved in the same way across nations. National traditions, histories, ethnic composition, and homogeneity embedded in institutional arrangements get their way and eventually find an expression in a "national formula" or strategy of responding to outside challenges.[14]

Figure 2.1. The Process of National Identity Formation

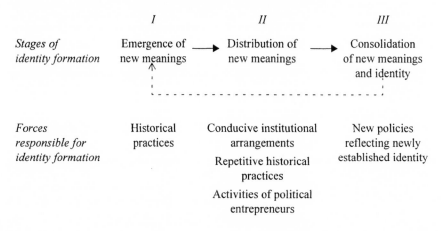

	I	II	III
Stages of identity formation	Emergence of new meanings ⟶	Distribution of new meanings ⟶	Consolidation of new meanings and identity
Forces responsible for identity formation	Historical practices	Conducive institutional arrangements / Repetitive historical practices / Activities of political entrepreneurs	New policies reflecting newly established identity

Change

Identity change comes as a result of increased tension between old and newly created meanings (this is often referred to as identity crisis). It can be classified in terms of the change's form and substance. By its form, national identity change can be both incremental and revolutionary. Incremental change comes as a result of a country's adaptation to domestic/international pressures of relatively low degree. Revolutionary change, on the other hand, occurs when a society must respond to environmental pressures that are formidable in their potential effects. Revolutionary change comes as a result of social revolution, war, or any other event directly challenging the previously existing national image of the Self. The illustrations of revolutionary change in national identity may include Russia's transition from a relatively open economic system to economic autarchy after the First World War and the October 1917 revolution, or Japanese and German transitions from mercantilist-type systems after the Second World War. On the other hand, Chinese economic reform since 1979 may illustrate incremental change, as it undermines—slowly-but surely—the country's communist identity and creates its new entrepreneurial and capitalist image that is increasingly reflected in the country's institutions. Identity change can also be classified in terms of substance. For example, depending on one's evaluative standards, national identity can change in a more progressive way (learning) or in the opposite direction (regression). With some notable exceptions, the discussion of these issues has yet to come to the international relations (IR) discipline.[15]

National Identity of the Postimperial Nations

Applying these insights about national identity to the postimperial nations requires a certain modification. It is this historical experience of being effectively deprived of sovereignty for a relatively long time that makes them special and affects, in crucial way, their sense of identity and community. Both the unity and distinctness dimensions of national identity have been affected. National unity has been undermined and weakened as a result of imperial efforts to make those nations think and act as if they share the identity of the empire without having an identity of their own. National distinctness was also decreased and formed almost exclusively vis-à-vis the empire. With no sovereignty—a fundamental attribute of national security—nations' identities came to be heavily dominated by concerns about their survival or security. Without being satisfied, those concerns became exacerbated, pushing many other important concerns off the agenda, such as preserving the linguistic and other cultural specifics of a nation.[16] Not surprisingly, the question "how are we different from/similar to other nations?" in the imperial context sounds like "how are we different from the empire?" To put it the strongest way, for the postimperial nations, identity *is* security,[17] and they are likely to perceive all other problems, including those related to their economies, in the light of their concerns about the survival of national community.

Postimperial nations, of course, are not homogeneous. While sharing the same imperial legacy, they differ across various dimensions relevant for understanding their national identities. Scholars of empires, imperial disintegration, and postimperial nationalism suggest a long list of such dimensions, which includes, among others, pre-imperial historical experience with nationhood, degree of peripheral elite's incorporation into the empire, level of economic development, ethnic homogeneity, stability of geographic borders, and linguistic and religious differences from the metropole.[18] All these differences are likely to affect the extent to which aspirations for sovereign nationhood are shared across a society and how strongly a society identifies itself with the ex-empire and the ex-metropole. Depending on how strongly the meaning of community is established and how pronounced national (that is, non-imperial) feelings are, various societies may identify themselves externally in a very different way.[19]

At least two groups of nations can be identified.

The people of one group may have had some experience of independence and, therefore, some sense of national identity before they had been incorporated into the empire. If this independence experience was lengthy enough and the domestic institutions of sovereignty grew relatively strong, these people also developed a strong connection, both physical and symbolic, with the world of sovereign nations. All this became imprinted on these nations' national memories and led to perceiving the metropole as more threatening to their security and the outside world as less threatening or even potentially friendly.[20] Assuming the absence of other powerful actors with strong imperial ambitions, the nations of this group after the imperial disintegration will be unlikely to make positive external identification with the ex-metropole. Rather, they are likely to identify with various parts of the world of sovereign nations, assuming the growing strength and the only alternative this world represents to the old imperial order in terms of the authority principles.[21] On the other hand, one can imagine the group of people who did not have any historical record of independence and had been incorporated into the empire without a well-developed sense of their political identity. This lack of ability to identify themselves with a country or region outside the empire (weak external identification) led them to perceiving the metropole as neutral or potentially friendly and other parts of external environment as threatening to their security.[22]

Thus, due to their special nature, the postimperial nations may find themselves between at least two different systems of authority relationships that are associated with an empire and the world of sovereign nations-states, respectively. The choice the postimperial people will be making then is a choice between these two significant Others,[23] a choice of identifying with only one of those at the expense of another. These significant Others then are likely to exert fundamentally different influences on the process of identification among postimperial nations depending on the degree in their national identity strength. More specifically, by accepting the qualities from one significant Other, a nation will be likely to perceive another significant Other as neutral or even threatening to its survival.

National Identity Effects on Policy Making

I now turn to the effects of an acquired identity on the Self's behavior. Because I am interested in the effects, rather than the process by which the Self relates to the Other and acquires its identity, I will now treat identity as a relatively stable rather than a constantly changing phenomenon.

Four Effects of National Identity on Policy Making

I propose to consider four possible effects of national identity on behavior, or policymaking. A developed sense of national identity can serve as a guide in interpreting the political situation, determining policy objectives and choosing among policy options. It can also provide policymakers with additional resources for mobilizing necessary social support.[24]

Determining how the political situation is interpreted by the actor is the first step in the analysis and should precede other steps in determining the actor's behavior. Many rational choice approaches rush to estimating potential costs and benefits of a political act without bothering to reveal on just what scale of meaning the cost/benefit calculations should take place. This makes the estimate fundamentally flawed, as the social situation and the political situations are never value-neutral or objective, and individual actions always take place in the context of meanings attached to them.[25] National identity, as collective emotion, is an important key to considering politics in a "web of significance."[26] As with other components of culture and social institutions, it plays the role of constitutive norm or the norm that constitutes, creates, or revises the actors or interests rather than explicitly regulating the actors' behaviors.[27] It guides individual interpretation of reality and helps policymakers to make sense of the political situation.[28]

As individual policymakers share collective socially constructed meanings, they should be expected to determine policy objectives consistently with those meanings (other things being equal). Depending on how strongly these meanings are shared, the determination of a policy objective at any given moment can be a more or a less easy business. Accordingly, in choosing among various options a policymaker is likely to accept those that in his or her view meet the established national goals and national self-image and to reject those that do not.

To illustrate how national identity can be crucial in interpreting the political situation and setting a certain policy behavior, let us briefly consider two examples. The first example considers Japanese and German foreign policies since the Second World War. In coping with external threats, both countries eschewed violent state practices and did not pursue militarist goals, in striking contrast to their national histories between the 1880s and 1945. One major reason was these countries' changed identities under the decisive influence of multilateral security institutions, such as the UN, NATO, or the more limited bilateral context of the U.S.-Japanese Security Treaty.[29] The two countries also agreed to participate in the Marshall Plan, having perceived it as being in accord with their new identity posture. On the other hand, Soviet Russia refused to participate in the arrangement despite U.S. invitations. Its identity was formed by the 1917 Socialist revolution and the revolution-related hostility toward the Western world, and its cultural perception of the Marshall Plan has been entirely different from that of Germany or Japan.

Cultural meanings, however, are not always shared in an equally strong way.[30] Often, a sense of national identity is not developed sufficiently to make a decision quickly and firmly. Contradictory influences on a nation's identity can be exerted from both inside and outside. In this case, a conflict of influences is likely to generate a conflict of interpretations. In the words of March and Olsen, social rules do not eliminate conflict:

> Rules and their applicability to particular situations are often ambiguous. Individuals have multiple identities... Situations can be defined in different ways that call forth different rules... Consequently, describing behavior as rule-following is only the first step in understanding how rules affect behavior.[31]

The third step is to understand what particular rule is likely to be evoked. Generally speaking, it is likely to be the rule that reinforces the initially developed image that a nation has of itself. Conversely, when an influence runs counter to the existing image of a nation, it is likely to be perceived by the nation as threatening to its security. The more fundamental the challenge to values and traditions on which the nation is built, the more likely it is that a nation will perceive the challenge as a threat. Or alternatively, in situations of identity crisis, a nation may invoke the rule that has been recently used or recently revised in response to crisis and, therefore, comes to its attention first.[32]

Finally, as an intersubjectively shared structure of meanings, a strong national identity can also provide policymakers with additional resources for mobilizing necessary social support. Again, depending on how strongly a nation as a whole feels about a particular political decision, mobilizing support might be relatively more or less difficult. If the policy decision is perceived as corresponding with a society's identity, a political coalition favoring the decision is likely to be able to overcome opposition and to obtain the necessary social support. If otherwise, a society is likely to be split, with little chance for the decision to be implemented. European countries in the wake of new technological challenges, such as rapid innovation in computer and other industries, might serve as an illustration. France, in the words of a French political scientist, has not yet "found the way to modernize while preserving our imagined community." As a result, with the political left and right, socialists and conservatives have become increasingly indistinguishable, while the racist, extreme-right National Front party of Jean-Marie Le Pen had swept to a series of victories in municipal elections and had generally increased its showing to 15.2 percent in the 1995 presidential election.[33]

National Identity Effects on Policy Making in the Postimperial Nations

The previously made points can be applied to the newly independent nations and their policy making. First, preoccupation with issues of security and survival—political, economic, and cultural—is likely to guide policymakers' interpretations of reality and to constitute their policy interests and behavior. Second and related, security is likely to become the major policy objective for the postimperial nations. Depending on their national identities, some will view security in terms of reuniting with the ex-metropole, while others will pursue the goal of nation building and reaching a full-scale sovereignty. Third, depending on the way in which policy objectives are defined, policymakers are likely to accept those policy options that meet the established national goals and national self-image, as these are defined, and to reject those that do not. Finally, the extent to which the defined policy goals (reunification with the ex-metropole or full national independence) are shared across a postimperial nation may or may not provide policymakers with additional resources for mobilizing necessary social support.[34]

Turning to the issue of foreign economic policy making in the postimperial nations, we may be able to formulate the following points. Depending on how strongly people in those nations disassociate themselves from the ex-metropole and identify with the world of sovereign nations, the policymakers may view the goals of survival in a fundamentally different way. A strong national identity challenges the institutional legacies of the former empire, and thereby broadens a state's options in choosing an optimal strategy of international economic adjustment. The ex-imperial nations will, therefore, vary in their economic policies depending on their abilities to challenge the inherited imperial institutions for the purpose of assuming control over their policies or, in other words, depending on the strength of their national identities (other things being equal).

The difference in policy objectives suggests differences in policy tradeoffs. To those with stronger national identities and senses of being threatened by the ex-metropole, survival is likely to mean establishing independent political institutions and assuming control over economic policy making even at the cost of economic benefits from cooperating with the ex-metropole. Conversely, those with relatively weaker national identities may view their survival in terms of close economic cooperation with the ex-metropole, even at the cost of their sovereignty and national independence. Holding other things constant, those with a stronger sense of national identity and disassociation from the empire are likely to be mobilized faster and be more supportive to policymakers' efforts of protecting national independence. A strong national identity is therefore likely to be employed by policymakers as a lever in pursuing more independent policy. One can expect that the stronger a country's national identity, the more likely that country's government will be to perceive economic cooperation with the former metropole as threatening to its security and the more likely that its policy will run counter to the old, empire-initiated economic pattern (again, other things being equal).

The simple matrix below (see figure 2.2) hypothesizes four levels of policy deviation from maintaining the old economic pattern that may be expected in the postimperial states, based on the interaction of identity and economic motivations. The incentive to pursue a policy of economic reorientation will depend on two factors: the strength of the society's national identity and assessments of its economic viability.[35] The stronger the national identity and the higher the perceived threat from the former metropole, the greater is the need for policy deviation from maintaining the old economic pattern. Similarly, the more cost-efficient the economic deviation, the greater is the impetus to achieve it for development purposes. When the political and economic conditions differ in their strength, either security or economic motivations may prevail (square 2 and 3 compared). Finally, when a society's identity and the threat perception are low along with its economic viability, the government is very unlikely to adopt a policy of economic deviation from the old imperial pattern (square 4).

Capturing the Strength of National Identity and the Sense of Threat to It

The discussion above suggests the necessity to account for at least two forces in capturing the strength of national identity and the sense of threat to it: historical practices and institutional environment. It is through historical practices and their repetition that a nation becomes more or less susceptible to newly created meanings and interpretations, and these may eventually be incorporated into its identity. Institutions are also important in capturing the strength of identity because they provide space in which meanings emerge, spread, and are consolidated. Both historical practices and institutions can be more or less conducive to identity consolidation and can therefore be analyzed in terms of their ability to capture the strength of national identity and the sense of threat to it.

Figure 2.2. Expected Deviation of the Postimperial States' Economic Policies from the Former Empire

		Strength of National Identity	
		strong identity	*weak identity*
Economic	*cost-efficient*	1. High deviation	2. Medium deviation
Viability	*cost-inefficient*	3. Medium deviation	4. Low deviation

Since national identity is often defined in terms of citizens' sense of common origins or common destiny,[36] it is important to find ways to measure the "commonness" of a nation's historical experience in order to account for its historical practices. This characteristic can be seen in both qualitative ("what kind of experience?") and quantitative ("how strongly does the national experience differentiate nation from empire?") terms. Nations and ethnic groups may be united by a variety of historical events; their sense of unity is developed in the process of being ruled by common leaders, under the umbrella of common political and social institutions, and in the course of fighting against common enemies. For the postimperial nations, one reasonable way to capture a commonness of their historical experience is to look at their experience with independent nationhood before the incorporation into the empire. It is through this experience that nations might have developed—in various degrees—the sense of commonness and distinctness. Quantitatively, it may be measured, among other ways, by the number of years of independence a nation experienced before its incorporation into the empire. Qualitative measurements can be developed by analyzing the various challenges a nation faces during times of relative stability versus instability.

As for nations' institutional arrangements, the relevant literature suggests at least four institutions that provide space for (and therefore affect) the process of national identity formation. These four—geographic territory, state, national economy, and culture—can be more or less conducive to maintaining a nation's cohesiveness and distinctness from the outside world.[37] Each of them can be measured in a number of ways.

Territorial unity fosters emotional attachment and sense of unity.[38] Asking questions about the length of maintaining territorial unity, the scope and types of change a nation's territorial boundaries have undergone, and about the peripheral territory's geographical distinctness (climate, location, etc.) from that of the metropole may help to obtain additional quantitative and qualitative characteristics of national identity.

Commonness of political institutions also deserves to be considered by national identity scholars. It is particularly through political institutions that an ethnic group eventually turns into a nation. In the words of Karl Deutsch, "nationalities turn into nations when they acquire power to back up their aspirations."[39] For the postimperial nations, the institutions that enforce peripheral distinctness from the empire are of particular relevance.[40] Some of these might have been created before the imperial incorporation and have simply outlived the empire while maintaining the periphery's sense of distinctness.[41] Others might have been established by the imperial rulers themselves, as it was with the Soviet federalism that put some ethnic groups in a privileged position, but not others.[42] Another example may be Russia's attempt in 1815 to allow a more liberal constitution for Poland than in Russia itself, which eventually led to the Polish national uprising and subsequent violent repression on Russia's side.[43]

Other things being equal, a nation's identity may also become stronger after a nation reaches a certain level of economic development. As with political institutions and territoriality, a developed economy helps to foster the sense of national unity and "belongingness," as well as the sense of a nation's relative distinctness.[44] A variety of more and less aggregated variables can be used for measuring the level of a nation's economic development.

Finally, a nation's distinctness and degree of homogeneity in terms of religion, language, customs, and racial appearance can also become relevant for national identity formation. These cultural features are often referred to as "primordial"[45] because they change much slower than many other historically contextual national characteristics.[46] Although primordial or ethnic features do not by themselves constitute the sense of nation and national identity, they may become relevant to the nation-building process if peripheral nations and their elites choose to exploit their primordial distinctness in anti-imperial mobilization.[47] Nations' primordial qualities can be captured through various measurements of the periphery's cultural (linguistic and religious) distinctness from the metropole, the level of cultural homogeneity, and the extent to which those characteristics change over time (for example, as a result of the imperial efforts to incorporate the periphery).

Variation in Strength of National Identity and Cultural Perception of Threat

Historical practices and institutional arrangements should not be assumed as equally important in defining the degree of national identity strength. Primordial features, for example, may not matter as much if taken out of their social and historical contexts. Most modern nation-states are multiethnic, multilingual and multireligious, which does not preclude them from relatively peaceful existence and development. Nor will territoriality or degree of economic development, taken individually, necessarily foster a nation's anti-imperial identity.

Following the above-developed logic of identity formation, I assume the primary significance of historical practices in establishing national identity of the postimperial states. It is through historical practices that the new meaning of sovereign nationhood emerged and eventually became a part of domestic political discourse capable of challenging the traditional imperial practices and authority structures. It is also through historical practices that a nation's sense of external threat(s) gets established and articulated in domestic memory and discourse. Institutions, however important, are seen here as being of secondary importance and only indirectly responsible for challenging the imperial authority structures and determining the relative strength of the periphery's nationalist feelings.[48] They provide a space for meaning distribution, but they do not produce meanings on their own. History, that is, historical practices do.[49]

On the basis of this assumption, one can construct the following variation in strength of identity and sense of threat[50] among the postimperial nations. Some nations may emerge out of empire with a well-preserved memory of national independence they had experienced before their incorporation into the empire. Their sense of commonness would be relatively well developed. Externally, they would also identify strongly with a country/region outside the empire. The institutional factors responsible for shaping the identity of these nations may vary: they may weaken the sense of national identity somewhat as well as make it stronger. The other group of postimperial nations may be weak in its national identity dimension. These nations may vary in terms of factors of secondary importance, but they would have commonly weak national identities and low senses of threat from the ex-metropole due to their lack of historical experience with independent statehood. Finally, one can imagine nations falling somewhere between the two groups in terms of strength of national identity. Although the people of this group might have some experience with independent statehood in the past, they would still differ from the first group in terms of its significance for preserving their national memories.

The above typology can be illustrated with the example of the fourteen post-Soviet nations.[51] Baltic nations (Latvia, Lithuania, and Estonia) exemplify nations with relatively strong identities and senses of being threatened by the ex-metropole (Russia).[52] Despite some variation within the group, they are similar in many important respects. They all enjoyed a quarter-century period of independent statehood before they had been incorporated into the Soviet empire in 1939. During this period they developed a particularly acute sense of belonging to the European civilization of sovereign nations, and established close economic and cultural ties with Western and Northern European nations. All this led Baltic nations to perceive their incorporation into the Soviet empire as a threat to their security and maintain a sense of their own identity, even during the Soviet occupation and despite the efforts to incorporate them culturally, not only politically and economically.

At the other extreme are Belarus, Moldova, and the five Central Asian nations. While different in many dimensions, these nations are similar in having no historical experience with independent statehood and relatively low sense of threat from the ex-metropole. These seven emerged as republics in the late 1930s, relatively late compared to other post-Soviet states, and under the initiative of Moscow. In other respects, the nations of this group vary. For example, some have difficulties in distinguishing themselves from Russia and the Soviet empire because of linguistic and religious similarity (Belarus); others have relatively large proportions of Russians residing in their territories (Kazakhstan, Kyrgyzstan, Moldova); still others are relatively homogeneous ethnically (Tajikistan, Uzbekistan, Turkmenistan).[53]

Finally, Armenia, Georgia, Ukraine, and, to a lesser extent, Azerbaijan would seem to fall somewhere between those two poles. Compared to Baltic nations, the experience of these nations with national independence was rather short-lived and fragmented, but it proved to be sufficient to develop and retain— even through the period of the Soviet empire—a set of historical myths glorifying the idea of national independence. For such reasons these nations, along with the Baltics, are sometimes referred to as "historic nations."[54] Ukraine, for one, may refer to a Cossack state that existed in the seventeenth and eighteenth centuries, as well as to a brief period of independence between 1917 and 1920, after which Moscow created the Ukrainian Soviet Socialist Republic. Georgia and Armenia may build on the period before they became a Russian protectorate, as well as on the period of their short-lived independence after the October 1917 revolution. Finally, Azerbaijan, too, was briefly independent before the Soviet incorporation. Thus, on the scale of historical experience with national independence, these four fall roughly in the middle group.[55]

Domestic Structures

Domestic structures is a variable that has been employed by scholars of foreign economic and security policies.[56] Specifically, the approach emphasizes political institutions and societal structures. Domestic structures are an important addition to the national identity variable in answering our research question for at least two reasons. First, it allows us to trace the process of interrelations between national identity and trade policy outcomes thereby checking whether this correlation is really causal, and not spurious.[57] Second and related, by tracing the process we get closer to identifying the agency through which national identity energy gets transmitted into state policies.[58] Thus, in my analysis the domestic structure is a variable that provides us with important details about the process of state economic policy formation in the former USSR, thereby allowing us to learn more about the "how" as well as the "why" aspects of the research question.[59]

Main Elements of Domestic Structures

I emphasize two main elements of domestic structures, society and state, linking the first two together in terms of their impact on policy outcomes.[60]

Society

The domestic society and its structure has various economic and cultural components. Traditionally, following most influential comparative studies of the 1950s and 1960s, the domestic society has often been studied in terms of the structure of its economic and class actors.[61] The focus on various economic actors in conceptualizing society remains in many ways central to studies of economic and political development,[62] and it was this focus that was borrowed by and remains most influential in international political economy.[63] In other areas of international studies, however, society recently came to be analyzed in terms that go beyond a composition of class or interest-based groups. In security studies, for example, explanations from the idea- and culture-based structure of society have recently become popular.[64] Overall, scholars seem to be on their way to rethinking the Weberian insight that any understanding of society should not be reduced to interest-based explanations, and that culture and culture-based coalitions are as important if we are to interpret societal process adequately.

Societal structures can vary along many dimensions, producing variations in policy outcomes. The question that is relevant for our investigation is to what extent a society is capable of generating support for a government's economic policy. We ought to know in particular the degree of societal economic and cultural polarization, the strength of social organization, and the degree to which social pressure can be mobilized in favor or against certain policies. How homo- or heterogeneous is the society in terms of ideological and/or class cleavages, and how well developed are social coalitions and organizations in their abilities to express grievances and raise demands? These are the central questions of our study.

State

For the last fifteen to twenty years, the state has been treated by many social scientists as an autonomous political actor relatively independent from social pressures in determining policy outcomes.[65] The state is now associated with instrumental institutions capable of influencing and structuring society (the state apparatus), rather than with a system that is subjected to that apparatus.[66] This narrow definition of state, with its emphasis on political institutions, came to be the most influential focus of analysis.

As with society, state can vary along many different lines relevant for understanding political outcomes. One important dimension is the state capacity or ability to mobilize required social resources in support of a policy decision which, in turn, depends on the degree of its centralization and legitimacy. The former refers to the nature of political institutions: Is executive power concentrated in the hands of one decision maker who controls the bureaucratic infighting among governmental agencies? To what extent can the government control the legislative process?[67] State legitimacy, on the other hand, refers to a symbolic dimension of capacity to extract social resources.[68] State capacity should not be confused with state strength or the degree of state intervention in the society. State capacity, as John Ikenberry has demonstrated, is about state flexibility in controlling policy outcomes. The ability to reimpose the market, for example, can be as powerful an indicator of state capacity as the ability to intervene in the economy.[69]

Depending on societal and state characteristics, they can be linked in different ways and have differing impact on policy. The relevant question here is who—society, or state, or both—is capable of setting the agenda of decision making and, therefore, controlling policy outcomes. For example, in countries with centralized political institutions but polarized societies and rather weak social organizations, the policy networks are likely to be *state-dominated*. The policy-relevant coalition building would then be restricted to the political elites and would more or less exclude societal actors. On the other hand, *societal control* of the policy networks may be expected in countries with comparatively homogeneous societies and a high degree of societal mobilization but less centralized state structures. The policy-relevant coalition building would take place among societal actors; accordingly, societal actors and public opinion would play a major role.[70]

Domestic Structures of the Postimperial Nations

Postimperial nations as a group, as argued in the previous chapter, are different from all other nations due to their lack of experience with sovereign statehood. This sovereignty deprivation leads policymakers to perceive all major problems confronting the newly independent nations, including economic ones, in the light of their preoccupation with survival or security from threats posed by the ex-metropole. In terms of postimperial domestic structures, this suggests that, at least in some cases, security-based social cleavages might be more important than purely economy-based cleavages.

Security self-determination should not be understood as having the same substance in different societies. Rather, as I have argued, it is a variable that is determined by various cultural perceptions of security threats, particularly by various national identities. This makes the Weberian insight about significance of culture-based coalitions especially relevant for adequate interpretation of policy-making processes in the postimperial societies. Simultaneously, this suggests that economic classes/interest groups-based typologies of society, still popular in international political economy, must be complemented by the analysis of culture-based cleavages. In the postimperial nations, an important social cleavage may emerge between those seeing security as national self-determination and nation building and those who argue that security cannot be provided without saving the empire and bandwagoning with the former metropole. This division between "nation builders" and "empire savers"[71] may, of course, be partly determined by elites' perceptions of political objectives and chosen strategies of achieving those objectives.[72] However, it can also be traced to the perceptions of the general public. The latter suggests the involvement of social factors, such as national memory and cultural perceptions of threats.

Earlier, I hypothesized that postimperial nations vary in their economic policies, depending on the strength of their national identities and senses of threat to
their security. After introducing domestic structures to the analysis, the process of
causality becomes clearer. Strong national identity means that people en masse
have gone through the process of mental disassociation from the empire and
identification with the separate nation. With the decline of the empire, this sense
of national difference and national Selfness gives additional stimulus to a rapid
development of movements supporting national independence or nationalist
movements.[73] Nationalists get involved in a political process of competing with
empire savers for mobilizing sufficient social support. If such support turns out to
be sufficient, nationalists have good chances of replacing the old pro-imperial
elite as a result of a coup or democratic elections and setting the agenda of economic decision making.

A state structure is another important element in our "equation," and policy
outcomes are not determined by exclusively societal pressures. States, of course,
maintain and exercise certain policy autonomy and, therefore, have room for
maneuvering in response to societal pressures. At the same time, they have to
deal with social pressures whether states are completely subject to these pressures (low-centralized state) or merely supportive of social demands in setting
the policy agenda (highly centralized state).

Types of Variation in Postimperial Domestic Structures

Applying these points requires a modification of the above-formulated typology of domestic structures. Depending on the degree of national identity strength,
domestic society can be either nationalist or empire oriented.[74] Strong national
identity produces relatively homogeneous societies mobilized around nationalist
demands and policy agenda. Conversely, a weak sense of national identity leads
to the emergence of pro-imperial societies that are likely to be particularly sensitive to calls for political and economic reintegration with the former metropole.
Lastly, a moderate degree of national identity is likely to produce a society that is
considerably less certain about its future economic and political identification
than the previous two societal types. In this society, a balance between those
favoring nation building and those in favor of maintaining the closest political-
economic relations with the former colony is likely to be generally maintained
without prevalence on either side.

To illustrate these theoretical expectations, I draw some examples from the
post-Soviet region. It should be emphasized that these examples serve the purpose of nothing more than illustrating the above-formulated typology. Baltic people may present a relatively obvious example of homogeneous nationalist-oriented society. During the first years of their independence, they had relatively
weak, low-centralized states due to the process of fundamental transformation in

their political systems. Mass-based nationalist movements, such as Popular Fronts in Latvia and Estonia and Sajudis in Lithuania, were particularly active and won a majority of seats in the national legislatures. A new, nationalist-oriented elite came to power for conducting the policy that was outlined while in opposition to the communist regime. The activists of nationalist-oriented movements have rapidly advanced to become prime ministers and presidents. The policy networks, therefore, were primarily society controlled. State, loosely speaking, can be considered low-concentrated, especially during 1990-1992 when the main institutions of communist rule were in the process of their dismantling and new ones, such as a constitution and presidency, were only emerging. State power became more consolidated and concentrated as the Baltics moved in the second half of the 1990s and stronger divisions between legislative and executive power emerged.[75]

Belarus during 1992-1994 can help to illustrate the "weak pro-imperial society/low-concentrated state" combination. Due to the weakness of nationalists, Belarus was much less persistent in its independence drive, and the dissolution of the Soviet empire caught the republic by surprise. The parliament was dominated by conservative politicians whose mindsets were formed during the Soviet era. This was somewhat compensated for by Belarus's first leader, Chairman of the Supreme Soviet Stanislav Shushkevich, whose personal political stance was that of centrism, or moderate nationalism. However, with no presidential authority established, Shushkevich lacked the ability to control a policy-making process. In 1993, his efforts to develop Belarus' institutions of independent statehood were opposed by the pro-empire-oriented Prime Minister Vyacheslau Kebich. With the support of the largest parliamentary faction, the conservative *Belarus* and the government under his control, Kebich was increasingly capable of challenging Shushkevich, making the overall policy-making process ineffective and eventually leading to Shushkevich's forced resignation in favor of active supporters of Belarus's reintegration with Russia.[76]

Ukraine may serve as a relatively good illustration of the "polarized society/highly centralized state" domestic structures. It falls between the Baltic states and Belarus in terms of degree of societal nationalist orientation. Nationalist movements such as Rukh were quite active during the Perestroika era and managed to secure nearly one-third of the seats in the 1990 elections to the republican Supreme Soviet. The nationalist ideas were eventually seized by the republic's political leadership, although the Ukrainian state has never been completely supportive of nationalist demands. The Ukrainian state proved to be much stronger compared to Belarus during 1992-1994. A presidency was established very early, with the former Supreme Soviet Chairman Leonid Kravchuk winning 62 percent of the vote in December 1991.[77] Despite a number of ethnic tensions, the state building and the concentration of presidential authority in Ukraine have generally been successful.[78]

Foreign Economic Policy

With some notable exceptions, previous studies of foreign economic policy over-looked the central question asked by this study. At least four bodies of IPE litera-ture can be identified: studies of government preferences for protectionism or trade openness; studies of strategic trade and industrial policy; studies focusing on international economic orders and the reasons for their openness or closure; and, finally, studies of economic regionalism. Each is useful yet insufficient for answering the question addressed herein.

Scholarship explaining government use of trade restrictions[79] studies how government actions were designed to facilitate or, conversely, inhibit the external flow of goods and services in general, from any country/group of countries. Build-ing on this scholarship, my study proposes to further explore how governments facilitate or inhibit external trade with one country/group of countries at the expense of the other, not of the outside world in general. In addition, it goes beyond considering unilateral government policies, such as imposing trade restric-tions, and looks at a broader set of relevant actions aimed at restructuring state economic activities, including negotiating bilateral and multilateral agreements.

The studies, which focus on strategic trade and industrial policy,[80] are also devoted to an essentially different subject. The issue here is national industrial competitiveness in the world of increasingly globalized economic relations and the extent to which government—by supporting temporary, potentially competi-tive industries and upgrading their resources and capabilities—should intervene in the process of domestic adjustments to international demands. Competitive-ness can certainly matter for national ability to restructure the external trade from one region to another, but only indirectly and with the use of additional govern-mental efforts.

The literature on openness/closure of international trade regimes[81] explains the degree of international cooperation, particularly among advanced industrial-ized countries. It is relevant for understanding domestic and systemic conditions favoring such cooperation, although much less so for understanding the reasons behind states' decisions to restructure patterns of trade activity. The literature as a whole is about international cooperation—it does not study the formation of for-eign economic policy at the national level. By focusing on international arrange-ments, it tends to disregard the fact that the attitudes of state-participants toward these arrangements are variables that should be studied on their own terms.

Finally, there is a rapidly growing body of research devoted to the political economy of regionalism,[82] which asks the questions of international cooperation as they arise in distinct geographical contexts. In particular, scholars of regional-ism are interested in learning about the reasons for the contemporary prolifera-tion of regional arrangements in Europe, Latin America, and Pacific Asia, as well as of diversity of various regions' institutional forms and degrees of trade diver-

sion rather than trade creation.[83] However, the question why some states participate in a regional arrangement while others do not has yet to be specifically
addressed by scholars of regionalism. The motivations behind states' decisions to
change or maintain their regional economic orientations still await their systematic investigation.

There are exceptions. Various foreign policy analyses addressed the research
question asked by this study, albeit in a rarely systematic way and without any
attempt to generalize the results beyond the small number of cases selected.[84] Kal
Holsti selected postwar Japan and Finland for a qualitative comparison of their
policies of restructuring trade patterns for the purpose of generating the hypothesis that "the survival or autonomy of the political community is a more fundamental value than economic maximization."[85] Holsti concluded that the two
states' economic policy options reflected the two states' preferences for military
alliances. More recently, Stephen Shulman argued that national consciousness
and nationalist movements in Quebec, India, and Ukraine may push peoples and
their states toward greater economic cooperation, rather than autarchy.[86]

My study attempts to investigate the issue further. It refers to foreign economic policy as *state action aimed at shifting a country's international economic
activities from one country/group of countries to another.* As a result of such policy, a country is expected to increase its economic activities (trade, investment,
financial capital, production) with a new country or group of countries at the cost
of decreasing it with the old one, or vice versa. By their very nature, state actions
will thus be more favorable toward some countries and less favorable toward others. For the purposes of this study, I will focus mainly on state *trade* activities
and exclude from consideration issues of redirecting investment, financial capital, labor movement and production patterns. Foreign economic policy, or a policy of economic orientation, can vary from a relatively low to a relatively high
degree of government support to deviate from a traditional pattern.

The objectives of foreign economic policy can be achieved through a number of policy instruments. The instruments available to policymakers can take the
form of unilateral as well as bilateral and multilateral actions providing the basis
for a country's increased economic cooperation with another country/group of
countries at the expense of the third side. The following list of foreign economic
policy tools is proposed in table 2.1.

Some of these instruments might be more important than others in accomplishing foreign economic reorientation. International economic agreements can
vary in terms of fostering cooperation and integration among the signatories. Both
bilateral and multilateral agreements can promote various levels of international
cooperation and integration including removing tariff and nontariff restrictions to
trade in goods and services among states (free trade agreement), to accepting a
common external tariff against nonpartners (customs union),[87] and, finally, to
completely liberalizing movements of factors of production within the union

Table 2.1. Main Foreign Economic Policy Instruments

Unilateral actions

Trade policy instruments

On import side.

1. Import quotas. By imposing high quotas on imports from country A and low quotas on imports from country B, a state encourages B and discourages A to export, thereby redirecting its commercial activities from A to B.
2. Import subsidies. By subsidizing those who import from B and not those who import from A, a state contributes to redirecting its economic activities towards B.
3. Tariffs. By imposing high tariffs in trade with country A and low ones with country B, a state encourages B and discourages A to export, thereby redirecting its commercial activities from A to B.

On export side.

4. Export quotas. By setting high quotas on exports to country A and low quotas on exports to country B, a state encourages trade with B and discourages trade with A.
5. Export subsidies. By subsidizing exporters to country A, but not to country B, a state contributes to redirecting its economic activities towards A and away from B.
6. Taxes. By setting higher export taxes in trade with country A than with country B, a state encourages trade with B and discourages trade with A. For example, by introducing VAT on exports to countries of the former Soviet Union exclusively, a country contributes to redirecting its trade away from the former Soviet republics.

Monetary instruments

7. Abandoning previously established currency regime and currency area. By abandoning previously established currency regime with country A, a country B makes financial transaction with A more complicated, thereby contributing to redirecting its economic activities away from A. An example might be an introduction of national currency and leaving a previously existed common currency regime.
8. Setting more/less favorable prices for trading. Setting higher prices in imports from country A and lower on B's goods should contribute to economic reorientation towards B and away from A, others being equal. For example, by switching from relatively low regionally set prices and introducing hard currency only transactions with the previous economic partners, a country redirects its economic activities away from the old region and towards countries beyond it.

Bilateral and multilateral actions

---

1. Negotiating quantity of commodity supplies (barter). By negotiating supplies of goods with country A and not with country B, a state redirects its trade away from B and towards A.
2. Negotiating reduction of import/export restrictions. By negotiating reduction of trade restrictions with countries A and B, but not with C and D, a state increases its commercial activities with A and B at the expense of trading with C and D.
3. Negotiating common external tariff that is higher than before. By negotiating common external tariff with countries A, B, and C, a state increases its economic activities with A, B and C and against the rest of the world.
4. Negotiating a regime for currency and payment cooperation. By setting mechanism of currency and payment coordination with countries A and B, a country increases its economic activities with A and B and against the rest of the world.
5. Negotiating reduction of capital/labor movement restrictions. By reducing restrictions for capital/labor movement in relations with countries A and B, a country increases its economic activities with A and B and against the rest of the world.

(common market). In terms of market access and restructuring external economic activities, free trade, customs union, and common market agreements, for example, are relatively more important than deal-specific types of agreements.[88]

Foreign economic policy can vary depending on state efforts to reorient a country's economic activities. Variation in a state's external economic policy can be observed via the use of the above-considered policy instruments. This study proposes that a country, geographically located between country/group A and country/group B, will redirect its commercial activities toward A and away from B if it adopts all or a substantial portion of the above-listed measures in a way preferential toward A and discriminatory toward B. More specifically, a country redirecting its commercial activities toward A and away from B may do some of the following:

1) set relatively low import quotas and tariffs in trade with A, and high with B;
2) offer subsidies to domestic producers exporting to A, but not to those to B;
3) set relatively high export quotas in trade with A, and low with B;
4) set relatively low export taxes in trade with A, and high with B;
5) abandon a previously established currency regime with A;
6) set relatively low prices for trading with A, and high with B;
7) negotiate barter supplies of goods with A, and not with B;
8) negotiate the reduction of trade restrictions with A, but not with B;
9) negotiate a common external tariff with A, but against B and the rest of the world;
10) negotiate a currency and payment regime with A, but not with B; and
11) negotiate a reduction of capital/labor movement restrictions in relations with A, but not with B.

Foreign Economic Policies of the Post-Soviet Nations

How can the previously formulated propositions be applied to the ex-Soviet nations? In addressing the question, I emphasize objectives and instruments available to policymakers as well as suggest a way of observing varying economic policy outcomes in the former Soviet region.

Before the Soviet collapse, the republics were forced to trade primarily with one another, rather than with countries outside of the Soviet borders.[89] After the breakup, the fourteen newly independent nations emerged to become international actors and, logically, faced some strategic options. First, a republic might have pursued a policy of restructuring away from the traditional area, i.e., Russia and the Commonwealth of Independent States (CIS). Second, it might have made all efforts to maintain the previously established economic ties at the expense of new partners beyond the ex-Soviet region. Finally, some intermediate strategies could have been advanced too, with measures aimed at diversifying a country's previously heavily concentrated economic ties, but without the intent of breaking away from the traditional area of economic activities.

Each of these policies or strategies requires certain policy instruments. In the former Soviet region, the following tools became widely used for accomplishing the identified goals. These tools can be loosely structured as those minimizing economic ties with some partners at the expense of others; finding potential new partners and establishing necessary domestic institutions for switching trade toward new partners; and securing relations with new partners (see table 2.2). Each of the three above-identified economic policy patterns can be found in the former Soviet region among the ex-Soviet republics.

Some nations directed their economic activities primarily toward Russia and other former members of the Soviet state. They showed little desire to search for alternative trading partners and instead committed themselves to transforming the CIS into a regional economic union. Belarus, Kyrgyzstan, and Kazakhstan represent this group.

Other nations choose to become full-fledged members of the world economy and to find new, primarily Western partners. Despite being closely connected with Russia and other ex-Soviet republics, and even economically dependent on them (oil and gas dependence on Russia is the most obvious aspect), these nations became the strongest proponents of economic reorientation away from traditional partners and toward new ones. The Baltic nations became the strongest proponents of this type of policy. By 1993-1994, Lithuania, Latvia, and Estonia had signed a number of trade agreements with northern European nations

Table 2.2. The Ex-Soviet Republics: Foreign Economic Policy Instruments

---

For minimizing economic ties with A:
1. Setting relatively high restrictions for imports from A
2. Setting relatively high restrictions for exports to A
3. Banning barter trade and abandoning previously established currency regime with A
4. Abstaining from entering preferential economic agreements with A as a participant

---

For establishing domestic institutions for market-oriented activities:
1. Lifting trading quotas and restrictions
2. Macroeconomic stabilization, which includes liberalization of prices and establishment of a foreign exchange system

---

For maximizing economic ties with B:
1. Setting relatively low restrictions for imports from B
2. Setting relatively low restrictions for exports to B
3. Negotiating bilateral preferential agreements with B
4. Negotiating multilateral preferential agreement with B (but not A) as a participant
5. Negotiating barter and specific-deal arrangements with B

---

and established the necessary domestic institutions for launching successful market-oriented foreign economic activities.

Finally, there were nations falling between those two poles in terms of their foreign economic policies. They saw the reorientation as strategically important, but unfeasible in a short-term perspective. Accordingly, the policy course eventually chosen was one of a "lesser evil"—cooperation with Russia and other CIS members, while gradually preparing to become a competitive participant in the world economy. These nations maintained their relationship with Russia and the CIS and, while not committing themselves to the CIS as a customs union, they stressed the importance of good relations with Russia and other CIS members. Also unlike the Baltic nations, they were slow in establishing domestic economic institutions necessary for shifting their economic patterns toward Western countries. Ukraine, Azerbaijan, Turkmenistan, and some other nations may be seen as falling into this category.

For the purpose of observing the republics' policies and their outcomes, this study will look separately at their policies vis-à-vis Russia and the CIS, on the one hand, and countries beyond the ex-Soviet area, on the other. The objective basis for judgments about the extent of the ex-Soviet republics' reorientation will be the amount of restrictions maintained by them in economic relations with the Russia/CIS pole and established as a result of negotiated bilateral and multilateral preferential agreements or unilateral governmental actions. Additionally, the study will consider the efforts undertaken by the ex-Soviet republics to establish domestic institutions for conducting market-oriented activities.

Notes

1. For other more recent efforts to adopt a national identity perspective in international studies, see, especially, Lapid and Kratochwil 1996; Katzenstein 1996; Krause and Williams 1997; Prizel 1998.

2. Here and elsewhere, I distinguish between "nation" and "state" as units of analysis. Whereas "nation" refers to identity of a nation as a whole, "state" is associated mainly with bureaucratic apparatus or institutions capable of influencing society. The "Domestic Structure" section returns to this point.

3. Almond and Powell 1966, 50; Mackenzie 1978, 12; Dijkink 1996. The affective orientations should be distinguished from other dimensions of political culture: cognitive orientations (knowledge and beliefs about political objects), on the one hand, and evaluative orientations (judgments and opinions about political objects), on the other (Almond and Powell 1966, 50).

4. Further clarification of relationships between *national* and *ethnic* deserves a more extended treatment and should be a subject of special analysis. For our purpose, it is sufficient to emphasize the *national* dimension of political identity. It is important to note, however, that *national* and *ethnic* have points of similarity and cannot be entirely separated from each other. The sense of nation is rarely shared across various ethnic groups in

equal amount. Especially at earlier stages of society building, one or a few ethnic groups can exert a particularly strong influence on the rest of a society, thereby playing a strategic role in establishing an "imagined political community."

5. Anderson 1991, 6.

6. Weber 1978, 903. See Smith 1993, 14; Tamir 1995, 425; Haas 1997, 23 for similar constructivist definitions.

7. I borrow this formulation of inclusiveness versus exclusiveness from Migdal 1997, 230.

8. A good place to go to learn more about identity as a highly contested concept is David Laitin's (1998) recent study *Identity in Formation*. The author argues that the Russian-speakers in the post-Soviet republics are facing a radical crisis of identity because these republics' center did not hold.

9. Historical practices are referred here as various facts, events and experiences nations go through during their development.

10. Something that some scholars referred to as "double backing of social process" (Alker 1997, 390) and others as "repertoires of social categories" (Laitin 1998, 17).

11. My thinking about process of identity construction was influenced by Martha Finnemore's and Kathryn Sikkink's (1998) theorizing about a norm's "life cycle," as well as David Laitin's (1998) study of ethnic identity crisis and formation.

12. For good overviews of various insights of psychological and social psychological literature, see Berger and Luckmann 1966; Bloom 1990; Neumann 1997.

13. Some scholars suggested that the Other in nations' identity formation is the discourse of international politics as anarchy (Ashley 1987; Walker 1988; Der-Derian and Shapiro 1989; Wendt 1992, 1999). Others related the nation's identity process with its state's foreign policy practice and foreign policy debates (Todorov 1984; Dalbi 1988; Campbell 1992; Neumann 1996).

14. Some scholars studied how national political integration and nation-building has been formed in the process of solving the tasks of economic and political modernization (For overviews, see Huntington and Dominguez 1975; Ross 1997). Others traced varying national strategies of adjustment to international economic change. (See, for example, Katzenstein 1977; Ikenberry 1986; Simmons 1996.) Still other studies drew attention to the contested nature of the nation-building process by revealing its conflicting implications for various social and cultural groups. (See, for example, Charlton, Everett, and Straudt 1989; Tickner 1992; Elshtain 1995.)

15. Exceptions include the volume edited by Adler and Crawford (1992), as well as the literature on learning, in which the issue of progressive identity change has been considered ("complex learning" as contrasted to "simple learning"), albeit in a brief, unsystematic way and with no reference to the "national identity" problematique (see, for example, Nye 1987; Breslauer and Tetlock 1991; Mendelson 1993). One promising way to develop a research agenda for studying identity change is to incorporate insights from recent constructivist literature (Finnemore 1993; Klotz 1995; Katzenstein 1996a; Finnemore 1996) into the learning (regimes and epistemic community) literature. For a noteworthy attempt to move in this direction, see Knopf 1998.

16. These are the issues that some West European nations are especially concerned with while considering joining the European Union. Rather than being worried about the physical survival of their national entities, the Europeans are preoccupied with maintaining

their cultural and institutional specifics in a highly complex and increasingly globalized web of political and economic meanings.

17. This is not to say that the postimperial nations necessarily seek security from the ex-metropole. Assuming the existence of other powerful actors in world politics, the postimperial or newly independent nations may be subjected to other equally threatening influences as far as their newly acquired sovereignty is concerned.

18. On this, see Eistenstadt 1963; Eisenstadt 1967; Seton-Watson 1977; Doyle 1986; Laitin 1991; Smith 1993; Kaiser 1994; Dawisha and Parrott 1997.

19. I am well aware of the limitations related with attempts to trace variation in national identity in terms of its strength. National identity is a variable rich in qualitative substance. It is a variable that is fuzzy, complex, and multidimensional. Yet, in my opinion, this is true of any ideational phenomena and should not preclude us from trying to emphasize those dimensions that are of particular relevance in learning about causal connections. It is in the interests of being more socially scientific that we must not limit ourselves to a discussion of exclusively qualitative or quantitative dimensions of national identity.

20. The literature on identities widely accepts the proposition that there is an important relationship between identity and construction of the threat (see, for instance, Bloom 1990, 32-53; Connolly 1992; Campbell 1992; Neumann 1992; Katzenstein 1996, esp.19-26, 37-49, 403-413; Weiver et al. 1997).

21. Ever since the Peace of Westphalia, the system of international relations has been in the process of its progressive development toward the global ascendancy of national sovereignty and away from traditional imperial polities (see, Seton-Watson 1977; Giddens 1985; Motyl 1992b; Dawisha and Parrott 1997). Not surprisingly, for the former imperial nations, the world of empires and the world of sovereign nations are fundamentally conflictual, and perhaps incompatible, as long as an empire "denotes a dominant society's control of the effective sovereignty of two or more subordinate societies" (Parrott 1997, 7). Conceptually, this conflict between the two systems of authority relationships was recognized by many scholars of empires, nationalism, and state building. (See, for example, Seton-Watson 1977, chaps. 6-8; Doyle 1986; Strange 1996; Dawisha and Parrott 1997; Barkey and von Hagen 1997.)

22. This can only be true holding many other things equal. Some nations that had a little experience with independence may still perceive the metropole as threatening if they are fundamentally different from the metropole on some other dimensions. If given historical chance, these difference may play out against the metropole and contribute to the process of national identity formation. The example might be cultural differences between the metropole and periphery (language, religion, etc.) which may help to explain why some parts of an empire succeed relatively early while others stick to the metropole until its very breakdown. For instance, the fact that Greece won its independence from the Ottoman empire as early as in 1829 while Romania and Bulgaria did so almost a half century later (Rustow 1997, 190) may have more to do with the relative strength of Greek *ethnic*, anti-Turkish identification, and less to do with the Greek national independence experience.

23. It is worth emphasizing that the world of sovereign nations itself is far from homogeneous, and a postimperial nation, that feels threatened by the ex-metropole, faces a choice with whom to identify externally. The decision regarding such identification is likely to be infuenced, in part, by history of the nation's relations with various countries outside the empire.

24. For earlier attempts to study policy making, particularly economic policy making as driven by nationalist aspirations, see Breton 1964; Johnson 1965, 1967. For more recent analysis, see Shulman 2000.

25. This observation goes back to Weberian central insight that social action can only be understood if investigators take into account its meaning for those involved (Weber 1978). For attempts to add to rational choice approaches to economic policy by accounting for effects of individual, rather than socially held, beliefs, see especially Odell 1982, 1988; Hall 1989; Goldstein and Keohane 1993; Woods 1995; McNamara 1997.

26. The expression is taken from Geertz 1973.

27. For a more extended theoretical discussion of the constitutive versus regulative norms, see, Wendt 1999. Valerie M. Hudson offered a somewhat similar way of conceptualizing the effects of culture on foreign policy by distinguishing among culture as shared meaning, culture as value preferences, and culture as a template for human action (1996, 7-19). For empirical applications, see especially Klotz 1995; Finnemore 1996; Katzenstein 1996a, 1996b.

28. For a theoretical discussion of sensemaking in organizational studies, see March and Olsen 1989, 39-52; Weick 1995.

29. Berger 1996; Katzenstein 1996b; Duffield 1998.

30. Martha Finnemore and Kathryn Sikkink suggested that cultural norms can have different influences depending on what stage of their "life cycle"—emergence, cascade, or internalization—they are in (1998, 895-96).

31. March and Olsen 1989, 24.

32. *Ibid.*, 25.

33. *New York Times*, February 11, 1997, A6.

34. The next section will consider this issue in more detail, classifying postimperial nations with well-developed, poorly-developed and an intermediate sense of national identity in terms of their domestic structures and coalition-building processes.

35. To a certain degree, such assessments of economic viability will be culturally based, as well.

36. See, for example, Emerson 1960, 95; Weber 1978, 903; Bloom 1990, 52; Smith 1993, 11.

37. Of course this differentiation in no way implies a nation's exclusiveness or isolation. A nation interrelates with others in variety of ways: it trades, fights, communicates via mail and traveling, allows migrations and cultural exchanges, etc., thereby developing its external identification (Deutsch 1979, 1981). A nation also reaches out externally when its primordial cultural characteristics (especially language and religion) are shared across the board (Brubaker 1995; Huntington 1996). The originally established cohesiveness and distinctness, however, allows a nation to maintain its identity in a highly complex web of international ties.

38. Stalin [1905] 1994; Smith 1986, 163; Taylor 1989; Kaiser 1994; Coleman 1995; Dijkink 1996.

39. Deutsch 1966, 105.

40. For the argument that distinct political institutions are critically important in mobilizing periphery and determining the stage of its independence, see Doyle 1986, 92-95, 369-71.

41. An example might be the independence of a peripheral Church from the metropole which, others being equal, can facilitate the rise of peripheral nationalism. For an account of how this may occur, see Levi and Hechter 1985.

42. For various accounts of the Soviet federalism and its effects on the republics' identity and the system's stability, see Lapidus 1984; Gleason 1990; Roeder 1991; Slezkine 1996; Brubaker 1996, 23-55.

43. Doyle 1986, 370.

44. Many scholars endorse this argument. For examples, see Gurr and Harff 1994, 91; Coleman 1995, 12; Wintrobe 1995, 65; Barkey 1997.

45. The term comes from Geertz [1963] 1994.

46. It is worth noting that even primordial features are not exactly primordial. They do change over time and in response to certain historically contingent events. Not surprisingly, primordial features are often invoked in a struggle of nationalists for mobilizing social support for their historically and socially constructed claims for the right of having "their own" state. For the argument that ethnic identity is a reflection of autonomous political choice, see Armstrong 1988. For the analyses of exploitation of primordial features and of religion and language-based nationalisms, see Laitin 1991, 1998; Van Evera 1994; Juergensmeyer 1996. For extending primordial, mainly religion-based argument to the analysis of civilizations, see Huntington 1996.

47. For the argument about importance of ethnicity and cultural unity for understanding consequences of Ottoman, Habsburg, Russian and Soviet empire and imperial break-up, see Barkey 1997.

48. Peripheral nationalists may not be united along ethnic lines and still share their anti-imperial feelings. On the other hand, after winning independence and at earlier stages of society building, the role of one or several ethnic groups may be particularly important in establishing an "imagined political community." At later stages, however, the sense of nation, although still rarely shared across various ethnic groups in equal amount, may become more evenly distributed across the nation as a whole.

49. Ethnic identity, for example, does not yet constitute national identity, it simply implies a combination of shared territorial and primordial characteristics.

50. For the work that emphasized the sense of threat from the dominant ethnic group in development of postimperial nationalism and national identity, see especially Shulman 2000.

51. All of the former Soviet republics, with the exception of Russia. As the former hegemon, Russia is incompatible with the NIS in its institutions and perceptions of the outside world and is therefore excluded from the analysis. In constructing my classification, I found useful typologies of post-Soviet and post-Communist nations offered in the following works: Rakowska-Harmstone 1974; Armstrong 1988; Brzezinski 1989/1990; Szporluk 1992; Suny 1993; Dawisha and Parrott 1994; *RFE/RL RR*, 1993-95; Chinn and Kaiser 1996; Bremmer and Taras 1997; Brzezinski 1997.

52. Arguably East European nations, the former Soviet bloc members can be also considered part of the group if one wishes to extend the analysis beyond the former Soviet republics. They are comparable with Baltics in having a significant historical experience beyond the Soviet empire and identifying strongly with the European civilization of sovereign nations and Europe as a region. In addition, they exercised more control over their domestic policy making and, while their domestic political institutions varied substantially

(Comisso and Tyson 1986), overall these institutions were distinctly stronger than those of the ex-Soviet republics.

53. For data from 1989, see Bremmer and Taras 1997, 706-707.

54. Brzezinski 1997, 128. For the argument about Ukraine as a historic nation, see Bilinsky 1992; Burant 1995.

55. On other dimensions relevant for national identity formation, they differ. For example, Ukraine is similar to Russia in terms of language, religion and appearance; Georgia and Armenia are Orthodox countries, as is Russia, but Azerbaijan is predominantly Muslim. Azerbaijan and Armenia are also much more ethnically homogenous than are Georgia and Ukraine.

56. The literature that analyses the foreign policy outcomes as a function of domestic politics is rapidly growing. See, for example, Migdal 1974; Katzenstein 1978; Hall 1986; Gourevich 1986; Evangelista 1988; Mastanduno, Lake, Ikenberry 1989; Snyder 1989; Ayoob 1991; David 1991; Risse-Kappen 1991; Milner 1992; Checkel 1993; Evans, Jacobson, Putnam 1993; Rosecrance and Stein 1993; Risse-Kappen 1995; Peterson 1996; Milner 1997; Knopf 1998.

57. On process tracing and the analysis of "mechanisms" that enable causes to produce effects, see, George 1982; Yee 1996; Van Evera 1997, 64-67.

58. This may reduce the limitation of recently developed norms and identity explanations of state behavior. For criticism of these approaches on the grounds that they of attention to agency, see Kowert and Legro 1996, 492-95; Checkel 1997.

59. These two sides are, in my opinion, intimately related and can only be meaningfully separated on a highly general epistemological level. When it comes to empirical investigation, however, a causal analysis is incomplete without telling the "how" side of the story. On the other hand, well-performed and empirically oriented interpretive investigations are always suggestive in terms of further causal analysis and can be viewed as complementary rather than hostile to positivist-like investigations. (For the argument contrasting these two approaches, see Taylor 1977; Hollis and Smith 1991; Neufeld 1993; for the argument about their complimentarity, see Weber 1977; Price 1994; Price and Tannenwald 1996, 124-26, 151-52.)

60. My approach to domestic structures has been particularly influenced by Thomas Risse-Kappen's framework (1991, 1995), which encompasses both institutional structures and coalition-building processes.

61. Many scholars traced how the composition of societal actors may affect the growth trajectories, paths to modernization, stability of political institutions, and types of political system. (See especially, Lipset 1960; Gerschenkron 1962; Moore 1965; Huntington 1968.)

62. See, for example, Mares 1985; Robison 1988; O'Donnell 1988; Przeworski 1991; Poznanski 1992; Silva 1993; Olsen 1993; Haggard and Kaufman 1995; Maravall 1997.

63. See especially Katzenstein 1978; Gourevich 1986; Ikenberry 1986; Rogowski 1989; Keohane and Milner 1996.

64. Snyder 1991; Jonston 1995; Chilton in Risse-Kappen 1995; Peterson 1996; McAdam, McCarthy, and Zald 1996; Herman in Katzenstein 1996.

65. This notion of state autonomy was first introduced by Max Weber in his well-known definition (1978, 54), but was later abandoned in favor of elite- (Mills 1956; Putnam 1976) and systems-based (Parsons 1963; Easton 1965) analyses. Since the late 1970s, the state has been brought back in (Katzenstein 1978; Krasner 1978; Skocpol 1979; Nor-

dlinger 1981; Evans, Rueschemeyer, and Skocpol 1985) and is now widely considered to be an important addition to society-based explanations (and not something subsumed by those explanations).

66. Biersteker 1990, 180.

67. Katzenstein 1977, 3-22, 295-336; Risse-Kappen 1991; Peterson 1996, chap. 1.

68. In part, legitimacy is linked to institutions, but more often it implies degree of social trust given to these institutions, to a state leader personally and to policies that are implemented within established institutional framework (Weber 1978; Fukuyama 1995). Barry Buzan's distinction between the idea of the state and the institutional expression of the state is relevant here (see Buzan 1991, 65).

69. Ikenberry 1986, 133, 135. Besides, state intervention in the economy varies widely. Thomas Biersteker, for example, identified six forms of such intervention: influence, regulation, mediation, distribution, production, and planning (1990).

70. Risse-Kappen 1991, 486; Peterson 1996, 31.

71. Roman Szporluk formulated the distinction for the analysis of domestic divisions in Russia, the metropole. "Empire savers" equate Russia's greatness with domination over neighboring people while "nation builders" believe that Russia should reconcile with the loss of empire and achieve its proper place by concentrating on domestic needs (Szporluk 1989). The distinction, however, has wider implications and may be applied for the post-imperial nations in general, including those that have broken away from the metropole.

72. For various analyses of national elites' political strategies vis-à-vis the ex-metropole and the external environment in general, see Rogowski 1985; Snyder 1991, 1993; Posen 1993; Snyder and Karen Ballentine 1996; Treisman 1997.

73. One of the most popular definitions of nationalism links it with a doctrine claiming that the state and the nation should be congruent (see Gellner 1983, chap. 1; Rogowski 1985).

74. For the sake of focusing discussion on national identity-based cleavages, I abstract from other social cleavages, such as those ethnically and income-based ones. It is worth noting, however, that such homogeneity of a society in sharing commitment to national independence does not exclude its heterogeneity in many other respects. A society, for example, can be mobilized around nationalists and yet divided along socioeconomic lines.

75. An example of such divisions can be debates over citizenship laws in 1997-98 in Latvia, with parliament pushing for more discriminatory regulations vis-à-vis Russian speakers and president defending a more moderate version of the law.

76. See, for example, Markus 1995a, 47.

77. Motyl and Krawchenko 1997, 269.

78. *Ibid.*, 258-59.

79. Schattschneider 1935; Milner 1988; Lake 1988; Eichengreen 1989; Goldstein 1993; O'Halloran 1994.

80. Milner and Yoffie 1989; Richardson 1990; Porter 1990; Prestowitz 1992; Tyson 1992.

81. Krasner 1976; Ruggie 1982; Yarbrough and Yarbrough 1987; Grieco 1990; Gowa 1994.

82. See especially Frankel and Kahler 1993; Stalling 1995; Mols 1996; Mansfield and Milner 1997.

83. The formulation of trade diversion versus trade creation in the context of studying the issue of economic regionalism goes back to Jakob Viner's seminal work on customs unions (1950).

84. See, for example, Burant 1995; Kulinich, 1995; Webber 1997.

85. *Ibid.*, 669.

86. Shulman 2000.

87. If tariffs and other trade restrictions are applied it is crucial to know in this case what particular country/region this policy is discriminative against. It is this knowledge of geographic orientation that becomes of particular relevance rather than simple knowledge of how "high" or "low" trade restrictions are.

88. In addition to those listed above, there might be instruments aimed at encouraging or discouraging trade in services (banking, financial capital, foreign direct investment) with certain countries, regulating cross border labor movement, or reorienting production structure away from one region and toward another. In principle, all of them qualify for conducting policy of restructuring economic activities and can therefore be included into the list of foreign economic policy instruments. For the purposes of this study, however, I limit myself to the previously listed items relevant for restructuring foreign trade activities.

89. The share of inter-republican trade comprised up to 85-90 percent of the republics' total trade (Bradshaw 1993, 29.)

Chapter 3
Latvia

Latvia was one of the first of the ex-Soviet republics to choose to become a full-fledged member of the world economy and to find new, primarily Western, economic partners. Despite being closely connected with Russia and other ex-Soviet republics, even economically dependent on them (oil and gas dependence on Russia is the most obvious aspect), Latvia chose against entering the Russia-dominated CIS or directing its trade toward Russia and CIS countries. Instead, by 1993-1994, Latvia, accompanied by other Baltic nations, designed an ambitious strategy to establish close economic relations with the Western European nations. As a result, by 1996 its trade with European Union (EU) members comprised 47 percent of total trade, while its trade with Russia decreased from about half to only 21.5 percent (see table 3.2 on pages 60-61). To understand the sources and the nature of Latvian economic policies, I begin with the analysis of Latvian identity formation as reflected in its history. I then turn to the effects of the republic's national identity on domestic politics and—through it—on international economic policies toward Russia and CIS states, on the one hand, and the nations beyond the ex-Soviet region, on the other.

National Identity

National identity, as argued in the previous chapter, is a product of a country's external and domestic history. Latvian identity was formed around its experience with independent statehood during the interwar period, and it is this experience that primarily, although not exclusively, accounts for the relatively high degree of strength of the country's national identity. It is during this period that Latvia makes significant progress in internalizing the norm of sovereignty and identifying itself with European sovereign nations, while at the same time disassociating itself from its last imperial ruler, Russia. Latvia's other characteristics—relative stability of geopolitical borders, (sub)political institutions, economic cohesiveness, and cultural features—affected the acquired sense of identity in their own way serving as domestic filters transmitting the influence of the sovereignty norm.

The Experience with Independent Statehood and the Persistent National Memory

When Mikhail Gorbachev came to power and initiated the policy of perestroika, the "point of departure" for Latvian nationalists in their struggle for independence was "the fact of the existence of the Republic of Latvia, an independent state that had been demolished in 1940."[1] Indeed, unlike most of the ex-Soviet republics, Latvia was independent during the interwar period. It became independent in 1918, in the aftermath of the Russian Revolution. Before then, Latvia was for almost two centuries a province of the Russian empire. The cultural influences of Northern and Central European countries—most notably Germany and Sweden—that had previously ruled parts of Latvia[2] persisted, however, and in the late nineteenth century it was in part those influences that gave rise to demands for autonomy within the empire. In November 1918, after the fall of the Russian empire, the Young Latvian Movement, Latvia's most active nationalist movement, which promoted Latvian autonomy within the confines of the Russian empire, initiated the declaration of the independent Republic of Latvia. By 1922, despite armed resistance from the Bolsheviks and local Germans, the independent government of Latvia managed to win full control of the country. All attributes of nationhood, including international recognition, a constitution, an electoral system, the state's official language, and an independent foreign policy, were established.[3]

In August 1940, however, Latvia's, as well as Lithuania's and Estonia's, period of independence was also terminated following the signing of the Nazi-Soviet pact in August 1939. The pact's secret protocols defined respective spheres of influence, with the Baltics falling within Moscow's area. Fifty years of colonial status led to dramatic changes in Latvia's domestic economy and composition of trade. Together with other nations, Latvia was remote from the decision-making process at the center and could hardly influence its policies at the regional level.[4] The Soviet regime also did its best to pursue policies of Russification and Sovietization. Mass deportation of Balts to Siberia and the large-scale influx of Slavs were examples of this policy.

Yet the sense of a Latvian national identity was by no means eliminated. For Latvia, the twenty-year period proved to be sufficient to internalize the international norm of sovereign nationhood and develop a sense of its own national self. The flagrant manner in which Latvia was incorporated into the USSR could not abolish the fact that it had developed identification with European independent nations, and not with Russian empire (of which it was a part before the October Revolution). Consistent with identification theory, Latvia had absorbed a socially relevant knowledge and meaning from its significant Other (European independent nations) and could only perceive the incorporation into the empire as a threat to its acquired identity. Not surprisingly, the incorporation caused many attempts at resistance to Soviet rule[5] and only exacerbated the Latvian sense of "non-Russianness" or "non-Sovietness." The irony, as one analyst observed, was that "the period of Soviet occupation strengthened nationalism among the Baltic people to a degree it never would have attained under independent political existence."[6]

> For the Baltic peoples... it is not only a fact that the inter-war years symbolize the fulfillment of their nationalist dream of self-determination. The brutal Communist regime after 1940 has made that period stand out in contrast as the golden era of freedom and progress... Rather than producing an identification with the Soviet state, fifty years of Russian Communist rule in the Baltic states had resulted in an identification with an almost mythical Europe. Russia and the Soviet Union came to stand for all things evil, Europe for everything that was good and worth striving for.[7]

There are many examples indicating Latvia's resistance to Sovietization and language Russification. For one, Latvia was relatively successful in resisting pressures of Russification, a direct threat to its cultural identity. Despite the large influx of Russian speakers during the years of occupation, Latvia did significantly better than Moldova, Ukraine, and Belarus in preserving its own language (see table 3.1). But perhaps even more telling are historical attempts of Latvians to restore the "historical justice" and to return the "freedom" from the empire. Two of those attempts deserve a special mention; they reflected the existing strength of national memory, but also contributed to it by the very fact of their existence.

The first attempt came in 1941, with the outbreak of the World War II being used by Latvia, as well as Lithuania and Estonia, for the purpose of restoring independence from the Soviet empire. Two separate quasi-governmental bodies, the Central Organizing Committee for Liberated Latvia and the Provisional State Council, were formed and tolerated by the newly established German regime. At one point, Latvian politicians were ready to collaborate with the Nazis and proposed the formation of a Latvian army to fight the USSR in exchange for the establishment of a formally independent nation entity, albeit one with somewhat circumscribed sovereignty.[8]

Table 3.1. Linguistic Situation in Latvia, Ukraine, and Belarus, 1989

	Latvia	Ukraine	Belarus
Ethnic Russians (percent)	34	22	13
Russian as mother tongue for persons of titular nationality (including diaspora in other republics) (percent)	5	18.8	28.5
Kindergartens with Russian as the language instruction (percent)	38.8	40.2	72.7
Students in schools with Russian as the medium of instruction (percent)	47.6	51.8	79.2
Library collections (percent)			
Russian	47	61	82
Titular nationality language	46	38	16
Newspapers (number of copies per issue, in thousands)			
Russian	764	8,044	3,579
Titular nationality language	2,008	15,682	1,773
Book published (number of copies, in thousands)			
Russian	3,518	91,683	48,133
Titular nationality language	13,110	95,231	9,404

Sources: Prazauskas 1994, 152-153; Bremmer and Taras 1997, 714-15.

In the aftermath of Stalin's death, Latvians again tried to mobilize national sentiments and implement more independent economic and political policies using a period of the regime decentralization. Led by Eduards Berklavs, Deputy Chairman of the Council of Ministers, Latvian authorities attempted to assert more control over the republic by slowing the influx of Slavic settlers, promoting native cadres, expanding the use of the Latvian language in the education system and in party affairs, and increasing republican autonomy in management of the economy. The attempt was terminated in 1959, when Berklavs was charged with "bourgeois nationalism" and purged from the party and the country.[9]

Latvia's interwar experience with independence in many ways thus determined how the people of Latvia situated themselves vis-à-vis the empire, on the one hand, and the outside world, on the other. The period served as a basis for internalizing the sovereignty norm. More than twenty years of practicing independent domestic and foreign policies established a certain cultural context that could not have been destroyed by a forceful incorporation into the empire. Feelings of being culturally alien persisted and proved to be strong enough to generate powerful nationalist sentiments that were quickly mobilized with the decline of the empire.

Other Factors Affecting Latvian Identity

The experience with independent nationhood, however important, was not the only factor affecting how strongly Latvians identified with their nation. To obtain a more complete picture of Latvia's identity formation, one must look at how the externally imbued cultural meanings traveled domestically, particularly after Latvia had been subjected to the imperial rule. To do that, the nation's domestic institutions—territorial, political, economic, and cultural—should also be considered. Some of these institutions strengthened Latvia's identity while others weakened it. A detailed analysis of these institutions' evolution and effects on national identity formation would constitute the subject of a separate study; for our purposes, a brief review will suffice.

As an ethnic group, Latvians have had relatively stable geopolitical borders since the eigteenth century. Two events essentially contributed to the emergence of "territorial Latvia." In the early eighteenth century, the southwestern part of Latvia was annexed by Russia as a result of Peter the Great's victory over the Swedish army, and in 1773 eastern Latvia was also incorporated into the Russian empire.[10] Since then, for over 200 years Latvia's territorial borders have remained generally unchanged,[11] creating a sense of territorial belongingness and distinctiveness.

Latvia was much less lucky in preserving its political institutions. During the interwar years, Latvia made considerable progress in developing its own political institutions (e.g., constitution, national government, and political parties). The incorporation into the Soviet empire, however, meant a breaking point in Latvia's political institution building. Its national institutions were replaced with those typical of the Soviet regime. Moscow imposed its control over foreign and domestic affairs through the Communist party networks. Yet, as significant a setback as it was, Soviet rule did leave some room for preserving Latvia's institutional autonomy. Soviet federalism gave privileges to ethnic Latvians,[12] and quasi-political institutions (republican governments, Supreme Soviets, flags, etc.) helped the republic to maintain a sense of a quasi-state unit, thereby providing institutional room for preserving Latvia's national memory.

Economic development was another important factor affecting Latvia's national identity formation. It played a paradoxical role, however. On the one hand, the fact that Latvia was one of the most urbanized and industrialized republics in the USSR helped to transform the society into a more cohesive and uniform national entity. On the other hand, economic modernization in Latvia undoubtedly undermined its ethnic identity, as it was largely designed by Moscow planners, without any respect to its ethnic composition and with the use of extensive influx of ethnic Russians.[13]

The latter leads us to yet another potentially important factor in the formation of Latvia's sense of unity/distinctness—its ethnic and religious composition. The large influx of Russians, the "imperialists," has negatively affected

Latvia's sense of national unity. In 1991, ethnic Latvians comprised only 52.5 percent of the population, while 34 percent were ethnic Russians (see table 3.1).[14] It is no accident that Russians, by and large, decided against participation in Latvian nationalist organizations and instead preferred either to stay neutral or even add their support to empire-saving voices. A poll taken in late 1988 indicated, for example, that 48 percent of Russians in Latvia believed there was a need for Interfront, an empire-saving organization, compared to a mere 6 percent of Latvians.[15]

To summarize, Latvia's national identity was built around its experience with independence during the interwar period. By the time of its incorporation into the Soviet empire, the people of Latvia had already acquired a coherent sense of being different. It was unified and distinct as an independent nation with clear territorial borders, strong political institutions, and, at the time, a relatively homogenous ethnic population. Furthermore, its close geographic proximity to Europe and historically extensive foreign ties with European, particularly North European countries, created a distinct dynamic of external identification with Europe rather than with Russia. The experience of being part of the USSR in some ways undermined, but in others strengthened, a sense of distinctness among the people of Latvia. By the time of Gorbachev's perestroika, these feelings of distinctness and alienation from the empire were vastly exacerbated by Latvia's perceived economic backwardness relative to Sweden and Finland, countries that before World War II were at a relatively similar level of development.[16] The strength of Latvia's national identity helps to illuminate the domestic political dynamics of Latvia in the late twentieth century, particularly how and why nationalists managed to gain control over the policy-making process.

Domestic Structures

In Latvia, nationalist-oriented movements proved themselves to be capable of mobilizing the society and eventually gaining control over the policy-making process. In contrast, the empire savers had relatively weak social support and little ability to influence policy making. Before nationalists came to power and began implementing their foreign economic policy vision, they had had to mobilize the society and defeat the empire savers in the domestic struggle.

Society

Latvia's late-twentieth century society can be seen as composed of two main groups, each with distinct political orientations: the nationalists and the empire savers.

Nationalists

Nationalist-oriented movements, or the movements committed to Latvia's full-fledged independence from the USSR, started to emerge in Latvia in 1988, when Moscow-initiated reforms were well under way and an unofficial grass-roots activism had gained prominence.[17] Two major organizations were established: the national Independence Movement and the Popular Front.[18] The more radical Independence Movement immediately pronounced the restoration of the independence of the Republic of Latvia founded in 1918, thereby making itself the target of attacks by hard-line Communists and the Soviet press.[19] The Popular Front was established a few months later than the Independence Movement, and with more modest goals. Its first program spoke of "sovereignty" for the Latvian Soviet Socialist Republic rather than the restoration of the independent Republic of Latvia.[20] The variation in pursued goals stemmed in part from the two movements' social bases. While the Independence Movement was formed by people who had previously worked in the political underground,[21] the Popular Front was more mainstream and had strong support among the Party members. Symptomatically, in October 1988 when the Front emerged, one-third of the delegates of its founding congress were members of the Communist Party.[22]

The fact that Latvian nationalism emerged relatively early and pursued a relatively bold agenda (when compared with other non-Baltic republics) had a lot to do with support given to it by society during the Soviet era. In one way or another, various social stratums were supportive of broadly defined nationalist goals. In the words of historians,

> Dissent—disagreement with or opposition to the system—was, almost by definition, endemic within the Baltic republics... A whole spectrum of individuals, encompassing a major portion of the Baltic populations, could be characterized as falling within this group, and their general goal was shared by, among others, passive nationalists seeking to preserve and maximize the national forms of the Soviet system, members of the intelligentsia striving to enrich the national cultures and thus make them attractive and immune to denationalization, and even some national Communists. All seemed to be striving for an improvement within the system.[23]

Gorbachev's Perestroika became a great opportunity for nationalist-oriented movements. Many of them viewed the twentieth century as the "age of decolonization" and, thus, as strong evidence in the case against the continued existence of empires, including the Soviet one.[24] One of the first nationalist activities was the organization in August 1987 of mass demonstrations on the anniversary of the Nazi-Soviet pact. In two years, the Popular Front of the Baltic republics arranged the "Baltic chain" as a symbol of protest against the pact, which led to the long-awaited official Soviet acknowledgment of the existence of the secret protocols.[25] In October 1989, the Popular Front declared the goal of "complete independence"[26] and, in March 1990, nationalist movements achieved victory in the elections to the Latvian parliament, winning about 70 percent of the seats.[27] It was a clear sign that, as one of the Popular Front's leaders said, "the demand for independence is not confined to extremists, but is shared by the majority."[28]

Not only were the nationalists able to influence the policy-making process, but they were actually determining the policy agenda after 1990. As a result of the growing popularity of nationalist ideas,[29] nationalist-oriented politicians dominated the national legislature. Ivars Godmanis, one of the Popular Front's leaders, was appointed prime minister, with 131 deputies voting for him, 46 against and 6 abstaining.[30] This put the nationalists in control of the executive process as well. Subsequent referendum and nationwide elections generally confirmed the notion that all the mainstream forces in the society shared the values of national independence. Although, with the beginning of painful economic reforms, popular support for nationalist-oriented groups declined somewhat, nationalist ideas became institutionalized, thereby preserving their fundamental importance in the policy-making process.

Empire Savers

As a reaction to nationalist activities, the movements supporting Latvia's colonial status within the empire, or the empire-saving movements, emerged. In January 1989, a Russian-dominated Internationalist Front of the Workers of the Latvian SSR (Interfront) was established with the agenda of upholding the leading role of the Communist party and protecting the Russian-speaking community from the ethnic claims of Latvian nationalists.[31] The main support for the movement came from hard-line forces in Moscow, conservative Communist party members, retired military officers, and workers and managers in the military-industrial complex.[32] The Interfront also maintained ties with the leaders of the Baltic Military District, the KGB, the pro-Soviet parts of the Ministry of Interior and the Prosecutor's Office,[33] and—not surprisingly—shortly after its appearance, it became a center of resistance to Latvian independence.

Unlike nationalist movements, however, the Interfront enjoyed little popularity in Latvian society. Even ethnic Russians, allegedly the empire-savers' main pillar, were far from enthusiastic about supporting the Interfront. During the March 1991 referendum on the issue of independence, 74 percent voted in favor, implying that from 38 to 45 percent of Russians supported independence, apparently with the belief that it would bring prosperity.[34] The turnout at demonstrations in support of the Interfront's goals was typically low, and "most of the activities of the pro-Soviet forces were organized by traditional Soviet power holders rather than by participants themselves."[35] It was these Soviet power holders, such as Minister of International Affairs Boris Pugo in Moscow and a leader of the Interfront, Colonel Viktor Alksnis in Riga, who were standing behind the National Salvation Committee during the anti-independence coup attempts in January and August 1991.[36] Accordingly, with the disintegration of the USSR,

Interfronts in Latvia and other Baltic republics had effectively lost most of their organizational resources.

As a result, influence of the empire savers' policy continued to decline. The institutional channels could hardly be mobilized, with centrist and nationalist party representatives dominating the national legislature and executive bodies. In 1994, a new Latvian Socialist Party claimed to reflect the interests of the Latvian Russian population, which had only six members in the parliament (6 percent of the seats) and claimed a membership of about 1000 people. Another leftist party, the National Harmony, received 13 percent of the vote and, accordingly, elected 13 members to the Saeima.[37]

State

The institutional structure of Latvia's state was defined by nationalists with their rise to power in 1990. Until the nationwide election of the President, the state, while possessing policy-making tools, was relatively low-centralized. The state was legitimate, and it owed the legitimacy essentially to the popularity of the nationalists.

Degree of Centralization

At this time, Latvia's state was relatively low-centralized when compared with many other presidential democracies in the former Soviet region. After achieving the independence, Latvians adopted what an expert called "the extremely egalitarian" constitution of 1922. According to the constitution, the head of state was to be elected by the parliament, and his or her government would lack any veto against parliamentary decisions. Parliament fixed the budget, confirmed the cabinet, and fixed the strength of the armed forces in peace and war.[38] The parliament was therefore the "core institution," whereas the president—before Guntis Ulmanis's election in 1993, at least[39]—was assigned an essentially ceremonial role.[40] Paradoxically, for those supporting a strong presidency as an optimal institution for conducting economic reforms, Latvia's low-centralized state, with the parliament providing the political basis for reforms, proved to be highly successful. This implies that, under certain conditions, a "strong executive does not necessarily guarantee a more coherent and determined implementation of the first phase of economic reforms."[41]

Legitimacy

One of those conditions is, of course, legitimacy, or a high level of public trust in the executive power. Such a level of trust assumes that the executive power is created by a society with a relatively homogeneous system of policy preferences. Various studies suggest that, at least during its first years, Latvia's executive bodies were, indeed, highly legitimate. The extremely high level of mobilization during the confrontation with the old system produced a parliament with relatively homogeneous policy preferences in favor of national independence, with about 80 percent of deputies who were either members of the Latvian Popular Front and the Independence Movement, or those sympathetic to these two nationalist movements. Predictably, after being elected the Supreme Soviet passed a resolution stating as the ultimate goal of its work the eventual achievement of full independence and confirmed a cabinet committed to the accomplishment of this goal.[42] Although the government's legitimacy declined soon after its confirmation, mainly because of pressing issues of the economic and ethnic situation,[43] the rating of confidence in the presidency remained at a consistently high level.[44]

As a result of the combination "homogeneous society—low-centralized state," the policy-making process in Latvia may be characterized as society-dominated. Changes came primarily as a result of national elections through which the society, mobilized by nationalist movements, gained comparatively easy access to the decision-making process. The idea of gaining genuine independence from the disintegrating empire preoccupied the minds of Latvian politicians, and it was hardly surprising that after the nationalists' victory in the 1990 elections, Latvia pursued even more aggressive policies toward assuming control over its domestic and foreign affairs. It terminated the "leading role" of the Communist Party. The 1940 annexation of Latvia by the Soviet Union was declared illegal by the Latvian parliament; the constitution of 1922 was reinstated and so was the official name of the republic—the Republic of Latvia. All these taken together provided nationalists with an institutional basis for advancing a policy of economic reorientation away from the metropole.

Foreign Economic Strategy

Logically, a policy of economic restructuring assumes accomplishing three tasks: 1) minimizing economic ties with old partners; 2) finding potential new partners and establishing necessary domestic institutions for switching economic activities toward new partners; and 3) signing economic agreements, both bilateral and multilateral, with new partners. A policy of economic restructuring is observable in each of these three dimensions.

Russian Pole

I consider Latvia's foreign economic strategy along two of the following lines. First, I analyze Latvia's attitude toward multilateral economic institutions with Russia as a participant, most prominently the CIS. Second, I turn to Latvian bilateral policies with respect to Russia. Specifically, I focus on Latvia's decision to introduce national currency and its trade policy vis-à-vis the ex-metropole.

The "Economic Autonomy" and Economic Independence Drive

Latvia's attitude toward multilateral arrangements in place of the USSR was clearly demonstrated by its active participation in the so-called "economic autonomy" effort during 1988-1990. Latvia's nationalists sided firmly with their Estonian and Lithuanian counterparts in demands, at first, for more "economic sovereignty," and in late 1989 for "full economic and political independence" within the USSR.[45]

The "economic autonomy" program was originally drafted by a group of Estonian politicians and economists with the hope of seizing the momentum of Gorbachev's perestroika and to transform the Soviet federation into a system with more rights for non-Russian republics, particularly for the three Baltic nations. In late 1987 some basic first principles were drawn up for a program of Estonian economic autonomy within the USSR. It is worth quoting those principles at length, both because they constituted the core of the program and because, within about a year, they were embraced by Latvia in its economic claims.[46] Although the program never had a chance to actually be implemented, its principles, in an important way, highlighted the general philosophy underlying further Latvian policy-making in economic affairs. The following nine points constituted the basis for the program:

1. The law of value and the commodity-money relationship form the basis for steering and planning the economy.
2. Economic institutions and enterprises on Estonian territory should be under Estonian control.
3. Trade with the other Soviet republics should be based on market principles and on direct relations between producer and consumer.
4. A convertible ruble should be established as an international currency and should form the basis for economic relations with enterprises and economic institutions in other parts of the Soviet Union.
5. The republic as a whole accepts its share of the burden of the Soviet budget, as it is determined by the all-Union Supreme Soviet, but separates its own local budget from that of the Union.
6. There is to be complete economic self-determination in the whole republic, in all economic spheres.
7. Economic pluralism ensures competition between producers, in the best interest of the consumers, and promotes different forms of economic organization.
8. Labor mobility between Estonia and other parts of the union is controlled by special rules, designed to achieve a rational use of labor resources.
9. Steering is based on economic principles, with independent enterprises, and controlling bureaucracies are abolished.[47]

The program's *leitmotif* was that of autonomy, the meaning of which had nothing to do with special economic zones within the USSR.[48] Such arrangements, the authors argued, would only perpetuate Russia's domination over the Baltics. Instead, autonomy was supposed to save the republics from the status of "exploited colonies."[49] It required that the republics have the right to enter into various economic arrangements with foreign firms without consulting Moscow. In June 1988 the program was echoed in the resolution adopted by the extended Plenum of the Latvian SSR Writers' Union, the organization that later gave birth to the Popular Front.[50] In September of the same year, following the program, the state planning (Gosplan) directors of Estonia, Latvia, and Lithuania jointly demanded that the republics have exclusive control over republic property and the right to decide all issues of economic development, price formation, taxation, wages, and economic incentives.[51]

The center's reaction to the republics' economic autonomy drive was that of limited acceptance of their demands. In part this coincided with Gorbachev's own plans to reorganize the Soviet federation, pushing him toward defining these plans in a clear way. Moscow's responses—first, the March 1989 draft program on republican autonomy by the USSR Council of Ministers and the November 1989 USSR Law on Economic Autonomy of the Lithuanian, Latvian, and Estonian Socialist Republics[52]—were, however, inadequate. The crucial issues, such as the treatment of property rights in land and natural resources and in the "all-Union" systems, were not decided; many formulations were vague, and the price control and supply system remained in Moscow's hands.[53] In the words of an observer, "the Balts cannot obtain economic sovereignty through these reforms, which promise no more than a kind of semi-autonomy. This will not satisfy them, to put it mildly."[54]

The events that followed proved the accuracy of this observation. The center's suggested reforms were met with increased efforts to establish economic and political bases of the republics' independence. In August 1989 the leaders of Popular Front of Latvia stated the goal of total economic independence, not just economic self-financing, the significance of which was predicated by the fact that at the time the Front largely determined "the current political situation in the republic."[55] Anticipating the difficulties of further negotiations with Moscow, Latvian academics began a discussion of Latvia's economic survivability "under emergency conditions." Sensing the possibility of Moscow ordering an economic blockade against Latvia the day after "Latvia has acquired full independence," they nonetheless urged policymakers to continue the independence drive as a way to eventual salvation.[56]

Latvia's empire savers responded with severe criticism of the Popular Front recommendations and projections. A Latvian Communist, a military officer and a leader of the Interfront, Viktor Alksnis, for example, made a case for republic economic interdependence arguing that

A nationalist mind is being placed beneath *perestroika* essentially negating the development of the republic within the USSR... [Latvia was] producing expensive industrial output from cheap raw materials essentially through the heavy labor of Uzbek children and women. But what if our egocentrism permeates to Tyumen, which supplies us with oil and gas for next to nothing; what if it also raises the question of bringing [oil] prices in line with world prices?[57]

Apart from Moscow, however, the empire-savers' voices were weak, and the republic doubled its efforts along the chosen path. Even the actual attempts by Moscow to impose an economic blockade against the neighboring Lithuania and Estonia,[58] and the subsequent Moscow-orchestrated military coups in Latvia and Lithuania of January 1991[59] could not have stopped Latvia and other Baltic nations from pursuing an independence path. Against the expectations of Russia, such attempts only strengthened Latvia's reorientation drive.[60]

The CIS Stance

Unlike many other republics, Latvia was explicit about its intentions not to participate in drafting a new Union treaty, which was the Gorbachev-initiated attempt to preserve the unity of the increasingly diverse republics. While sending an observer to forums discussing such a treaty, the Latvian government adopted a special declaration to prevent any attempts of involving the republic in the process of drafting a treaty. The declaration stated that, because of Latvia's May 4, 1990 declaration of independence, the government would neither take part in the drafting of the Union treaty, nor sign any treaties that did not recognize the May 4 declaration. Latvian policymakers were convinced that, as deputy chairman of the Supreme Council of Latvia and observer in a meeting of the Federation Council Andrejs Krastins said, "Judging from Gorbachev, the new treaty will be a facade behind which the unitary system of government will be strengthened."[61]

By the time the CIS came into existence and replaced the Soviet Union in December 1991, Latvia was already on the fast track of distancing itself from Moscow. After the bloody clash with Moscow in January 1991, Latvian voters voted overwhelmingly (73.7 percent) for independence in the March referendum of the same year, and the nationalists' efforts to minimize ties with Moscow were considered to be both necessary and legitimate. It was hardly surprising to anyone when Latvia and other Baltic nations decided against joining the CIS, despite the invitations of the new Russian regime. As Latvian Prime Minister Ivars Godmanis said, "Our membership in a Union of any type is excluded. We could only conclude a specific agreement with an economic union as a whole, of course, if it is created." Instead of entering multilateral arrangements in place of the former USSR, Latvia's leaders said it would aim to join the European Community.[62]

Politically, this became evident in the exercise of control over Latvia's borders and the replacement of old Soviet passports with Latvian ones. In addition, Latvia was the second of the Baltic republics (after Estonia) to introduce a visa requirement for the CIS citizens.[63] On the domestic scene, the fear of maintaining ties with the CIS and Russia resulted in a discriminatory citizenship policy toward those Russians who happened to reside in Latvia.[64]

Economically, Latvia's response to the formation of the CIS was a decision to deal with CIS members on a strictly bilateral basis and not to engage in any collective arrangements. One form of this came through bilateral Most Favored Nation (MFN) agreements. During 1992 Latvia concluded MFN agreements with a number of former Soviet countries, establishing lower import tariffs for Latvian goods, excluding agriculture. The other form of bilateral dealings with CIS members was in barter agreements that served to compensate for the sharp decline of trade among them, partially the result of their messy transition to new currency systems.[65]

Bound by economic needs and a deep level of integration into the economy of the former USSR, Latvia could not simply turn its back on the ex-Soviet republics. But proposals for searching for solutions to economic problems on a cooperative basis[66] were not acceptable for Latvian policymakers either. The prevailing mood was that dealings with the former Soviet republics—members of the CIS—should be treated as a temporary solution, that by no means could it be considered the best solution, but rather a necessary "evil" of Latvia's transition away from Russia's authoritarianism and socialism, and toward Western freedom and capitalism. The fact that Russia was also moving away from capitalism and authoritarianism was viewed by many Baltic politicians as something potentially problematic and unnatural for Russia that would eventually lead to total breakdown in the East. Thus, the primary task of Latvia, as well as other Baltic nations, "was to sever as many links [with Russia] as possible so as not to be dragged into the maelstrom."[67] Dealings with Russia and other CIS members on a bilateral basis seemed to be a compromise acceptable to Latvian politicians.

Currency Cooperation with Russia

In Baltic nations, national currency was overwhelmingly given special consideration among many other attributes of national sovereignty. In Anatol Lieven's words,

> No symbol of independence was more ardently desired in the period 1990-92 than the restoration of the pre-1940 Baltic currencies. It was believed that these would bring economic miracles, and politicians, like prophets, repeatedly promised the Appearance of the Kroon, the Litas and the Lat, and anathematized each other when it failed to materialize.[68]

Captured by the "economic autonomy" ideas, politicians and policymakers viewed currency independence as a prerequisite for gaining distance from Russia and other traditional economic partners.[69]

In the early 1990s the ideational rationale for introducing national currencies was reinforced by pressing economic considerations. As a result of Moscow's short-term economic embargo in 1990,[70] Latvia was experiencing the deficit of goods and products outlets. Accompanied by deteriorating economic and political conditions in the rest of the former USSR, this produced rapidly growing inflation in Latvia and other Baltic nations (see table 3.2). Tight monetary policy might have allowed policymakers to reduce inflationary pressures, but the Latvian government had no control of its monetary policy and was entirely dependent on the use of the ruble as a medium of exchange.

Latvia and the other Baltic nations faced a tough dilemma. To be sure, it was becoming increasingly less sensible to continue staying in the ruble zone given the above-listed developments. At the same time, breaking with the ruble might have led to a number of negative consequences, especially the possibility of an inevitable decline in trade activities with the former Soviet region.[71] Latvia's trade with Russia and other republics comprised up to 90 percent of its total trade before the Soviet disintegration, causing many players inside and outside the country to worry about the consequences of currency reform. Inside the country, opposition came from leaders of industry who were terrified that the reform would deprive them of the required supplies from the rest of the former USSR. Latvian leaders themselves were aware of the problems the currency introduction might have brought with it.[72] Outside Latvia, the International Monetary Fund (IMF) and World Bank, for example, were highly skeptical of the value of an early introduction of national currencies, and warned in particular against breaking links to markets in the East.[73]

Under these conditions, in May 1992, the Latvian leadership made a compromise decision by introducing a provisional currency, the Latvian ruble. Latvian rubles coexisted with Russian rubles as legal tender, and—due a series of liberal policy measures[74]—were accepted and preferred to the Russian rubles by Latvians. As early as late July, all the negative inflationary influences from Russia and other republics were repressed, and the Latvian ruble became the sole legal tender within the Latvian market. Originally pegged at a 1:1 rate, by mid-1993 one Latvian ruble could have bought as many as five Russian rubles.[75] This strengthening of Latvian currency undoubtedly reinforced Latvia's general reorientation drive, as Latvian goods were becoming increasingly less competitive on Russian markets.[76] Finally, in October 1993, the Latvian ruble was replaced with Latvia's own currency, the *lats*.

The currency reform was thus successfully implemented, despite some domestic and outside opposition to it. Nationalist beliefs constituted the ideational environment in which the reform could have been carried out: "Monetary independence ... meant freedom from Moscow's rule and a natural part of shedding the Soviet identity and 'returning to Europe.'"[77] Reinforced by immediate economic concerns, such as the necessity to cope with growing inflation, those beliefs worked against the option of staying in the ruble zone. For example, the political roots of Latvian State Bank Chairman Einars Repse were on the radical

Table 3.2. Latvia, Ukraine, and Belarus: Basic Economic Data, 1991-1996

Real GDP growth (%)

	1991	1992	1993	1994	1995	1996
Latvia	-8.3	-33.8	-11.7	2.0	-2.0	3.3
Ukraine	-11.9	-17.0	-14.2	-24.3	-11.8	-10.0
Belarus	-1.2	-9.6	-11.6	-20.2	-10.0	2.8

Sources: EIU, *Quarterly Economic Reports* 1996; EIU, *Country Profiles* 1998-2000.

Consumer price inflation, annual average (%)

	1991	1992	1993	1994	1995	1996
Latvia	125	951	109	37	27	18
Ukraine	91	1310	4735	891	377	80
Belarus	84	969	1188	2220	709	53

Sources: EIU, *Quarterly Economic Reports* 1996; EIU, *Country Profiles* 1998-2000.

Unemployment rate (%)

	1991	1992	1993	1994	1995	1996
Latvia	n/a	n/a	5.3	6.5	6.1	7.1
Ukraine	-	0.3	0.3	n/a	0.4	0.9
Belarus	0.2	0.5	1.4	2.1	2.7	3.2

Sources: IMF, *Republic of Belarus* 1998, 83; IMF, *Economic Review, Ukraine* 1993, 102; IMF, *Ukraine—Recent Economic Development* 1997, 70.

Average dollar wages

	1991	1992	1993	1994	1995	1996
Latvia	n/a	29[a]	76.5	139.6	186.1	189.8
Ukraine	n/a	19.5	14	27.3	48.5	68.6
Belarus	n/a	27.5	23	23.9	65.1	88.9

[a] State sector only.
Sources: 12; Michapoloulos and Tarr 1994, 12; IMF, *Republic of Latvia—Recent Economic Development* 1996, 81.

Table 3.2—Continued

Total trade, exports and imports ($ billions)

	1991	1992	1993	1994	1995	1996	1997
Latvia							
exports	n/a	0.77	1.04	0.99	1.28	1.42	1.67
imports	n/a	0.69	0.96	1.24	1.65	2.10	2.47
Ukraine							
exports	n/a	1.51	3.95	9.53	14.93	16.32	16.11
imports	n/a	1.94	3.96	11.08	20.10	23.76	26.89
Belarus							
exports	n/a	3.44	1.94	2.46	4.65	5.15	7.38
imports	n/a	3.40	2.47	2.98	5.51	6.81	8.69

Sources: EIU, *Country Profiles* 1992-1998; EIU, *Country Reports* 1994-1997; IMF, *Direction of Trade Statistics Yearbook 1998* 1999.

Trade with Russia, exports and imports (% of total)

	1990[a]	1992	1993	1994	1995	1996	1997
Latvia							
exports	50.0	26.1	28.6	28.1	24.9	23.2	20.1
imports	52.4	29.7	28.1	23.5	21.6	20.3	15.6
Ukraine							
exports	65.9	n/a	n/a	40.1	40.3	34.8	22.5
imports	74.1	n/a	n/a	54.1	37.8	35.1	29.6
Belarus							
exports	57.7	41.3	40.7	47.1	44.4	58.8	62.7
imports	62.6	54.0	45.9	62.9	56.1	51.7	53.3

[a] Share of interrepublican trade with Russia (Watson 1994, 375-76).
Sources: EIU, *Country Profiles* 1992-1998; EIU, *Country Reports* 1994-1997; IMF, *Direction of Trade Statistics Yearbook 1998* 1999.

nationalist side of politics, helping to adopt the tight money policy dictated by the IMF and to resist pressures from Russian managers and workers to increase their wages. Institutionally, this became possible because of the State Bank's constitutional independence from political control.[78]

Trade Cooperation with Russia

Latvia's trade policy thinking was essentially similar to that behind currency reform. Trade reorientation away from Russia and toward Western markets was widely perceived as a crucial prerequisite for achieving economic self-reliance and complete national independence. The issue, as one observer put it, "was seen first and foremost as one of security—a major instrument to preserve and strengthen the state's sovereignty."[79] Russia, on the other hand, was increasingly seen as a sinking ship that had been activating all the leverages available to continue extracting benefits from the Baltic economies and, therefore, further blocking them from development. Breaking away from Russia was therefore viewed as something in the economic interests of Baltic nations.

At the same time, most Latvian policymakers were well aware that, due to heavy economic dependence on the other ex-Soviet republics, the reorientation could not be accomplished without immediate losses. These losses could only be recovered with the passing of time. For many years, up to 90 percent of industrial concerns in the Baltics were run solely or jointly by all-Union authorities.[80] Before the Soviet disintegration, almost all of Latvian trade was with the Soviet Union, primarily with Russia. In 1991, for example, 95 percent of Latvian exports went to the USSR and a similar proportion was imported. Russia accounted for about 50 percent of total trade[81] (see table 3.2). Latvia was particularly dependent on Russia's supplies of energy and Russia's transit to the West via Latvian territory.[82] These complex considerations were well summarized by a Latvian policymaker:

> Our economic situation is determined by the economic crises in the eastern market upon which we were made to be dependent. Now we have become an independent country. Russia still wants us to be part of its sphere of influence. Moscow uses policies trying to make us dependent. Our biggest market was and still is to a marked measure Russia. We have to have alternative economic relations [other than with Russia]; otherwise we will continue to be dependent on it. This has to be done quickly.[83]

To reduce the immediate losses from the reorientation policy, it was proposed that Russia be seen as an important, albeit a short-term, partner. Economic ties with the East, while not a strategic priority, should be maintained for the sake of smoother reorientation toward Western markets. A series of bilateral agreements was supposed to help to maintain those ties, while Latvia's mid-term objectives were to be reached by gaining memberships in Western multilateral institutions.[84]

In 1992, after Moscow's recognition of the Baltics' independence, Latvia signed a number of trade agreements with Russia.[85] Barter agreements were a particularly common form. In April 1992, for example, an agreement was signed according to which Latvia was provided with a certain amount of energy resources in return for food supplies to Russia. The other form of bilateral dealings with Russia and other CIS members was in Most Favored Nation (MFN) agreements. During 1992 Latvia concluded MFN agreements with a number of former Soviet Union countries, establishing lower import tariffs for Latvian goods, excluding agriculture.[86] In October 1992 a similar agreement was signed, although not ratified, with Russia.

Such an approach, however, did not prove to be sufficient for reviving trade. In the winter of 1991-1992, Latvia experienced a particularly sharp decline in trade with the CIS states, largely as a result of the Soviet disintegration. In 1992 Latvia's trade volume fell dramatically, by about one-third, and the decline continued in 1993.[87] At the time, Latvia was still largely isolated from the world economy, which accounted for the decline.[88] The MFN agreement with the former Soviet states, despite being signed, did not come into force until mid-1994.[89] The critical example was the October 1992 agreement signed between the Latvian and Russian governments. In the agreement, the two sides pledged to extend MFN status beyond 1992 and gradually establish a free trade agreement. However, the Russian parliament did not ratify the agreement. As a result, even the previously arranged MFN agreement collapsed: Russia applied double-MFN tariff rates (30 percent) on Latvian goods, and Latvia applied 20 percent tariffs rather than 15 percent.[90] Even deal-specific bilateral agreements with Russia, many of which had been signed, went unfulfilled. Latvia was particularly affected by Russia's failure to provide previously negotiated amounts of raw materials and parts[91] and by Russia's threats to switch to world prices in its trade with the newly independent states.[92] So acute did the problem become that it was described by some Latvian officials as "economic warfare by Russia against Latvia."[93]

Russia's tough and noncooperative stance vis-à-vis Latvia was, at least in part, politically motivated. Moscow complained about violations of human rights of the Russian-speaking population in Latvia[94] and about the Latvia's unilateral decision to nationalize the oil pipeline, and was even considering economic sanctions against Latvia and other Baltic nations. At the time, Russian President Boris Yeltsin singled out the Baltic nations and Ukraine as countries that should be forced to pay hard currency for their energy deliveries, due to their differing economic and political policies.[95]

As a result, opposition to governmental policy was growing. Large state enterprises, in particular, wanted closer relations with the East.[96] The workers in those enterprises united in the Union of Free Trade Unions of Latvia were strongly behind this idea. In January 1992, for example, the organization issued an appeal to the governments and trade unions of the Commonwealth of Independent States in which it argued that

> the whole of the historically formed economic relations within industry—and the entire national economy of Latvia—is oriented toward close links with the economy of the former USSR ... Only together will we be able to overcome this difficult time, economic hardship, and everything which was left to us as a legacy from totalitarianism.[97]

The view also found some support in the growing private sector, where many people shared a past in the communist apparatus or the communist youth organization Komsomol.[98] The situation was pressing the government to go beyond the originally designed approach in economic relations with Russia.

Despite all the difficulties, Latvia did not consider making political concessions or changing its policies vis-à-vis Russia and the CIS in a fundamental way. Faced with collapsing trade, Latvian leadership kept pressing for MFN treatment by Russia while activating a series of tools to make the reorientation real and to compensate for the recent losses.

First, in mid-1992, after Latvia abolished all Soviet-era export quotas and licenses and replaced them with export taxes, it used the taxes as a lever to encourage the reorientation to the West. Although, in principle, using the export taxes might have discouraged exports, setting different tax rates on exports to different areas may have served the purpose of reorientation. In particular, in order to encourage exports to the West, Latvia set higher export tax rates on exports to nonconvertible currency areas (including Russia) and on barter trade than on exports to areas outside the former USSR.[99] Second, import tariffs were also discriminatory against Russia and other CIS countries with whom Latvia did not have trade agreements in effect.[100] With a new law covering import duties entering into force in March 1994, the new tariff structure maintained the discriminatory pattern.[101] Third, Latvia actively used energy and other raw material reexports from Russia, taking advantage of the relatively low prices at that time.[102] Finally, Latvia was actively working on the marketization of domestic economies in preparation for market-oriented commercial activities and the eventual breakthrough in establishing economic relations with the West. The next section returns to this.

Commercial reorientation away from the ex-metropole was due to the same nationalist beliefs that gave birth to currency reform. These beliefs can be traced at least to the "economic autonomy" program, which first conceptually linked successful development with control over the national economy. As Seija Lainela and Pekka Sutela wrote, Latvia and other Baltic nations have demonstrated "an almost religious devotion to currency convertibility and trade reorientation," which were seen "as essential elements of the escape from the former Soviet Union and a return to Europe":[103]

There was the feeling of an overwhelming national mission, and this explains the relative weakness of lobbies and vested interests in Baltic politics. If industrial lobbies would have decided the issue, the reorientation of trade from Russia to the West would certainly have been much slower... In principle, the lobbies may become more powerful when politics normalizes as the national mission is fulfilled. But by then traditional lobbies will have been much weakened by economic and social change.[104]

The post-1996 period has essentially demonstrated continuity in the identified patterns of foreign economic policy of Latvia. The country's leaders became somewhat more favorably disposed toward economic cooperation with Russia and expressed their willingness to overcome mistrust and alienation in relations with the ex-metropole.[105] At the same time, they made clear that Russia's economic sanctions would not result in any political concessions on Latvia's part; such measures, had they had been undertaken, would only have accelerated Latvia's reorientation efforts.[106] Latvian policymakers viewed the economic relations with Russia in terms of the relative gains and security risks involved. The attitude was best summarized by Latvia's foreign minister, Valdis Birkavs: "Let the volume of trade with Russia increase, but let the relative share of Russia in our total trade decrease."[107]

Domestic Economic Institutions

While shifting the economy away from the former Soviet Union was overwhelmingly considered in Latvia to be an important precondition of national independence, the reorientation toward Western countries was economically impossible because of incompatibility with their economic systems. Latvia inherited from the Soviet Union a highly centralized, immobile economy with only minor market incentives for development. A series of measures were necessary for Latvia to prepare for market-oriented foreign economic activities. Two crucial and particularly significant conditions are usually identified—macroeconomic stabilization and lifting trading quotas and restrictions.[108] These conditions are normally recommended by leading Western economic agencies, such as the World Bank and the IMF,[109] both of which Latvia joined in April 1992. Impatient to become a part of the West and encouraged by the Western financial assistance that had already been received by that time,[110] Latvia's nationalist coalition began to implement a package of economic reforms.

Macroeconomic stabilization efforts began with price liberalization reform in December 1991 and January 1992. It was accompanied by an immediate economic recession (see table 3.2), as later became the case in the rest of the USSR. Only a highly popular government could afford to launch this kind of reform. In December 1991 farm procurement and food retail prices were fully decontrolled. In the following month gasoline and diesel prices were fully liberalized. Finally, in July 1992 price ceilings for oil, liquefied gas, and coal for industrial uses were also eliminated. By mid-1992 price liberalization was completed.

Another important part of the stabilization program was the establishment of a coherent foreign exchange system, which took Latvia about two years to complete (see the previous section on trade cooperation with Russia).

The nationalist coalition also deserves credit for beginning the process of changing the Soviet-era trade regulations. All state orders, export quotas, and licenses were abolished in mid-1992 and replaced by export taxes ranging from 0 to 100 percent. The Tariff Council was established for dealing with trade issues on a permanent basis. As a result of its activities, the tariff regime was modified. In September 1992, for example, the Tariff Council abolished export taxes on most goods. Duties remained only on timber and wood products, metal and metal products, leather, furs, and some other products.

Domestic reforms proved to be a politically costly enterprise. As a result, the nationalist government lost some of its credibility. As Latvia plunged into a recession, the Godmanis Popular Front's government became increasingly unpopular, and a series of ministers departed or were forced to resign. In February 1993 the Popular Front, becoming less popular and less cohesive, ceased to exist as a ruling coalition and was replaced by a more credible, right-of-center grouping, Latvian Way (Latvijas Cels), established by the acting president and chairman of the Supreme Council, Anatolijs Gorbunovs, and a number of leading politicians.[111] The shift of forces was reflected in new elections that took place in June 1993 and brought a victory to the new coalition.

The fact that the nationalists lost some of their credibility was also reflected in their inability to liberalize the tariff regime completely. The system was still structured to favor domestic industry and agriculture. Latvia kept a relatively high import tariff, especially on agricultural products. The standard tariff rate was 20 percent, and a tariff rate of up to 45 percent was imposed on goods that could be produced locally.[112] Those tariffs were applicable to all countries, including the other Baltics, but in the spirit of nationalism, agricultural goods from Russia and Ukraine were subject to higher tariffs. Domestic pressures on the government, particularly from the agricultural sector, remained strong after 1992. In March 1993 specific import duties were imposed on grain, flour, and bread. A new series of import tariffs on agricultural products was introduced in 1994[113] and 1995 to protect domestic farmers. Those pressures were reflected in the October 1995 parliamentary elections that produced a divided parliament, with leftist and left-of-center protectionist parties controlling about 40 seats in the 100-seat chamber.

With parliamentary seats divided between parties of leftist and left-of-center protectionist orientation and nationalists favoring more openness, Latvia became a less homogeneous society, somewhat slowing its move toward national independence. The reforms, however, in no way stopped the formation of independent economic policies in the country. By the time the new ruling coalition emerged, price liberalization was fully completed and currency reforms were well under way. As a result of price liberalization and the establishment of a new foreign exchange system, annual inflation dropped from 950 percent in 1992 to 37 percent in 1994 (see table 3.2). Similarly, the fact that the nationalist-oriented policy of foreign trade liberalization was abandoned did not slow Latvia's development significantly. Rather, it can be considered as the country's way of catching its breath on the rapid move toward the Westernization of its markets. The main barriers for launching market-oriented trade activities, such as quotas and surrender requirements, were removed. By the end of 1993, with the completion of its currency reform, Latvia was well on the track toward gaining membership into Western trading institutions. This was accomplished, in the words of Latvian prime minister, because "national identity and firm confidence in the necessity of building an independent state were especially meaningful for a successful start and further development of economic reform."[114]

Looking beyond Russia

Among other post-Soviet nations, Latvia was one of the most active promoters of its independence and of establishing economic and political ties outside the Soviet Union. In a sense, the creation of independent foreign policies in the Baltic republics actually began before they gained independence in August 1991.[115] Gaining access to Western markets and economic institutions was perceived to be a strategic priority, in fact, goal in and of itself. Latvia and other Baltic nations thought of themselves as "returning" to Europe, where they belonged historically, culturally, and geographically.

Originally formulated that way, the intention of joining Western economic arrangements was reinforced by Soviet and, later, Russia's behavior. First, the Moscow coup of August 1991 and the ensuing Soviet break-up in December facilitated the process of alignment with Western European countries. In the eyes of Latvian politicians and Balts in general, the coup had only confirmed Russia's aggressive imperialist intentions and left no chance for the once-entertained idea of the Baltic nations as a gateway between East and West.[116] If anything, the coup pushed the Baltics toward the West and away from the East. The West was perceived as friendly and sufficiently stable, whereas the East was seen as much less predictable and inherently hostile. Russia, too, was perceived as a threatening, potentially expansionist nation. Russia's tendency to view post-Soviet nations as within the natural sphere of its influence, demands to grant dual citizenship to ethnic Russians living in these countries, and other behaviors were widely considered in Latvia as indicators that Russia remained a threat to Latvia's independence.[117]

In their wish to become Europeans, the Baltic authorities undertook measures toward rapprochement with Western European countries. They started with efforts to pursue bilateral cooperation with those countries. After winning wide international recognition of its independence and becoming a member of the United Nations, the IMF, and the World Bank, Latvia launched a series of bilateral free-trade agreements (excluding agriculture) with European countries. During 1992, such agreements were signed with Sweden (March), Norway (June), Finland (November), and Switzerland (December).[118]

Latvia's major goal, however, was perceived as entering into Western multilateral arrangements, primarily the European Union. At least three main reasons were listed by Latvian politicians and observers for attributing the highest priority to multilateral forms of cooperation with Western countries: such cooperation was seen as capable of giving the Baltic nations a new stimulus for advancing their economic reforms in the market direction; it was supposed to provide them with access to alternative markets; and it would have given tangible security benefits.[119] However surprising it may sound, nationalists were not worried about losing Latvia's national identity by joining another union. "European-ness" did not seem threatening to their identity. In fact, they wholeheartedly embraced the idea of joining Europe. Eager to overcome Russia's damaging influences, nationalists perceived the membership in the "European family" as a way to bolster Latvia's nonimperial identity and to pursue their nation-state.[120]

Latvia's efforts to participate in alternative multilateral international economic arrangements can be analyzed as advancing in three directions. First and foremost, Latvia wanted to establish close relations with Western European countries, most notably through the European Union and the European Free Trade Association. Second, it participated actively in forming the inter-Baltic economic union, with Lithuania and Estonia as additional members. Finally, it expressed an interest in cooperating with those of the former Soviet republics who were eager to reduce their economic dependence on Russia.

Striving for the EU Membership

Despite some early advantages,[121] accomplishing the goal of becoming Europeans proved to be much more difficult than was originally expected. As one Baltic leader sardonically remarked, "joining" the USSR was easy; joining the EU was proving to be a long and complex process.[122] Pushed in the Western direction by their original cultural priorities and increasingly heavy-handed Russia's policies, Baltics faced tight trade restrictions as much as the other post-Soviet nations. Nonetheless, it seems clear that Latvia and other Baltic nations were firmly supportive of eventually becoming EU members.

Latvia revealed interest in joining the EU from the very beginning of its national independence drive. With the European Community's (now the European Union) recognition of Latvian independence on August 27, 1991, the channels of mutual interaction were open. The first steps toward access to the EC markets were made in May 1992, with the signing of trade and cooperation agreements with the European Community and obtaining MFN status from the EC. Latvia and other Baltic nations also signed a political declaration with the EC, declaring their shared ideals and pledging foreign policy coordination.[123] This was a critically important step for both advancing further cooperative relations with the EC and facilitating domestic economic reforms.

Progress toward joining the EC became more concrete in 1993-1995. In June 1993, Latvia and other Baltic nations applied to become EC associate members.[124] Government commissions were formed in the Baltic countries to develop the bases for eventual integration. In April 1994 Latvia became the first former Soviet republic to initial a preliminary free-trade accord with the European Union[125] that took effect in January 1995. The opening of the European market[126] came as both an opportunity and a challenge, since not all Latvian goods were competitive. The results of entering the competition, however, proved to be rewarding. During 1995-1997, Latvian exports to and imports from the EU countries increased by 1.6 and 2.2 times, respectively.[127]

In the fall 1995, Latvia's European drive was somewhat undermined, with the populist Movement for Latvia and the Party of Unity gaining 24 out of 100 seats in the parliament. A combination of anti-European[128] and pro-Russian views undermined the country's pro-European orientation. The episode, however, became an additional push for the leadership's European drive. On October 13, Latvia's President Guntis Ulmanis used his power to call for an extraordinary meeting of the Cabinet of Ministers with only one point on the agenda—the formal application for full EU membership. The ministers unanimously supported the application and, on October 27, Latvia became the first post-Soviet country to apply for full membership in the EU. In support of the move, the chairmen of all eleven political parties represented in the new parliament met with Ulmanis and signed a declaration expressing their positive attitude toward application for EU membership and asserting that admission into the EU was the most essential goal of Latvia's foreign policy.[129] Whereas Latvia's full membership in the organization is not likely before 2005, given the Union's own preoccupation with internal problems,[130] Latvia's trade regime,[131] and the Union's intention to admit the Baltics as a group rather than on an individual basis,[132] it certainly marked the interest of both sides in continuing economic cooperation.

The EU drive received overwhelming support in the society. In the words of one observer, many of those same nationalists who helped to bring about the demise of Soviet rule "are now among the prime advocates of EU membership."[133] In April 1995, when the parliament considered the foreign policy concept of Latvia with a clearly defined goal of eventual joining the EU, it stated "the EU is essential to the likelihood of the survival of the Latvian people and the preservation of the Latvian state."[134] Only a few abstained or voted against the concept. National surveys also amply illustrated the adherence of Latvian elite to the idea of entering Europe and gaining full membership in the EU.[135] The elites' attitude toward the EU was well expressed by Prime Minister of Latvian Republic Guntar Krasts, who said that "Integration of Latvia into European Union provides us, or—to be more precise—returns us, to our historical and geopolitical identity."[136] Finally, the general public was also quite receptive to the country's eventual membership in the EU.[137]

After 1996, Latvia has generally maintained its pro-European orientation and increased its prospects of becoming a full member in the European Union, Europe's major economic institution. In February 1998, the Europe Agreement entered into force. Replacing the Agreement on economic cooperation and fully incorporating the free-trade agreement with the EU, the Europe Agreement made explicit the intention of pursuing the gradual integration of Latvia into the organization.[138] Joining the WTO also facilitated Latvia's reorientation efforts.[139] Latvia also continued its domestic efforts to harmonize its national legislature with that of the EU.[140] Latvian leaders continued to view the country's full incorporation into European economic and security institutions as the number one priority on their policy agenda.[141]

As in the early years of independence, Latvia's post-1996 policy rested on broad social support. Until late-1998, Latvia was led by a coalition of nationalist-oriented parties, with a prime minister representing the Fatherland and Freedom and a foreign minister from Latvia's Way, and their movements dominated the parliament. After the October 1998 election, left and center-left parties became better represented in the parliament, but were still far from able to seriously influence, let alone control, the policy agenda. Latvian voters expressed a clear preference for pro-Western parties and, hence, for the policy of further reorientation toward European countries.[142]

Inter-Baltic Cooperation

Latvia's cooperation with other Baltic countries began even before the disintegration of the USSR, with the signing of the Agreement on Economic Cooperation with Lithuania and Estonia in April 1990, and with the adoption of the Declaration on Unity and Cooperation and establishment of a Council of the Baltic States to assist in the full restoration of independence.[143] The Baltics closely coordinated their efforts to gain the EU memberships.[144] Their trade and cooperation agreements with the European Community and the obtaining of most-favored-nation trading status from the EC in 1992 were concluded jointly, not individually. So, too, was a political declaration with the EC on shared ideals and foreign policy coordination. The Baltics' communiqué on applying for associate membership in the EC in June 1993 was also a joint one. Finally, the three Baltic nations signed association agreements with the EU almost simultaneously in June 1994.

After the demise of the Soviet Union, inter-Baltic relations continued to proceed smoothly, despite the appearance of some disagreements.[145] They announced their intention to set up a customs union as early as September 1991. The union, it was announced, would establish a common external tariff at approximately EC levels and allow free movements of goods, services, and people within it.[146] In September 1993, the three states reached a free-trade agreement, excluding agriculture,[147] and in June 1996, this agreement was supplemented with a long-sought treaty on free agricultural trade and plans for establishing common Baltic transportation and communication systems.[148]

Other Reorientation Efforts

In addition to its interest in joining the EU, Latvia advanced its efforts to establish closer relations with another European organization, the European Free Trade Association (EFTA). The EFTA unites all the European countries outside the EU, most of which had established yearly bilateral trade ties with Latvia as early as in 1992.[149] In November 1995 Latvia was the first of the ex-Soviet nations to initial a free-trade agreement with the EFTA, thereby taking another crucial step toward its Westernization.[150] Latvia also signed free-trade agreements with Slovakia, Slovenia and the Czech Republic.[151]

Other efforts to strengthen its position as a country free of Russia's influence included Latvia's attempts to establish economic ties with Ukraine and to support Ukraine in its efforts to establish better relations with the West.[152] These attempts began in 1995 and must be considered in the broad context of Latvia's search for favorable security arrangements and its desire to minimize Russian influence.

Notes

1. See, for example, the conversation with Ilmar Latkovskis, a leader of the Movement for National Independence of Latvia (*Atmoda*, 17 July, 1989, 5). The view was (and still is) widely shared in Latvian society (personal interviews, Riga, May-June 1999).

2. Lieven 1993, 44-46.

3. Misiunas and Taagepera 1993, 8-14; Lieven 1993, 54-74.

4. Prazauskas 1994, 160.

5. See Conquest 1986, 183-208; Muizniek 1997, 377-379.

6. Misiunas 1994, 94-95. Algimantas Prazauskas made a similar point (1994, 160).

7. Gerner and Hedlund 1993, 67-68.

8. Misiunas and Taagepera 1993, 48, 67.

9. Trapans 1991, 29; Muiznieks 1997, 339. In addition, 2,000 other native Latvians were removed from positions of higher responsibility, but the memory of the event proved very much alive. In 1971, for example, a letter from seventeen Latvian old Communists (who preferred to remain anonymous), addressed to several of the world's Communist parties, not only openly defended Berklavs's line but went further by vigorously denouncing Soviet policies in Latvia (Shtromas 1994, 100; Clemens 1991, 208).

10. Although the Baltic German nobility of western central Latvia continued to enjoy considerable economic and cultural autonomy and a special relationship with St Petersburg at this time (Smith 1996, 148).

11. The exception was a part of the Abrene district in the northeast, about 2 percent of the pre-war territory and population (Misiunas and Taagepera 1993, 74, xvi; Sergounin 1998, 49).

12. Gleason 1990; Roeder 1991.

13. Hiden and Salmon 1994, 126. The Moscow-designed industrialization meant the emergence of many defense-related plants in the Latvian economy (personal interview with a head of department at Latvia's Privatization Agency, Riga, June 1, 1999).

14. This ethnic composition contrasts with that one of the interwar time. In 1935, for example, Latvians and Russians accounted for 77 and 8.8 percent, respectively (Krickus 1993, 30). In terms of religion, Lutheran confession prevails in Latvia, with a significant minority of Catholic background. Yet, again, this only accounts for the non-Russian population. The local branches of Russian Orthodox Church constitute another source of religious influence, having a significant effect on the cultural and political attitudes of the local Russian population (Dawisha and Parrott 1994, 110).

15. Clemens 1991, 170.

16. The "point of reference for the Balts was not that Ukrainians, Jews, Kazakhs and even Russians have also suffered under Communist rule, and that democratization of the USSR within its established boundaries could be a solution to their problems. The perceptual framework of the Balts was instead patterned on what they know about the conditions in the pre-war independent Baltic states, and in contemporary Sweden and Finland" (Gerner and Hedlund 1993, 67).

17. Dreifelds 1989, 79-87; Muiznieks 1997, 382.

18. For a more detailed analysis of Latvia's popular movements, see Trapans 1991.

19. Karklins 1994, 75.

20. For the first program of the popular Front of Latvia, see *Sovetskaia Latvia*, October 19, 1988.

21. Its leader, Eduards Berklavs, was charged with "bourgeois nationalism" for attempts to reassert Latvian control in the aftermath of Stalin's death and subsequently expelled from the Party (Trapans 1991, 29).

22. Muiznieks 1997, 386.

23. Misiunas and Taagepera 1993, 250; see also Shtromas 1994 on this point.

24. See, for example, the article by Ianis Rukshans, "Is there an alternative to Latvia's independence?," which develops the argument about the inevitability of imperial disintegration due to the effect of the worldwide spread of the decolonization norm (*Atmoda*, August 21, 1989, 5).

25. Vares 1995, 167.

26. *Plan to Achieve Latvian Independence* 1990.

27. Muiznieks 1997, 400.

28. Clemens 1991, 212.

29. Both the National Independence Movement and, especially, the Popular Front acquired large memberships as early as 1989. The number of registered members of the Independence Movement grew from 600 in late July 1988 to over 11,000 by November 1989. And the Popular Front, at the time, claimed a membership of 250,000 people,

almost one-tenth of the country's total population (Karklins 1994, 75; Clemens 1991, 204).

30. *Latvian Information Bulletin*, "Ivars Godmanis—New Latvian Prime Minister," 1990, June, 3. Another example was the appointment of Einars Repse, a prominent activist of the People Front, as Head of the Bank of Latvia.

31. For the text of the Interfront's Declaration adopted at its constituent congress, see *Declaration* 1989.

32. Karklins 1994, 104; Muiznieks 1997, 386.

33. Gerner and Hedlund 1993, 113.

34. *EIU CP 1994-1995*, 25; Muiznieks 1997, 391.

35. Karklins 1994, 104.

36. *Ibid.*

37. Plakans 1997, 276-79.

38. Hope 1994, 48-49.

39. Ulmanis was seen by some analysts as seemingly desiring to enhance the role of the presidency (Nørgaard et al. 1996, 70).

40. *Ibid.*, 70.

41. *Ibid.*, 223.

42. Plakans 1997, 256; *RFE/RL Daily Report*, "Latvia Reaffirms Independence," August 22, 1991.

43. In addition, the government was severely undermined by allegations that three of its members had links with the KGB (Krickus 1993; Bungs 1994; *EIU CP 1994-1995*, 27).

44. Nørgaard et al. 1996, 107.

45. Clemens 1991, 107, 206. *Latvian Information Bulletin*, "Plan to Achieve Latvian Independence," 1990, January, 4-5.

46. Gerner and Hedlund 1993, 87.

47. *Ibid.*, 78-79.

48. Clemens 1991; Smith 1996.

49. The perception that Latvia, as well as other Baltic republics, had been exploited by Russia and some other republics was short of scientific evaluations, but nonetheless widely shared by mainstream politicians. A number of policymakers, including those strongly favoring Latvia's independence, expressed their frustration with the lack of professional discussion of the economic aspects of independence (personal interviews, Riga, June 1999).

50. Penikis 1996, 269-70.

51. Clemens 1991, 138.

52. For detailed analyses of those documents, see Tedstrom 1989; Bond and Sager 1990.

53. Tedstrom 1989, 8; Trapans 1991, Bradshaw et al. 1994, 169; Hiden and Salmon 1994, 170. For the reactions of the Popular Front activists, see *Atmoda*, July 17, 1989; July 31, 1989.

54. Trapans 1991, 98.

55. Clemens 1991, 208.

56. *Ibid.*, 209. The issue sparked a major debate between the Popular Front and its supporters, on the one hand, and those committed to economic autonomy within the Soviet Union, on the other. The former were writing for the newspaper *Atomoda*, the latter, such

as prominent economist Sergei Dimanis, mainly for the newspaper *Sovietskaia Molodiezh'* (personal interview with an economist and leader of the faction *Equal Rights* of Latvian parliament, Riga, June 1999).

57. *Ibid.*, 207. The point on world prices was also made by policymakers in Moscow. For example, in early 1990 Gorbachev, in his appeal to the three Baltic republics, said, "You get independence and switch to world prices, and you'll end up in the soup." Various calculations demonstrated the validity of the point. (See, for example, Hanson 1990.)

58. Hiden and Salmon 1994, 170-77.

59. Lieven 1993, 244-54; Gerner and Hedlund 1993, 147-52.

60. Given the perception of Latvia's insecurity vis-à-vis the ex-metropole, Russia's economic coercion could have hardly led to anything but feelings of further alienation among Latvian policymakers and politicians. Ironically, Russia in its own way greatly contributed to the formation of Latvia's reorientation policy (personal interviews with a head of department at Latvia's privatization agency and a senior specialist at the Bank of Latvia, Riga, June 1999).

61. *Latvian Information Bulletin*, "Latvia Rejects Participation in Drafting of New Union Treaty," 1990, October, 3; Clemens 1991, 213.

62. *RFE/RL Daily Report*, "Latvia Will Not Join Soviet Economic Union," October 10, 1991; *Moscow BALTFAX*, "Godmanis: We Will Only Join Economic Union," in FBIS-SOV-91-191, October 2, 1991, 57-58.

63. Misiunas 1994, 104.

64. See, Barrington 1995, 738-39; Krickus 1993, 29-34; Girnius 1993, 33.

65. For example, in 1994 barter agreements were signed with the Central Asian republics (EIU, *Quarterly Economic Report 1995*, 1, 30).

66. Many analysts suggested that the Baltics would benefit from participation in some kind of economic union among the former republics. One example was a proposal to create a "clearing arrangement or payment union" among them. (See Schroeder 1992, 561; similar thoughts were expressed in Nyberg 1993 and Bronstein 1993.)

67. Misiunas 1994, 103-104.

68. Lieven 1993, 355.

69. Shen 1994, 58. The goal of establishing Latvia's own convertible currency was first stated explicitly by the Popular Front of Latvia's second congress held on October 9, 1989 (*Plan to Achieve Latvian Independence* 1990, 4).

70. Shen 1994, 55; Shteinbuka 1993, 494. The embargo was especially severe in Lithuania and lasted for about two months, from the middle of April until the end of June (Senn 1997, 358).

71. Other difficulties with implementing currency reform are listed in Shteinbuka 1993, 495.

72. *Moscow TASS*, "Economic Confrontation with Russia Seen," in FBIS-SOV-91-209, October 29, 1991, 42.

73. Lieven 1993, 356-357; Krasts 1998, 31.

74. Shen listed six policy measures to boast the Latvian ruble's confidence. 1994, 59. Crucially, Latvia's currency reform was proceeded by rapid price liberalization and accompanied by liberal banking regulation (Lainela and Sutela 1997, 139).

75. Shen 1994, 58, 60.

76. Personal interview with a senior specialist at the Bank of Latvia, Riga, 2 June 1999.

77. Lainela and Sutela 1997, 124. Latvian prime minister Guntar Krasts made a similar point (1998, 29).

78. Lieven 1993, 360-61.

79. Bleiere 1997, 78.

80. Hiden and Salmon 1994, 171.

81. *EIU CP 1993/94* 1993, 34.

82. Rossiia i Pribaltika 1997, 4; Hiden and Salmon 1994, 192.

83. Shen 1994, 166; Similar thoughts were expressed by Latvian Supreme Council Chairman Anatolijs Gorbunovs in November 1991 (*RFE/RL Daily Report*, "Gorbunovs: Priorities for Latvia," November 8, 1991).

84. Shen 1994, 170-171; Ebel 1997, 183; Hiden and Salmon 1994, 192.

85. *Moscow BALTFAX*, "Clearing Settlements with Russia Suspended," in FBIS-SOV-92-005, January 8, 1992, 81; *RFE/RL Daily Report*, "Latvian-Russian Talks in March," February 27, 1992; "Latvian-Russian Economic Accord," July 23, 1992; "Latvia, Moscow Council Agree on Economic Cooperation," March 10, 1993.

86. The rate of MFN tariffs is 15 percent, 5 percent lower than a standard tariff. Agricultural goods, particularly those from Russia and Ukraine, were subject to higher tariffs. After June 1992 Latvia also had export tariffs which were applied to metals and metal products, timber and wood products, fur and leather (*EIU CP 1993/94*, 1993, 35; *Trade Policy* 1994, 54).

87. *EIU CP 1993/94* 1993, 34; *IMF Economic Review 1994*, 31.

88. Bradshaw et al. 1994, 174.

89. Nørgaard et al. 1996, 159; *RFE/RL Daily Report*, "Russia Gives Latvia Temporary Most Favored Trade Status," June 1, 1994.

90. *RFE/RL Daily Report*, "Latvian-Russian Economic Accords," October 29, 1992; *Trade Policy* 1994, 54.

91. At the end of 1991 one Latvian official was complaining that Latvia had supplied the republics of the former USSR with goods worth 1 billion rubles more than it received. Others argued that, while they had met their obligations to deliver products to Russia and other ex-Soviet republics on 80 percent, they only fulfilled their commitments on 30 percent (*Riga Radio Riga Network*, "Negotiator on Economic Talks with Russia," in FBIS-SOV-91-235, December 6, 1991, 45; *Moscow TASS,* "Economic Confrontation With Russia Seen," in FBIS-SOV-91-209, October 29, 1991, 42; *RFE/RL Daily Report*, "Russia Restricts Gasoline Supplies to Latvia," November 7, 1991; "Godmanis on Energy Crisis in Latvia," January 16, 1992; "Fuel Shortage Cuts Flights out of Riga," February 10, 1992; "Russia Wants Reduced Prices on Latvian Imports," March 25, 1992).

92. In the words of Yeltsin, the introduction of world prices in trade with the republics was a form of recognizing their independence (*Moscow BALTFAX*, "Yeltsin, Gorbunovs Discuss Economic Ties," in FBIS-SOV-91-211, October 31, 1991, 39. See also *Moscow TASS*, "Economic Confrontation With Russia Seen," in FBIS-SOV-91-209, October 29, 1991, 42; *Moscow BALTFAX*, "Russia Warned Against Hard Currency Deals," in FBIS-SOV-91-210, October 30, 1991, 58).

93. For example, leader of the People's Front faction, the majority faction of the Latvian parliament, Minister of State and the head of Latvian delegation for the talks with the USSR Janis Dinevics said on one occasion: "I have gained the impression that the USSR endeavors to specially delay their [talks'] start in order to weaken Latvia economi-

cally and to make it more submissive" (*Riga Radio Riga Network*, "Minister on 'Economic War' with Russia," in FBIS-SOV-91-227, November 25, 1991, 58. See also *Izvestiya*, "Accused of Economic Warfare," in FBIS-SOV-91-211, October 31, 1991, 39; *Riga Radio Riga Network*, "Negotiator on Economic Talks with Russia," in FBIS-SOV-91-235, December 6, 1991, 45).

94. In September 1992, Latvia drafted citizenship laws, in which ethnic Russians (33.1% of Latvia's population) were denied citizenship unless they or their families resided in the country before 17 June 1940 (Chinn and Kaiser 1996, 109).

95. *RFE/RL Daily Report*, "OMON Behind Petroleum Shortage in Latvia," December 6, 1991; *Moscow ITAR-TASS*, "Russia Introduces Double Taxation on Latvian Goods," in FBIS-SOV-93-023, February 16, 1993, 78; Drezner 1997, 105-106.

96. A department head at Latvia's privatization agency (personal interview, Riga, 1 June 1999).

97. *Riga Radio Riga Network*, "Trade Unions Appeal For CIS Solidarity," in FBIS-SOV-92-020, January 30, 1992, 75. See also *Komsomolskaya pravda*, "Trade Unions Organize Petition for Economic Demands," in FBIS-SOV-92-216, November 6, 1992, 71.

98. Samorodni 1993, 94; Nørgaard et al. 1996, 148.

99. Excluding specific rates, two-thirds of the taxes on exports in convertible currencies were below 10 percent compared with one-tenth of taxes on export in non-convertible currencies. This bias against exports in nonconvertible currencies was only reduced at the end of 1993 (Sorsa 1994, 147; *Moscow BALFAX*, "Tariffs Must Be Paid in National, Hard Currencies, in FBIS-SOV-93-029, February 16, 1993, 78)

100. Twenty percent duties were charged relative to 15 percent on goods from countries with trade agreements (*Ibid.*, 148; *Riga Radio Riga International*, "Government Introduces New Import, Export Tariffs," in FBIS-SOV-92-206, October 23, 1992, 73-74).

101. As Piritta Sorsa reports, the unweighted average duty for imports from trading partners with which Latvia had no trade agreements was 13.4 percent compared to 10 percent for those with agreements. Free-trade agreements with most of EFTA countries and with other Baltic countries, which granted duty-free entry to industrial goods, further intensified the discriminatory pattern (1994, 149).

102. Most of this was done illegally, via various processing schemes, which allowed private actors to bypass border taxes (Sorsa 1994, 145, 151). The government regulations were far from strict, and some evidence suggest that border service was heavily corrupted (*Moscow POSTFACTUM*, "Private Fuel Trade Ban May Be Lifted," in FBIS-SOV-92-025, February 6, 1992, 80; *Tallinn BNS*, "Officer Says Border Service 'Fully Corrupt,'" in FBIS-SOV-94-209, October 28, 1994, 43). Some Russian experts even argued that as much as 70 percent of Baltic exports to the West became possible due to re-export of Russian goods (Kuznetsov 1998, 8). Such estimates, while undoubtedly exaggerated, point to a source of economic reorientation. The reexport had been particularly beneficial until the mid-1993 when Russia moved closer to setting domestic prices of fuel closer to world market levels. Instructively, energy rexports by Latvia reached over $100 million of the first half of 1993, but plummeted to only $15 million in the second half of the year (*IMF Economic Reviews* 1994, 32).

103. Lainela and Sutela 1997, 140.

104. *Ibid.*

105. *Ibid.*

106. For instance, on one occasion Moscow threatened to introduce stricter trade restrictions and cut relations with certain Latvian enterprises accused of supporting Latvia's most nationalist movement, the Fatherland and Freedom/National Independence Movement. The purpose of the move was to stop Latvia in its quest for NATO membership. The reaction from Latvian officials, however, was the opposite from what Moscow might had expected. Guntars Krasts, prime minister and leader of the Fatherland and Freedom movement, responded that Russia's actions only demonstrated the risk of trade dependence on Russia and should spur Latvia to accelerate the reorientation of its foreign trade (*The Jamestown Monitor*, "Russian Blacklist of Latvian Firms Is Politically Motivated," June 10, 1998).

107. Birkavs 1999; *The Jamestown Monitor*, "European Union, Germany Surge Ahead of Russia in Latvia's Trade," October 22, 1998.

108. Macroeconomic stabilization establishes domestic preconditions for market activities and usually identified as inseparable from foreign trade transformation (Slay 1991, 8; Michalopoulos and Tarr 1996, 22). Lifting quotas and restrictions is essentially the continuation of the same process, as it reduces the state interference and encourages free exchange of goods and services.

109. See, for example, *Trade Policy Reform 1994,* 5-8, 19-23.

110. Schroeder 1992, 562.

111. A new coalition also took a more moderate stance on the status of Latvia's Russians, the largest minority (EIU, *Country Profile* 1995, 25).

112. EIU, *Country Profile* 1995, 39.

113. Dairy products and pork were subject to 55 percent duties, other meats 40 percent (EIU, *Quarterly Economic Report,* 1st quarter 1995, 30).

114. Krasts 1998, 29.

115. Vares 1995, 157.

116. *Ibid.,* 166. An opinion poll taken before the coup provided some support given to the idea of Baltic nations as a bridge between the West and the USSR (Liepins 1993, 200).

117. Misiunas 1994, 104; Sergounin 1998; Personal interviews, Riga, May-June 1999.

118. See "Annex" in *Trade Policy Reform in the Countries of the Former Soviet Union.*

119. Bleiere 1997, 61-70; Krasts 1998, 35; Logfren 1998, 47.

120. Shen 1994, 171; Logfren 1998, 48.

121. Some analyses indicated that Latvia, as well as other Baltic republics, were granted Most Favored Nation and Generalized System of Preferences statuses earlier than other newly independent nations (Kaminski 1994, 247). Baltics were also better situated culturally in the sense that many Western countries never recognized the legitimacy of Baltic incorporation into the USSR.

122. *Ibid.,* 46.

123. Vares 1995, 166; *RFE/RL Daily Report*, "Latvia Initials EC Trade Pact," February 6, 1992; "Latvia Ratifies Accord with EC," September 18, 1992.

124. The actual associate membership in the EU was gained in June 1995 (Vares 1995, 166; Ozolina 1998, 148; *RFE/RL Daily Report*, "European Parliament Ratifies Association Agreements with Baltic States," November 16, 1995).

125. Initially the agreement will benefit Latvia more than the EU, as the EU abolished all tariff barriers and allowed for the free movement of goods, services, and capital between Latvia and EU member nations, while Latvia has four years to bring its trade regime in

line with EU standards (EIU, *Quarterly Economic Report 1994*, 3, 31; *Ibid.*, 1995, 3, 25; *RFE/RL Daily Report*, "Free Trade Talks Between EU and Baltic States," March 4, 1994; "European Union toward Closer Ties with Baltics," June 24, 1994; "Baltic-EU Free Trade Accord Signed," July 19, 1994).

126. Europeans eliminated trade restrictions on most goods, although not on textile and agricultural products (Krasts 1998, 35).

127. Krasts 1998, 36.

128. The Movement for Latvia was led by right-wing German businessman and did not share Latvia's enthusiasm about entering the EU.

129. Even Socialist Party Chairman Filip Stoganov, whose party had been considered to be opposed to EU membership, signed with the understanding that, when it comes to that point, a national referendum over the joining the EU would be held (*RFE/RL Daily Report*, "Latvia Formally Applies for EU Membership," November 16, 1995; "Latvia Hands In Application to Join EU," November 30, 1995; Ozolina 1998, 109).

130. EIU, *Quarterly Economic Report 1995*, 3, 25.

131. Latvia can only be admitted to the EU after it brings its tariff structure in line with EU standards, which is going to take a while because of domestic, particularly agricultural, protectionist pressures.

132. One example of such an intention is the announcement by the European Parliament Chairman Klaus Haensch on April 10 and 11 in Vilnius and Riga that the European Union will admit the Baltic republics as a group, not individually (*The Jamestown Monitor. E-Mail Bulletin,* April 11, 1995).

133. Jofgren 1998, 47.

134. Ozolina 1998, 148.

135. Connor et. al. 1995, 44-45; Bleiere 1997, 78; Ozolina 1998, 149.

136. Krasts 1998, 39.

137. In 1995, for example, when people were asked how they would vote if a referendum in EU membership were held at that time, as much as 80 percent of respondents in Latvia were ready to vote in favor of membership (of those who had the right to vote and knew how they would vote) (Bleiere 1997, 77). At later stages, some Euro-skepticism emerged in Latvia, but a majority of the population still viewed the prospects of the country's EU membership quite favorably. Ethnic Russians, too, were generally positively disposed toward the country's EU's drive (Personal interview with a researcher at the Latvian Institute of International Affairs, Riga, June 4, 1999).

138. *Europe Agreement* 1998.

139. *The Jamestown Monitor*, "Latvia Gains Admittance to WTO," October 15, 1998; Birkavs 1999.

140. Unlike Estonia, however, Latvia was not placed on the fast-track to accession negotiations and was expected to be invited to those negotiations by the end of 1999 (*The Jamestown Monitor*, "European Union Disappoints Latvia and Lithuania," November 5, 1998; "Latvia, Lithuania Retain Hope After EU Nondecision," December 15, 1998).

141. Ulmanis 1998; Birkavs 1999.

142. Nationalist parties—the People's Party, the Latvia's Way, and the Fatherland and Freedom—amounted to a 62-seat strong majority in the 100-seat parliament. On the minority side, the "centrist" New Party won eight seats, the left-of-center Social Democratic Alliance fourteen seats, and the leftist People's Harmony Party—whose electorate is

mainly Russian—sixteen seats (*Prism*, "As Latvia Turns So Turn the Baltics," October 16, 1998; *The Jamestown Monitor*, "Latvia Misses Chance to Form a Stable Majority Government," December 1, 1998).

143. The adoption of the Declaration renewed the Treaty on Unity and Cooperation and the resulting declaration signed by Estonia, Latvia, and Lithuania in Geneva on 12 September 1934, before they had been incorporated into the Soviet empire (Vares 1995, 158).

144. In a certain way, this was encouraged by the Union's officials (see fn. 132).

145. For example, Latvia established high import tariffs, particularly on agricultural products, and this was upsetting for agricultural exporters in Lithuania and Estonia, for whom Latvia is a key market (EIU, *Quarterly Economic Report 1995*, 1, 30).

146. Schroeder 1992, 561.

147. *RFE/RL Daily Report*, "Baltic Free Trade Agreement," September 14, 1993; "Baltic Free-Trade Agreement," February 17, 1994.

148. *The Jamestown Monitor*, 1996, June 16; *RFE/RL Daily Report*, "Baltic Prime Ministers Sign Free Agricultural Trade Agreement," June 17, 1996.

149. *Trade policy* 1994, 53; *RFE/RL Daily Report*, "Baltic States and EFTA," June 15, 1995.

150. *RFE/RL Daily Report*, "Latvia, EFTA Initial Free Trade Agreement," November 9, 1995.

151. *RFE/RL Daily Report*, "Latvia, Slovakia Sign Free Trade Agreement," April 22, 1996; "Latvia, Slovenia Sign Free Trade Agreement," April 24, 1996.

152. The presidents of Ukraine and Latvia, Leonid Kuchma and Guntis Ulmanis, respectively, said on a few occasions that they were interested in mutual support in foreign policy and cooperation within a "common economic space" from the Baltic to the Black Sea. For example, during Ulmanis's two-day visit in 1995, the two sides agreed to create a joint commission to implement agreements on mutual diplomatic support, trade, cooperation in the military-industrial sector, and in possible construction of a Black Sea-Baltic Sea oil pipeline. The notion that this constitutes a region in its own right, described as an "intermarium" (between the Seas) or as the Ponto-Baltic Isthmus, is traditional in European geopolitics. The idea of close cooperation among the peoples of the region stretching from the Baltic to the Black Sea dates back to the nineteenth century and the interwar period, as a plan to secure the region's freedom from Russian domination. The idea reemerged after the fall of Communism, but lost some of its strength after its main promoter and historic source, Poland, became eligible for NATO membership. Some elite groups in former western Soviet republics continue to view the Baltic-Black Sea region-wide cooperation as a means to ultimately reduce economic dependency on Russia, but the position of Belarus jeopardizes such plans. Moreover, Russian fears of a cordon sanitaire have forced the idea's promoters to move cautiously, if at all (*The Jamestown Monitor*, November 22, 1995; November 27, 1995; Samorodni 1993).

Chapter 4
Ukraine

In comparison with Latvia, Ukraine chose a moderate foreign economic course. Its government decided to join the CIS (although it has never been an active participant in the organization) and was, in general, more active in bilateral cooperation with Russia. While determined to diversify its economic activities toward Western partners, Ukraine has been much less successful than its Baltic neighbors. The Ukrainian leadership has also been much less decisive in maintaining its originally declared commitments to foreign economic reorientation, and its policy making during the period from 1990 to 1996 can be broken down into at least two subperiods, each following its own distinct patterns.

National Identity

Ukraine may serve as an example of a country with a moderate degree of national identity strength. Although Ukraine had some historical experience with independence and, hence, some memory of it, this memory has never had the opportunity to be consolidated. For the country as a whole, the experience with independence was simply too short and sporadic to internalize the norm of sovereignty and develop a strong identification with the world of sovereign nations to the same extent as Latvia. At best, the sovereignty norm has been internalized only partially and mainly among elites. National identity development, however, received additional support from the incorporation of western lands into the rest of Ukraine in 1939. Never previously a part of the Russian empire, western Ukraine displayed a strong resistance to the incorporation, serving as an "island" of diffusion of nationalist ideas and a source for strengthening the country's national identity. Paradoxically, some Soviet institutions also facilitated the formation of the Ukrainian national Self.

The Experience with National Independence and Unification

Unlike their Latvian counterparts, Ukrainian nationalists could not boast of significant historical experience with national independence. To support their calls for Ukraine's gaining sovereignty and leaving the USSR, they referred to two main attempts of Ukraine to establish national independence, both rather sporadic and short-lived. The first episode goes back to Ukraine's seventeenth-century experience with Cossackdom; the second emerged as a result of the early twentieth century breakdown of the Russian empire and the subsequent three years of independence and cultural reawakening in Ukraine.[1]

The Cossackdom emerged in the mid-seventeenth century when Ukraine was culturally and politically divided between the Polish-controlled Catholic west and the Moscow-oriented east. Recruited from rebellious serfs and peasants hiding from political authorities in the vast Ukrainian steppes, Cossacks defended their autonomy from Poles and Russians and pursued a distinct economic and political style of living. They were electing their leaders, or *hetmans*, and lived as free farmers and border patrolmen.[2] In 1648, under the leadership of Hetman Bohdan Khmelnytsky, an independent Cossack state was established, which lasted until 1654. Practically all strata of the Ukrainian population, dissatisfied with the harshness of Polish and Russian rule, sided with the Cossacks. Yet the difficulty of fighting simultaneously on three fronts against the Poles, Russians, and Tatars eventually forced Ukrainian leaders to seek an alliance with Moscow, formalized with the Treaty of Pereiaslav. Despite the original intentions of those signing the Treaty,[3] it effectively ended the short-lived Ukrainian independence and, for many years after, subjected Ukraine to Russian empire. The Cossackdom, however, became one of the key myths constituting the Ukrainian national idea and has always been very much alive among nationally conscious intellectuals.[4]

The next attempt to establish and consolidate national independence in Ukraine came with the decline and subsequent disintegration of the Russian empire. While at the time the idea of independence did not command wide support in Ukrainian society, it gained strength as the only way to preserve Ukrainian survival under the external and domestic upheavals. World War I, the Bolshevik revolution, and the Civil War posed a threat to the very survival of Ukraine as an autonomous unit and, by 1918, elites embraced the idea of independence as "the only option that offered them refuge from imperial collapse and Bolshevik takeover."[5] Yet internal turmoil and external circumstances made it impossible to build institutions of independent statehood. Fierce military fighting between the Bolsheviks and the Whites that was taking place on Ukrainian land, and the lack of an army and strong allies eventually led to mass social revolt in Ukraine and the deaths of millions of Ukrainians and Russians. No government could maintain order under these circumstances. Three short-lived governments succeeded each other until Ukraine was retaken by the Bolsheviks and, in December 1922, formally proclaimed a part of the USSR.

Although both episodes played an important role in fostering Ukraine's national memory (particularly among elites), their role was primarily symbolic: by themselves, they were not sufficient for internalizing the sovereignty norm and building an overarching sense of national identity. Nothing similar to what happened in Latvia took place in Ukraine. When Bolsheviks took over Ukraine in 1922, it was at its early stages of gaining the sense of being a nonimperial entity. Some strata of political elites felt attracted to the ideal of sovereign statehood, but the masses were ignorant, at best.

In the period of 1939-1945, however, Ukraine's identity formation received additional support from its western lands, which were never previously part of the Russian empire. As a result of the Ribbentrop-Molotov pact, the western territories[6] were incorporated into the Soviet empire and united with the rest of Ukraine. Although the western lands did not have the status as being formally independent and were parts of other countries, they had something important to bring to Ukraine's national identity formation. First and foremost, they had never been part of Russia[7] and, thus, were never subjected to policies of linguistic Russification that had been practiced before the Revolution. Instead, they enjoyed a reasonable degree of linguistic autonomy, as the Ukrainian language continued to be used in the press and in voluntary societies of various kinds. Second, the western lands preserved a strong nationalist underground that had operated throughout the Second World War years and continued to resist the Soviet authorities until after the war had ended. Third, despite large-scale emigration to the west, there remained a Ukrainian intelligentsia in west Ukraine, including the main city, Lviv.[8] All these points indicate that the western lands contributed greatly to the process of Ukraine's national identity formation, helping to diffuse nationalist ideas and preserve the legitimacy of the ideal of an independent nation.

Ukraine's historical experience with national independence and its unification with the western lands helped to build a sense of distinctness from the empire. While not as strong as in Latvia, Ukrainian sense of national Self persisted, even becoming stronger during post-1939 colonial existence. Two episodes from the Soviet period can help to illustrate the existence of Ukrainian national feelings. First, from 1939-1941, the population of Galicia, one of the western lands, supported Germany's attack on the USSR[9] in a bid for increased independence. During the war, Ukrainian nationalists continued to fight for independence from the Stalinist regime. The nationalist guerrilla warfare was doomed given the unfavorable conditions: the Soviet state was strong and consolidated; the German occupiers would not allow the formation of alternative state structures; and the Western powers were unable or unwilling to intervene.[10] Yet fighting continued through the mid-1950s.

A second attempt to reassert national rights came in the 1960s, under the leadership of Ukraine's first party secretary, Petro Shelest. In attempting to oppose the influx of non-Ukrainian cadres into the republic, far-reaching reforms in the educational system were proposed with a goal of gradual conversion to a completely Ukrainian-language education. The new elite also sought its own ideology, which, while coexisting with Soviet ideology, might have had the potential to undermine it.[11] By the 1970s, as some scholars have suggested, Ukraine was actually in the position of being capable of translating its symbolic sovereignty into genuine sovereignty.[12] Yet, as previously occurred with Stalin's rise to power, the process of "neo-Ukrainization" was abruptly interrupted with Brezhnev's ascension to power, tightening control over Ukraine and replacing Shelest with Kremlin loyalist Vladimir Scherbitsky.[13]

To summarize, by the time of the late-twentieth-century imperial decline, Ukraine did acquire a sense of its national distinctness from the empire and wanted to preserve it through specific policies. This sense of national Self was constructed from various pieces, such as some sporadic experiences with national independence and the incorporation of pro-Western lands, and was still lacking the strength and coherence that existed in Latvia. Various social and territorial strata were far from consolidated vis-à-vis the idea of independent nationhood, but the process of national identity formation did take off and went considerably far in the sense that there were serious forces sharing the idea of independence, as well as the networks for their activities.

Other Factors Shaping Ukrainian Identity

In addition to its historical experience with independence and national unification, Ukraine's identity formation was affected by its experience as a part of the Soviet empire. In a sense, the effect of relations with Moscow was more significant for Ukrainian identity than it was for Latvia, as Ukrainian national feelings were far less pronounced and widespread by the time of the country's unification within the Soviet borders (and, hence, much less able to preserve them). As happened in Latvia, though, the effects of Soviet experience reflected in Ukraine's domestic features—territorial, political, economic, and cultural—were ambiguous; some encouraged while others discouraged national identity formation.

The territoriality dimension did favor the strengthening of Ukrainian national identity; relatively stable geopolitical borders were acquired only in the mid-twentieth century, much later than in Latvia. Historically, at least since the sixteenth century, Ukraine has possessed a dual political and cultural identity as a result of the division between a European-oriented Catholic west and a Moscow-oriented Orthodox east.[14] Only in 1945, when Stalin annexed western lands, did Ukraine become a formally unified territory, having received an important attribute of nationhood.[15] This gave the nation a chance to start working on unifying its poorly integrated western and eastern areas.

As with Latvia, the establishment of the Soviet regime in Ukraine inevitably meant destruction of most of the previously existing indigenous political institutions and imposition of new institutional arrangements, with the task of subjecting republican life to Moscow's control. Yet in Ukraine, Soviet institution building arguably played a more constructive role than in Latvia. By the time of its reincorporation into the empire, Ukraine's basic political institutions were all but wrecked—the result of domestic and external turmoil—and the Soviet regime, in its own way, provided for their consolidation and strengthening. The shape of those subnational institutions—Supreme Soviets, governments, courts, army divisions, academy of science divisions, etc.—was, of course, decided in the Kremlin and, therefore, should have served the purpose of further stabilization of the empire. However, by supplying the republics, including Ukraine, with all these institutions, the Kremlin paradoxically supplied institutional channels that in principle could be mobilized by local politicians for resisting imperial policies.[16]

Economic development played a mixed role in Ukraine's identity formation, just as it did in Latvia. In part the result of Soviet industrialization, Ukraine became one of the upper-level developed republics, with its degree of urbanization one of the highest and its infant mortality rate one of the lowest.[17] It therefore unquestionably passed the test of creating necessary economic preconditions for making a successful transition from parochial loyalties to a nationwide sense of unity. At the same time, Ukrainian industrialization, as with that of Latvia, became possible due to a large influx of ethnic Russians, serving as a factor undermining the sense of Ukraine's ethnic cohesiveness.

Finally, Ukraine's cultural record and its change during the Soviet period had a mixed effect on the republic's identity formation. Historically, Ukraine had some features encouraging its cultural distinctness from the metropole and others strengthening Ukraine's similarity with Russia. For example, Ukraine does have its own distinct language, but is similar to Russia in its religion.[18] During the Soviet period, the religious link between the two nations came to the point of subjecting Ukraine's Orthodox Church to the formal influence of the Moscow Patriarch.[19] The religious nexus therefore strengthens Russo-Ukrainian cultural ties and complicates the process of Ukrainian postimperial nation building. The other problem is the degree of Ukraine's linguistic Russification, which is much higher than in Latvia (see table 3.1 on page 48). With some simplification, one can say that eastern Ukraine prefers to speak Russian, while western Ukraine speaks primarily Ukrainian.[20]

Overall, by the beginning of Gorbachev's reforms and the subsequent Soviet disintegration, Ukraine had acquired some important components of national identity. This identity was weaker than that of Latvia, mainly because of Ukraine's modest experience with national independence. The process of Ukraine's identity formation was also complicated by its late accomplishment of territorial unity and some cultural similarities with Russia. At the same time, Ukraine's historical experience with independence, however short-lived and sporadic, laid a foundation for belief in the distinctiveness of Ukraine as a nation apart from the Russian nation, a belief that was reinforced in the course of unifying the eastern and western lands. Ironically, the Soviet regime, too, in many ways encouraged Ukraine's national identity formation. It was the Soviet regime that had modernized the Ukrainian economy, granted Ukraine a national republican autonomy, established (sub)political institutions, and completed the process of territorial unification of eastern and western lands, thereby creating important preconditions for fostering Self-identification of Ukraine as an independent nation (national identity).

Domestic Structures

Unlike their Latvian counterparts, Ukrainian nationalists, over the course of five years of independence, did not manage to mobilize the society around their ideas and could not provide Ukrainian leadership with firm social support for implementing its policies. However, they did play an important role in domestic political struggle, offsetting the influence of empire savers and providing the ideological rationale for a continued nation-building process.

Society

Nationalists

Nationalists, or nation builders, were those committed to Ukraine's secession from the USSR and acquisition of a full-fledged national independence status. Nationalist groups emerged during the perestroika years and were particularly active in western Ukraine, with its well-preserved national memory.[21] Inspired by various dissent activities during the Soviet period, nationalist groupings emerged, in many cases as their direct continuation.[22] The largest of them were the Ukrainian People's Movement for Perestroika (Rukh), the Ukrainian Republican Party, and the Ukrainian Democratic Party.[23]

Before perestroika, nationalism in Ukraine did not enjoy wide social support and was mainly popular among some strata of humanitarian intelligentsia. Nationalist ideas only gained influence when the old communist beliefs were completely discredited in the course of Gorbachev's reforms and the so-called party of power decided to abandon them. In March 1990, nationalists, while hampered by the ruling regime, received about 17 percent of the vote to national legislature.[24] In Autumn 1990, their efforts were supported by student and worker protests in Kiev,[25] and in 1991 nationalism had gained a truly nationwide recognition, due mainly to support given to it by the newly recognized leader of the new *nomenklatura,* Leonid Kravchuk. In March 1991, in the referendum on the preservation of the USSR, the idea of independence received the support of close to 90 percent of voters in western *oblasts,*[26] and in yet another republican-wide vote in December, 90 percent of all Ukrainians gave their support to independence.[27] The triumph of nationalists, however, proved to be rather short-lived. After 1992, with economic recession and declining living standards, the ruling elite became less receptive to nationalist ideas and somewhat more sympathetic of empire savers' demands.

Beyond the ideational channels, nationalists had a few instruments with which to influence the policy-making process. The idea of independence could only reach masses when supported by the ruling elite.[28] After 1991, however, when the ruling regime withdrew its unequivocal support, nationalists were not nearly as successful in mobilizing mass support.[29] They could hardly set the legislative agenda in the left-dominated parliament and never actually controlled more than 15 percent of the seats.[30] Except for a few notable exceptions, they held no serious government positions.[31] The media was highly dependent on the state[32] and, therefore, could hardly be used by nationalists as a channel for mobilizing mass support in favor of their policy preferences. To summarize, Ukrainian nationalists had to rely on the support of the party in power and had no institutional means of challenging it.

Empire Savers

Empire savers were those willing to accept Russia's domination in one way or another for the sake of accomplishing other goals, primarily of a socioeconomic nature.[33] Politically related to parties of communist and socialist orientation,[34] they enjoyed wide social support among workers, industrialists, peasants, and bureaucrats feeling nostalgia for the "good old" Soviet system. Regionally, empire savers were concentrated in Ukraine's eastern oblasts, much more Russified and economically dependent on the ex-metropole. An opinion poll taken in May 1995 indicated, for example, that in Donetsk only 29.6 percent of residents identified themselves with the population of Ukraine as a whole, while 32.8 percent felt that they belonged to the "Former Soviet" category. For comparison, in Lviv (Galicia) the numbers were 75.4 and 8.5 percent, respectively.[35]

As in Russia, empire-saving forces in Ukraine were seriously defeated by Gorbachev's reforms and the subsequent Soviet collapse. They could hardly resist the state-building efforts pursued by the new nomenklatura during the first one or two years of independence. However, by the end of 1992, with Ukraine plunging into economic recession, the situation began to change. Communist and socialist-oriented parties reemerged.[36] More and more people felt that the country was going in the wrong direction: their percentage increased from 35 to 72 percent over the period from January 1992 to October 1994.[37] By 1994, despite the trauma of Stalinism, the percentage of those willing to trade their freedom for economic security was about the same as the percentage of those against it.[38] Various polls indicated that the country was torn between various economic and political alternatives,[39] and with their economy lagging behind Russia's, Ukrainian empire savers increased their political credentials and ability to influence the policy-making process.

Unlike nationalists, empire savers did not have new ideas to sell to the public and appealed mainly to people's nostalgia for economic security. To many Ukrainians, this nostalgia proved to be stronger than their feelings of national identity. The same people who voted for national independence in March 1991 supported close economic and political ties with Russia from 1993 on, which allowed empire savers to obtain a significant number of seats in the national legislature and to use strikes (particularly initiated by coal miners in eastern Ukraine) for putting pressures on policymakers. In addition, Ukrainian empire savers on various occasions obtained support (more moral than financial) from Russian politicians for the idea of Russo-Ukrainian union.[40]

Neither nation builders nor empire savers succeeded in setting the policy agenda during the five years of Ukrainian independence. Rather, each grouping had its own social support and its own way of influencing decision makers. Nationalists pioneered the ideas of independence, but were much less prepared to deal with negative, particularly economic, consequences of Soviet disintegration and offer a program for Ukrainian economic recovery. In their turn, empire savers maintained that economic security should not be sacrificed to national independence and that it could only be attained by restoring close ties with the ex-metropole.

State

Ukrainian state structures were less constrained by societal pressures than was the case in Latvia. As was theorized in chapter 2, in a polarized society such as Ukraine, the governing body would typically obtain more space for policy maneuvering than in a relatively homogeneous society. Not surprisingly, the Ukrainian state needed to develop an institutional capacity for mediating nationalists' and empire savers' demands. Overall, it succeeded: during the first five years of independence, the Ukrainian state possessed all the required instruments for conducting a consistent policy course and overcoming, when necessary, an excessive resistance from nationalist or empire-saving groupings.

Degree of Centralization

Ukraine's state was much more centralized than that of Latvia. The December 1991 election of Leonid Kravchuk, Ukraine's first president, was the first major step toward centralizing state authority required for overcoming excessive social pressures and conducting independent policies. In early 1992, a new constitution draft further strengthened the powers of the president at the cost of weakening those of the parliament.[41] In particular, the president could directly supervise the work of the government and issue decrees on various economic and political affairs[42] and, in the absence of the adoption of the constitution until June 1996, had maintained these powers.[43] Ukraine's parliament, too, took steps aimed at preventing nationalist and empire-saving parties from exerting excessive pressures. For example, in advance of the March 1994 elections, the parliament passed an electoral law that heavily favored incumbents and independents.[44] Finally, in the Soviet spirit, the state essentially retained control over the media.[45]

Legitimacy

Legitimacy, or the level of public trust, is another important dimension of state capacity. Ukraine's government was highly legitimate during 1991 and 1992, which was the result of its commitments to the widely popular ideas of national independence. Symptomatically, in the 1991 presidential election, Leonid Kravchuk received 62 percent of the vote.[46] In the referendum on independence, even in Russian-speaking Crimea and such regions as the Donbass, 54 percent and 84 percent of the turnout, respectively, voted "Yes," due largely to politicians' linking Ukrainian independence with hopes of prosperity.[47] State legitimacy declined, however, during the second part of Kravchuk's term and was only partially improved with Leonid Kuchma's election as the country's second president in July 1994. The fact that Kuchma had received only 52 percent of the vote and was closely followed by Kravchuk, with 45 percent, signified a relative decline of state capacity over the 1991-1994 period.

Ukraine's policy-making process was more state-dominated than that of Latvia. The Ukrainian state experienced constraints from various social poles and, hence, had a number of options to pursue in its policy. Logically, in a society divided between nationalists and empire savers, a state could choose among pro-nationalist, pro-imperial, and balancing strategies. The Ukrainian state, at various stages of its existence, exploited pro-nationalist and balancing strategies, having also given some consideration to the pro-imperial feelings of the eastern lands.

During 1990-1992, nation builders had the upper hand in influencing the policy agenda. At the same time, the state retained relative control over the policy-making process. Quite symptomatically, despite the widespread popularity of national independence, it was Leonid Kravchuk, a former high ranking Communist *apparatchyk*, who became a president and in charge of policy implementation. Vyacheslav Chornovil, a former dissident and leader of a key nationalist organization, Rukh, also ran for president, but received only 23 percent of the vote.[48] The Rukh movement had no choice but to announce its support for Kravchuk's policies. Kravchuk, too, made explicit his intention of cooperating with nationalists based on the idea of Ukraine's independent nationhood.[49] The change came in the second half of 1992, with some nationalists having withdrawn their support for the ruling regime. The Rukh split into two parts, and Chornovil announced his group's opposition to Kravchuk's course calling for accelerated economic reform, the creation of a federal state, and more cooperative relations with the CIS states.[50]

By 1994, the state realized the limitations of its pro-nationalist orientation and began to drift toward the empire savers. The change of policy orientation was particularly noticeable during a 1994 presidential election campaign in which both major competitors (Kravchuk and Kuchma) promised more cooperation with Russia and other CIS states, and the more Russia-oriented Kuchma defeated the more nationalistic Kravchuk.[51] An opinion poll taken in eight eastern and southern oblasts and Crimea in May 1994 revealed that as many as 47 percent of Ukrainians would have been against Ukraine's independence at the time if they were to repeat their December 1991 vote.[52] Against some expectations, however, Kuchma did not become a voice of the empire savers. Rather, under his leadership the state pursued a balancing strategy: the accomplishments of state- and nation-building period were preserved, while priority was given to accelerating marketization and improving relations with the ex-metropole and other CIS members. Instead of relying on either nationalists or empire savers, the state chose to build a social consensus and encourage the growth of political parties and movements with more "centrist" orientations and more supportive of nationhood, but not at the expense of economic reform.

Foreign Economic Policy

Russian Pole

The Belief in the Virtue of Economic Nationalism

By early 1990, Ukraine's political elite began to increasingly share a belief in the virtue of economic nationalism as a way to improve the republic's economic situation. The political vacuum generated by the decline of empire started to be filled with nationalist ideas, and the party in power finally gave in by embracing nationalist slogans and demonstrating its willingness to do what it took economically in order to build independent nation- and statehood.

At the core of the belief was the idea of Ukraine's colonial dependence on Russia, the metropole. Ukraine was commonly believed to possess the strongest economic potential of all the republics, including Russia. "At least we can feed ourselves—we will never starve" was a commonly shared sentiment, one also shared by most prominent economists.[53] Due to the size of its economic resources and its strategic geographic location, Ukraine was routinely compared with France and Germany, not with the other republics or countries of Eastern Europe.[54] It was argued that the reason why Ukraine did not become "like France" was that it was systematically exploited by the metropole. As a deputy head of Ukraine's parliament Ivan Plushch argued in December 1991,

> Why is it that our people have lived on their own land for a thousand years and still have not reach the level of the world civilization and in the wake of the 21st century, still have been doing dirty physical labor and unable to take a hot shower after work? That is because during many centuries, the Ukrainian people have never been masters on their own territory. We have always been alienated from the results of our own work.[55]

Since Ukraine, as was widely believed, was the richest republic within the empire and, in fact, was the one that had to "feed" Russia, it seemed only logical to further argue that Ukraine could prosper by leaving the USSR and restructuring economic activities away from the old partners. Indeed, many believed that should the old unfair and exploitative system be removed, Ukraine would quickly—in span of three to five years—become one of the largest economically developed European countries. Such beliefs almost inevitably led to the conclusion that it was the building of an independent nation that would be the key to solving Ukraine's economic problems and that the building of such a nation would be incompatible with any form of political, economic, and military integration with Russia.[56]

One can identify at least three sources of the emergence and the subsequent rise among Ukrainian elites of a belief in the virtue of economic nationalism. The first was the work of Ukraine's diaspora economists who had often advanced the "internal colony of the USSR" argument. In the 1970s, one of them concluded, for example, that "the Ukrainian population was forced to bear a heavy and greatly disproportionate burden in supporting the Soviet economy and the central government's activities by being forced to suffer a lower standard of living than otherwise would have been the case."[57] The second source was domestic and had to do with writings of Ukrainian nationalists such as Levko Lukianenko,[58] which later contributed to the Rukh's economic ideas. Finally, the belief in economic nationalism was supported by a Deutsche Bank study, according to which Ukraine had the best prospects in terms of integration into the European markets.[59] The study's conclusions were widely publicized domestically, with President Kravchuk and other politicians quoting them with pride as evidence supporting their policy course.[60]

Under conditions of political uncertainty, the idea of economic nationalism turned out to exert the strongest influence on Ukraine's policy community. The former Communist nomenklatura abandoned previously popular ideas of the enlightened socialism, but apparently was too conservative or economically illiterate to embrace market liberalism as a policy guide. In the meantime, the ideas of economic nationalism were already in the air and waiting to be adopted. They were available, increasingly popular, and sounded somewhat familiar to those already used to thinking about politics in zero-sum terms. Not surprisingly, having embraced those ideas, Ukrainian policymakers were eager to practically implement them.

The CIS Stance

Ukraine's attitude toward the CIS went through at least two major stages. During 1990-1992, a Ukraine, fascinated with the ideas of economic nationalism, resisted any Moscow-initiated attempts to create supranational institutions in place of the Soviet Union. However, particularly after 1993, this attitude changed somewhat, and the Ukrainian leadership publicly acknowledged that the CIS could serve some important purposes, such as economic cooperation among its members. The country's strategic orientation, however, remained a European one. Even with Kuchma as president, Ukraine continued to be a restrained participant in CIS affairs.

Ukraine's original attitude toward the CIS was in many ways predetermined by the resistance of Ukrainian leaders to Gorbachev-initiated attempts to negotiate a new Soviet treaty. Whereas this drive was not nearly as aggressive as the one by Latvia, it was distinctively persistent. Unlike some other republics, including Belarus, Ukraine firmly resisted many versions of a new Union treaty that were initiated one after another by the president of the USSR.[61] It avoided entering Moscow-initiated multilateral agreements and began pursuing its own economic policy, without Moscow as an intermediary. In November 1990, for example, Ukraine, together with Russia and Belarus, negotiated to coordinate price changes, thus demonstrating an attempt to enhance economic cooperation among the republics without the Soviet center.[62] Another example was the Treaty on Economic Community signed in October 1991 and intended to create a "common economic space" in which the republics would cooperate on economic policy, trade, and other matters. Ukraine refused to sign the treaty, viewing it as an obstacle to its independence. Explaining in a television address why Ukraine was staying out of the economic union, the deputy head of the Ukrainian parliament, Ivan Plyushch, declared, "History has given us a chance to become an independent nation, and we do not want to continue to be a colony."[63] The leadership's attitude was fully in accord with that of the nationalists. Rukh, for example, issued a statement calling the treaty a "real danger" to Ukraine's nationhood. The agreement, it said, was above all a political document aimed at salvaging the Soviet empire.[64]

Eager to become independent from Moscow, Ukraine, along with the new Russia's leadership, was directly responsible for the immediate breakup of the Soviet Union. The possibility of concluding a treaty still existed in the Fall of

1991, when Gorbachev had gone back to Moscow after the failed coup. Kravchuk insisted, however, that Ukraine would only consider entering into agreements "in which it does not lose a drop of its statehood."[65] In December 1991, the leaders of Russia, Ukraine, and Belarus met at Belovezhie. Kravchuk went along with Boris Yeltsin's proposal to sign a treaty about the establishment of what would soon become the Commonwealth of Independent States, because he shared Yeltsin's aspiration to eliminate the political center personified by Mikhail Gorbachev.[66]

The creation of a new union was, therefore, merely the fastest and most effective way to eliminate the old one. Ukrainian leadership did not see any future for a strong political center and viewed the newly emerged CIS as an "instrument for civilized divorce" with Russia and other ex-Soviet republics. This view was widely shared among political elites and was illustrated by the statement of Dmitrii Pavlychko, chairman of the Ukrainian parliament's Foreign Affairs Committee and a senior advisor to the Ukrainian president, who saw the commonwealth as a temporary system that would be discarded after Soviet nuclear weapons were destroyed. In Pavlychko's words, the commonwealth should have played merely a transitional role as the Soviet republics consolidated their independence and developed economic relations.[67] While nationalists were pushing to leave the CIS altogether,[68] the leadership was hoping the problem would be solved by itself, and the new union would disintegrate in the same manner as the old one.

This attitude began to change in late 1992, when Ukraine plunged into economic recession and hyperinflation (see table 3.2 on pages 60-61). The economic consequences of the Soviet disintegration, as well as Ukraine's own isolationist stance, hit the country badly. Coupon (currency) collapsed[69] and Ukraine experienced an extremely sharp decline in trade[70] (see table 3.2). Efforts to find alternative energy sources were far from successful, and the country was again forced to rely on Russia for its economic survival, though it was in no position to pay Russia back.[71] In addition, Ukraine faced severe problems with production supplies.[72] All these factors stimulated the decline of nationalist ideas and sharp criticism of the government's policies. The east-central region in particular gave national independence only conditional support and was not prepared to stand for independence at the expense of economic security. Led by newly emerged and reemerged parties of empire-saving orientations,[73] the east demanded to reverse the strategy of economic nationalism and to restore disrupted economic ties with Russia. Donbass's miners went on strike, and local governors of eastern oblasts began negotiating treaties directly with neighboring Russian cities "to restore the traditional, above all, economic ties."[74] These pressures soon took the form of territorial division, threatening to split the country along its "east versus west" line.

Under such conditions, the early illusions of a fast and relatively smooth integration with Western economic institutions began to fade, and the state launched a search for broader social support for its policies, beyond nationalist-oriented groupings. As a result, the original perception of the CIS as an organization with only temporary functions serving the "civilized divorce" of the ex-Soviet republics started to change, too. Instead, the CIS was increasingly viewed as able to serve some important functions and, therefore, as something that should continue to exist and not be disbanded in the same manner as the USSR. Confronted by severe economic problems, Ukrainian leadership felt that the CIS could and should have facilitated economic cooperation among the Soviet successor nations and that, should it have been disbanded, the situation in Ukraine would have become even worse.[75]

The year 1993 was a time of increased Ukrainian activity in CIS matters. At a CIS summit in Minsk in January 1993, Ukraine signed an agreement on interstate banking and, in July of the same year, the Prime Ministers of Ukraine, Russia, and Belarus issued a joint statement calling for the creation of a customs union and a single market in goods, services, and capital.[76] This spurred debate over the country's further participation in CIS economic affairs. In September 1993, Ukrainian leadership made a controversial decision to join the Economic Union agreement, albeit as an associate member only.[77] The agreement sought to achieve both economic and political goals. Economically, it was hoped that the agreement would help secure some dismantling of the trade barriers, which proliferated after 1991, between the former Soviet republics. The treaty was supposed to provide for a "gradual deepening of integration" through the progressive establishment of a free-trade zone, customs union, and a common market, as well as monetary coordination.[78] Politically, the leadership was making an effort to bandwagon a shift from the country's generally nationalist mood to one of "why do we need this independence?"

The signing of the Economic Union agreement preceded a heated discussion at home. Nationalists argued against Ukrainian participation in the treaty on the grounds that it served the interests of Russian domination over other CIS members. Empire savers, on the other hand, pushed for Ukraine's more active role in CIS matters. A roundtable of Communist and pro-Communist parties and groups, held in Kiev on August 20, urged that Ukraine form an economic union with its two neighboring Slavic nations. The discussion continued in the parliament.[79]

After much hesitation, Kravchuk supported the "economic union" agreement—drafted initially by Kuchma with the Russian and Belarussian governments—as a blueprint for a more integrated CIS. Speaking to the Ukrainian parliament on September 1, 1993, Kravchuk said it would be senseless for Ukraine to oppose economic integration, citing the example of Western Europe's single market and North American Free Trade Association (NAFTA) agreement. He called for a dispassionate calculation of the costs and benefits of economic union and, in a passage directed at nationalists, added: "On the basis of euphoria and emotions one can quickly take a decision, but the after-effects will be very complicated. It is time to learn something from experience."[80] The actual decision, however, had not been made until the Ukrainian delegation arrived in Moscow. Only there, after numerous discussions with Russia and other CIS members participants, did Kravchuk decide that Ukraine should join the controversial agreement, but only as an associate member.[81]

It seems very likely that the decision was motivated primarily by the desire to avoid further domestic polarization and even confrontation over the country's cultural identity. If so, it served its purpose well. Having arrived from Moscow, Kravchuk faced criticism from both sides of the political spectrum, and the ambiguously defined status of Ukraine in the CIS Economic Union helped him to withstand attacks for "betrayal of national interests" from both left and right. Upon returning home, he claimed, for example, that "we did not sign the agreement, because it was only signed by full members. That is to say we could not sign it even if we wanted to."[82] In early 1994, however, facing reelection and needing to confirm his willingness to cooperate within the CIS framework, he argued just the reverse—that Ukraine was in fact a full member in CIS economic matters.[83]

The 1994 election of Kuchma as president confirmed that Ukraine no longer believed in the virtue of breaking away from Russia and the CIS. In one of his speeches in Lviv, Kuchma declared that "the CIS countries and, first of all, Russia form a zone of our special interest. Here we have our main sources of raw materials, sales markets, close technological and cooperative ties."[84] At the same time, the earlier efforts of nationalists-led Kravchuk did not disappear without an effect; like his predecessor, Kuchma was committed to strategic goals of "returning to Europe" and protecting Ukraine's sovereignty. Like the nationalists, Kuchma wanted to practice economic relations with Russia and other CIS members on a bilateral basis and resented efforts to strengthen the CIS-based multilateralism. The actual difference between his vision and the vision of the early economic nationalists was that the goal of integrating with Europe was no longer defined in zero-sum terms as if it could only be reached at the cost of moving away from Russia and Eurasia. Instead, the new leadership proposed to view cooperation with Russia and the CIS countries as a *precondition* for establishing coherent economic foundations for Ukraine's independence and continued European drive.[85]

Ukraine, therefore, remained a restrained participant in CIS multilateral initiatives. For example, it maintained its reservations about participating in the CIS Economic Union and remained an associate (not a full) member of the arrangement. It also abstained from signing the Payment or Customs Union agreement among the CIS members,[86] and it remained highly critical of Russia for its desire to dominate in the former Soviet area and for its intolerance of other republics' sovereignty.[87] This policy stance remained at odds with Moscow's preferences for Ukraine's more active role in CIS affairs, but it served well in maintaining a domestic balance between pro-Russian and nationalist-oriented forces. On the one hand, Kuchma realized the importance of taking seriously the empire-saving demands and did move away from the earlier isolationist policies.[88] On the other hand, he remained open to nationalist pressures and did not become Ukraine's president "in order to become a vassal of Russia."[89] In early 1995, for example, Kuchma severely criticized the pro-Communist organizers of a campaign in favor of holding a referendum on the creation of a new political, economic, and military union with Russia, Belarus, and Kazakhstan. While visiting a military unit in the Chernihiv region, Kuchma told reporters that such a union would "do no one any good, including Ukraine" and warned organizers that, as the recently elected president of an independent Ukraine, he would not allow anyone to "rock the boat we are in" and would do his utmost to strengthen its independence.[90]

Currency Cooperation with Russia

A somewhat similar pattern of behavior was demonstrated by Ukraine in its bilateral relations with Russia. At earlier stages, Ukrainian leadership did not value cooperation with the ex-metropole very highly, viewing it as incompatible with the goals of establishing national independence. In late 1992, this attitude started to change, and normalization of economic relations with Russia was placed firmly on the policy agenda. Ukraine's policies in both currency and trade domains may illustrate how this patterned developed.

In the currency domain, Kravchuk and his supporters felt that the early intro-duction of *hryvna* (national currency) and a unilateral departure from the "ruble zone" were the key steps in bringing economic salvation to Ukraine.[91] Proposals to create a currency regime for the purpose of coordinating economic policies in the former USSR[92] were not given serious consideration. The belief in the neces-sity and urgency of introducing the hryvna was consistent with the ideology of nation builders who believed that the major priority was, as Stepan Khmara put it, "securing the self-sufficiency of the national economy and its independence from the influence of external economic competitors or political maneuvering."[93] Moreover, very few people realized that leaving the ex-Soviet currency area would require some serious sacrifices on Ukraine's part. In the words of an observer, "Cutting the economy off from Russia by leaving the ruble zone and trading at world prices was seen not as the price of political independence, but as an economic objective in itself."[94]

Consistent with the beliefs it held, Ukraine was one of the first in the former Soviet area to introduce its own, albeit temporary, currency (coupon). It did so in January 1992, in order to leave the ruble zone, but not necessarily to speed up its own economic transition. In fact, the step could be seen as hurting Ukraine's prospects so long as the Ukrainian leadership was not going to accompany it by other measures, such as price liberalization and inflation controls. Whereas in Latvia the introduction of national currency was part of a general package of economic reform measures, in Ukraine it was merely a way of reacting to Russia-initiated price liberalization and, inevitably, a sharp increase in prices in the area of ruble circulation. Since Ukraine could not print more rubles to offset negative consequences of the Moscow-initiated price reform (such a decision could only be made in Moscow), coupons were supposed to play the role. Salaries would be paid in coupons, and prices would remain government-controlled. Unlike Russian leadership, Ukrainian leadership did not see immediate price liberalization as a key step of economic transition and was hoping to protect its citizens from the increase in consumer prices. Further events confirmed that it was not the market reform Ukrainian leaders had in mind.

In March 1992, the Ukrainian parliament approved in closed session (with just 24 votes "against") a presidential program called "Foundations of Ukraine's National Economic Policy." This program considered national control over monetary affairs one of the key pillars of economic reform. In the words of the program's principal author, Oleksandr Yemelyanov, the main problem was that Ukraine was totally financially dependent on Russia:

> At a time when Ukraine has become an independent nation and the Union center has ceased to exist, our economy continues to be managed from afar, now through financial, monetary, and pricing policies. In practice, Ukraine has not taken, indeed, has not been able to take, any serious independent decision on the economy.[95]

The problem, labeled by the program's authors as the "extremely dangerous price race" (referring to Russia's liberalization reform), could only be solved upon the condition of "complete withdrawal from the ruble area and the swift introduction of a separate currency."[96] In November of the same year, Ukraine, acting consistently with the program's recommendations, unilaterally banned the ruble from circulation on its territory, thereby leaving the ruble zone. The official exchange rate allocated was one coupon to one ruble, despite the fact that in reality one coupon could only buy one-half ruble.

A further development demonstrated the shortsightedness of Ukraine's monetary isolationism. The policy of delaying price liberalization by assuming control over printing money proved to be a disaster for the country's economy. The lack of reform led to the outflow of goods to Russian markets, a development that could have hardly been stopped by the introduction of the coupon. The temporary currency was losing its real value relative to ruble[97] (see table 3.2 on pages 60-61), and Ukraine was further lagging behind Russia in living standards. As a result, the hryvna was introduced in September 1996, only after the government finally realized the importance of other reform measures. With a few isolated exceptions, Ukrainian economists did not foresee the collapse of their early introduced currency; politicians also believed in the strength of the political momentum built up behind the idea of establishing an independent currency and central bank.[98] All this suggests that, although the decision to leave the "ruble zone" was in part pushed by Russia's own isolationism,[99] its main origin was domestic and rooted in the elites' belief in the virtues of economic nationalism. The belief that Ukrainian "colonial status" was the main obstacle and that the key to prosperity was independence from the metropole, including the independence in monetary affairs, was widespread and proved to exert the strongest influences on policy making.[100]

Trade Cooperation with Russia

A somewhat similar, although distinct, pattern was demonstrated in Ukraine's trade relations with the ex-metropole. At earlier stages, Ukrainian leadership did attempt to limit commercial activities with Russia for the purpose of their reorientation toward other markets beyond the former Soviet region. In Ukraine, however, such a policy proved to be much less successful than in Latvia: already, by 1993, the policy of breaking away from Russia was largely reversed and Ukraine, instead, became the strongest proponent of establishing a free-trade area with Russia.

Ukraine's first reaction to the Soviet disintegration and calls to create an economic union among the CIS members was to restrict its relations within the former USSR to bilateral trade agreements. Most of these were agreements on barter deliveries of "vital" or "strategic" goods.[101] A similar policy was proposed vis-à-vis the ex-metropole, but the priority goal was to gradually reduce the dependence on trade with Russia. For that, a series of government measures were proposed. The aforementioned March 1992 economic program outlined the strategy of reducing Ukraine's commercial dependence. The introduction of national currency was to be accompanied by export and import restrictions and the establishment of customs posts at all borders, especially those with Russia. Along with the introduction of the coupon, commercial restrictions were intended to stop the growing outflow of Ukrainian goods abroad (mainly to Russia, where prices were higher due to their liberalization). Other measures aimed at trade reorientation included subsidies for domestic producers, banning barter trade and introducing a regime of hard-currency trade with the ex-Soviet republics, and lifting a ban on the reexport of goods from the countries of the ruble zone.[102] The presidentially initiated program was overwhelmingly supported by the parliament and recommended to be "taken into consideration" by various economic ministries.[103]

Economic agents and government agencies, however, took "into consideration" very few of those measures. Export and import restrictions had been in effect even before the program was designed, without making much progress in terms of maintaining the country's economic stability.[104] Subsidies for domestic producers were never applied,[105] primarily due to the government's lack of resources. Ban for barter-based trade operations and insistence on trade for cash also remained only on paper.[106] Given that as much as 45 percent of all Ukrainian trade was conducted in barter,[107] such a ban could have brought catastrophic consequences for the economy. Finally, while a ban on the reexport of goods from the countries of ruble zone (mainly Russia) was lifted, at the time it alone could not have produced the expected reorientation outcome. The very existence of such reexport indicated Ukraine's dependence on Russian markets and, without being accompanied by other measures, could not have brought strong reorientation effects.

Ukraine's lack of economic reform, as well as its heavy dependence on Russian markets[108] (see table 3.2 on pages 60-61), prevented a full-fledged implementation of the strategy outlined in the March 1992 program. From mid-1992 on, the potentially destructive outcomes of the strategy were increasingly obvious to Ukrainian leadership, and it began to realize—in a hard way—the significance of preserving close economic ties with Russia. A severe decline in trade and the collapse of the coupon generated social pressures and political resistance from striking miners and pro-Communist groups. Ukraine's trade unions, particularly those representing eastern oblasts, were explicit in their demands for stronger ties within the CIS and argued in favor of reestablishing broken economic links via coordination of actions with the CIS unions.[109] The leadership began losing its legitimacy and needed additional public support. Kravchuk acknowledged mistakes his leadership made in his overdue public statement of early-1993: "We obviously overestimated the potential of our economy. We overlooked the fact that it was structurally incomplete."[110]

A number of steps were undertaken to intensify trade cooperation between the two countries. First, Ukraine attempted to normalize bilateral relations. In late-1992, it initiated contacts with Russia's side and, as a result, a few economic agreements were signed. One of them pledged to coordinate the two sides' economic policies and introduce most favored treatment in mutual trading.[111] In order to deal with pressing energy problems and the country's rapidly increasing debt to Russia, a series of energy negotiations were launched.[112] The early 1993 meeting of Ukrainian and Russian presidents even announced the need to negotiate a bilateral treaty on friendship, partnership, and cooperation in the nearest future.[113] In addition to bilateral efforts, Ukraine made some unilateral steps to correct its previously isolationist stance. Import and export quotas were reduced or eliminated.[114] In August, the value-added tax and excise taxes on trade with Russia and other CIS members were eliminated.[115]

These steps were only partially helpful[116] and, in June 1993, under Ukraine's continued decline of trade, another bilateral agreement with Russia was concluded. This agreement again sought a revival of trade and provided both sides with MFN status, including the mutual exemption from import taxes. It again promised to establish a free-trade zone, liberalize banking regulations, and provide for the free movement of labor in five regions on each side of the border.[117] With Kuchma's arrival as Ukraine's president, the policy of establishing a free-trade area with Russia became one of the key directions of Ukraine's trade policy. Pushed from below, Kuchma, a former industrialist himself, wanted to give the enterprises a free hand in restoring the old links with Russia,[118] given Ukraine's trade dependency on the ex-metropole.[119] In February 1995, as a result of Kuchma's policy, the two countries were able to initial a friendship and cooperation agreement and sign a new trade agreement "On the mechanism of realization of the free trade agreement."[120] Russia, however, did not seem to be as interested in implementing the agreement, which, again, significantly reduced the practical effects of Ukrainian policies.[121]

Ukraine thus sharply reversed its original nationalist commercial policy toward Russia. As with the currency introduction, Ukrainian commercial intentions could not be fulfilled, partially because of their poor design and partially because of lack of efforts by the leadership to reform the domestic economy (the next section returns to this point). It is important to emphasize, however, that behind the idea of trade reorientation, as well as behind the ideas of breaking away from the CIS and leaving the "ruble zone," was the already familiar belief in the virtue of economic nationalism. As two Ukrainian scholars observed, "in Ukraine's political life, the motto 'Independence is above all other things' gained status of the most important one. Everything was sacrificed to it, and everything was justified by it."[122] The belief in economic nationalism had emerged before Ukraine gained independence, and it can be traced back to the nationalist programs and slogans of the late-1980s and early-1990s. After Kravchuk came to power, nationalist-minded intellectuals and government-affiliated economists worked closely to develop a Ukrainian foreign economic policy vision. To give just one example, the March 1992 program was prepared by Olexander Yemelyanov and Volodimir Shcherbak, both economists from a government agency (*Gosplan,* or State Planning Committee), but also with the involvement of the Rukh-affiliated economist, Vladimir Cherniak.[123] Defending the program, Cherniak described it as a "sharp turning point" and declared, consistent with the period's popular nationalist beliefs, that "following the Russian path would lead to a total collapse of the Ukrainian economy and total dependence of Ukraine on Russia."[124] Only in 1993 did the ideas of economic nationalism lose their early popularity among policy circles and various social groups.

After 1996, Ukraine had little choice but to continue to pursue a dual foreign economic course, thus responding to domestic pressures from both nationalists and integrationists. On the one hand, Ukraine continued to view the CIS as a strictly consultative organization "in which independent countries conduct bilateral relations with an emphasis on economics."[125] Despite empire-saving pressures, Ukrainian leaders refused to join the customs union of Russia, Belarus, Kazakhstan, and Kyrgyzstan, or the Russia-Belarus union.[126] On the other hand,

Ukraine continued to press for further development of bilateral economic relations with Russia. As was the case before 1996, the main issue concerned the establishment of a free-trade zone with the ex-metropole, something which never was fully implemented despite many previous attempts. Russia continued imposing various restrictions, and trade between the two kept shrinking.[127] In attempting to halt this development, Ukraine initiated the so-called "Big Treaty" on friendship and cooperation with Russia. Among other documents, the treaty included the Program of Russia-Ukraine cooperation until 2007 and promised to facilitate the development of trade and economic relations.[128] The treaty provoked criticism and encouragement on both sides,[129] but it was eventually ratified by Russia.[130]

The duality of Ukrainian society was obvious to the policymakers. Ukrainian parliament, unlike that of Latvia, was dominated by left and left-of-center forces, and nationalists were in no position to control parliamentary decisions.[131] On the other hand, the key executive positions were controlled by people either formally affiliated with Ukraine's nationalist organization or generally supportive of Ukraine's independent statehood and nationhood. In addition, a majority of the population continued to support independence,[132] the result of Ukraine's progress in its nation-building efforts. All these factors suggested that Ukraine's policy course could be successful only if it was careful and responsive to various social pressures. Examples of these pressures were plentiful. In September 1997, for example, eighty-six parliament deputies called for Ukraine to join the Russia-Belarus Union. The Treaty of Friendship signed by Ukraine and Russia also prompted a reaction from the right, and the Ukrainian Republican Party and an informal group known as Nation and State launched a campaign to begin impeachment proceedings against President Kuchma.[133]

Domestic Economic Institutions

As was argued in the previous chapter, reorientation of the ex-Soviet nations' international economic activities cannot be successful without conducting a series of domestic reforms, such as macroeconomic stabilization and dismantling the old trade regulation system, which was designed under the Communist regime. In Ukraine, however, the efforts aimed at gaining economic independence were not accompanied by decisive marketization at home, as was done in Latvia. Kravchuk's government announced its intention to liberalize prices, introduce its own national currency, and conduct privatization in early 1992. The best intentions remained frozen on a declaratory level until the end of 1994, which undoubtedly slowed Ukraine's progress in foreign economic reorientation. This section briefly reviews Ukraine's domestic marketization efforts, concentrating on price liberalization, the establishment of a foreign exchange system, and trade regulations.

Rather than decontrolling prices in a rapid and decisive manner, as was done in Latvia, the Ukrainian government followed a path of gradual and, supposedly, less painful partial price increases. By the time Leonid Kuchma became president and, in October 1994, announced a new and radical package of reforms, there had been at least five major increases in administered prices—three in 1992 and two in 1993. The government continued, however, to set prices on most basic food items, as well as energy, public utilities, housing rents, transportation, and communication.[134] These attempts at gradual price decontrol were halted in June 1993 when, after the fifth large increase of administered prices, the parliament imposed a moratorium on price increases on basic food items until October. Real changes only came as a result of Kuchma's intention to accelerate the pace of reforms. Due to these efforts, in early 1995, prices were freed at the producer level, with controls remaining only for natural monopolies and a small number of artificial monopolies. At the retail level, price controls remained on bread, public utilities, public transportation, and housing rent.[135]

Ukrainian efforts to establish a foreign exchange system faced similar obstacles. Despite the government's early announcements of an intention to introduce its own national currency, hryvna, this was not accomplished until a much later time. In November 1992, Ukraine left the ruble area and introduced the coupon, supposedly an interim step in introducing national currency. However the exchange rate of the coupon vis-à-vis the U.S. dollar and the Russian ruble has been constantly changing. For example, over the May-December period of 1993, the parallel market exchange rate increased from an average of 2,939 to 32,871, to the U.S. dollar.[136] The foreign exchange auctions were not functioning in a stable way and were abolished in November 1993 as a result of the dwindling of the National Bank of Ukraine's reserves. Thus there were two exchange rates for the coupon—official and market—a situation that ended only after Kuchma's reform package was introduced. Monthly inflation was extremely high—in November 1994 it reached the point of 72 percent[137]—and only went down in 1995, decreasing to 5.8 percent per month in May[138] (see table 3.2 on pages 60-61) A full-fledged national currency, the hryvna, was introduced in September 1996.[139]

Finally, Ukraine was slow in altering its trade regulations. In 1992, along with Latvia, Ukraine faced a sharp decline of trade.[140] Unlike Latvia's, though, the Ukrainian government tried different measures that often contradicted each other. For example, from 1992-1993 Ukraine had significant surrender requirements.[141] In mid-1993, however, in an attempt to both revive trade and join the World Trade Organization (WTO), the government cut import and export quotas in May and June 1993, and in August exempted enterprises that traded with the rest of the CIS from both value-added tax (VAT) and excise duty. Yet, instead of following this line of liberalization, the government announced that a VAT and excise duty must be paid on all imports after April 1, 1994. Importers had to pay a 28 percent VAT on goods at the borders *before* they were sold, while VAT had previously been paid after a sale.[142] In the absence of domestic economic preconditions and an effective administration for collecting duties, this measure did not give any significant positive effects. A fairly consistent trade restriction policy only came as a result of Kuchma's reform package in 1995. With the exception of some surrender requirements and a quota on grain, the export of all items was liberalized, although the introduction of import tariffs and nontariff barriers was likely, especially for food and agricultural produce.[143]

Ukraine was considerably socially constrained in conducting pro-Western domestic economic reforms; empire-saving attitudes in Ukrainian society were undoubtedly stronger than in Latvia. Yet the explanation for Ukraine's inconsistency in establishing domestic preconditions for market-oriented foreign economic policies would not be complete without considering the quality of its leadership. The reason why Kravchuk was not able to do what Latvian Popular Front leaders did—make a commitment to market-based domestic economic reform[144]—had in part to do with the fact that Kravchuk was a former Communist *apparatchyk,* with none of his own firmly established beliefs in the Western reforms. When, in 1991, the state embraced a nationalist policy agenda, there were no direct society-based obstacles to introducing the reform package at earlier stages instead of waiting until late 1994. In principle, the state could have initiated rapid marketization in the immediate aftermath of the Soviet disintegration, in the same manner as was done in the Baltic countries. The state was legitimate and centralized enough to do so. It could have found relatively broad social support for such reform, including among nationalists who initiated and led the reform in Latvia.[145] On the contrary, in the late 1994, it was in many ways more difficult to introduce the reform package: the society was split and tired of the unproductive and painful attempts of previous governments that led to a drastic decline in living standards and left little hope for future improvement. Trade unions turned into a well-organized political force whose demands for larger social spending[146] could no longer be ignored by the state.

To illustrate the point, let us consider for a moment what is perhaps Ukraine's most painful issue related to its efforts to diversify foreign economic activities—energy needs and dependency on Russia for supplies of oil and gas. Before 1991, Russia supplied Ukraine with about 85 percent of its oil and about 50 percent of its gas.[147] The government originally hoped to minimize this dependence by maintaining energy deliveries priced significantly below world levels for a few years, while intensifying its search for potential new suppliers of oil and gas and striking deals with them.[148] The success, however, was quite limited given rapidly rising prices for energy supplies from Russia and Turkmenistan and the deteriorating state of Ukraine's own economy.[149] Lagging on reform, Ukraine accumulated a huge energy bill: in 1994, its total energy debt to Russia stood at $1.7 billion—$1.5 billion for gas and $200 million for oil and oil products.[150]

Russia demanded payment in cash or in economic and security assets,[151] and Ukraine was forced to make some important concessions.[152] The situation improved in 1995 only when the Ukrainian government, instead of giving its assets away, started to apply other measures, including borrowing from international creditors, reducing energy consumption, and—most importantly—speeding up domestic reforms and cracking down on its domestic customers by holding them responsible for their debts. As a result, by the end 1996, Ukraine managed to pay Russia for 92 to 95 percent of its energy supplies.[153] In retrospect, this also could have been accomplished much earlier if Ukrainian leadership had moved more decisively with domestic marketization.

Looking Beyond Russia

The story of Ukraine's foreign economic reorientation efforts would be incomplete without learning about its attempts to establish alternative economic ties. I argue that Ukrainian attempts and successes in establishing alternative ties were much more modest than those of Latvia, yet greater than those of Belarus.

Like Latvia, Ukraine saw a vital necessity in reducing its dependence on Russia and the former Soviet area. Nationalist-oriented movements were worried that the CIS might eventually become an obstacle to Ukraine's broader integration with European economic and security institutions. As with their counterparts in Latvia, they did not see much of a threat to Ukraine's sovereignty in seeking closer ties with European multilateral organizations. In 1993, major nationalist-oriented organizations of Ukraine, such as the Congress of Ukrainian Nationalists, the Republican Party and the Democratic Party, stated, for example, that

> in the nearest future, the CIS may transform itself into an autarchic economic organization, the so called Euro-Asian area of economic cooperation, and it has already acquiring a clear political shape. It is in this light that one should view the attempts to pull Ukraine and Belarus into the CIS Economic Union, first of all on the side of Russia. Ukraine must make a historical choice: to play the role of a founder of this organization (as it has already happened in 1922 with the formation of the USSR) or find its way to direct integration with Europe—first, with the post-Communist countries of Eastern Europe—and, in the future, to learn its place in the united Europe.[154]

Both Kravchuk and Kuchma, in line with the views of nationalist-oriented forces, built their policies on the premise of economic diversification and developing closer ties with European countries. The European Union was perceived as being of particular significance. In addition, Ukrainian leaders attempted to develop closer relations with East European nations.

Attempts to Enter Alternative Multilateral Arrangements

Since the disintegration of the USSR, Ukraine's leaders were explicit about the country's strategic goal of eventually joining the EU.[155] Ukraine was the first CIS nation to initialize an agreement on partnership and cooperation with the EU and to reach such an accord in June 1994. The agreement liberalized some of Ukrainian-EU trade covering twenty-five areas. At the same time, a number of critically important restrictions on "sensitive goods"—including steel, coal, textiles, agricultural products, and nuclear materials—remained in force.[156] It was said the restrictions remained due in part to Ukraine's lack of progress with domestic reform. Article 4 of the agreement stated explicitly that further progress of Ukrainian-EU relations would be determined by Ukraine's commitment to continuation of market economic reform but, in 1998, the sides might begin negotiations about the creation of a free-trade zone.[157] All this generated hopes for further liberalization among the political class. Boris Oliynik, chairman of the parliamentary commission on foreign affairs and CIS relations, evaluated Kravchuk's signing of the agreement as an indicator that Ukraine was "returning to Europe." Anatolii Zlenko, foreign minister at the time, also expressed hope that Ukraine would gradually be absorbed into the "European economic zone."[158]

Unlike Latvia, however, Ukraine never managed to gain even associate EU membership and, by the end of 1996, its prospects for further liberalization of relations were still not very bright.[159] A Ukrainian analyst, a scholar of his country's foreign economic policy, summarized the major difficulties Ukraine was experiencing in its relations with the EU. He listed six major obstacles on the Ukrainian path to becoming an EU member. First was Ukraine's low progress in market economic reform, which had to do with its relatively late start.[160] Second, and related to the first, Ukraine's legal framework was still in many ways incompatible with that of the EU. Third, a number of Ukrainian industries, such as ferrous metals, agriculture, and light industry, while crucial for the country's economy, did not really "fit" the EU priorities for development. The fourth had to do with the low competitiveness level of Ukraine's enterprises, which would inevitably lead to their quick bankruptcy after the unified competition rules would have been adopted by the country. Fifth, Ukraine was not psychologically prepared to give up its national autonomy in economic decision making. Finally, the Ukraine's financial situation did not allow it to be a full-fledged contributor to the EU budget.[161]

Central European countries, too, were perceived by Ukraine as its geographically and historically "natural" partners.[162] Upon Ukraine's independence in 1991, its leaders pressed for membership in the Central European Initiative (CEI), created together with Poland and Hungary. The CEI, successor to the *Pentagonale* that was established in November 1989, currently includes Austria, Bosnia-Herzegovina, Croatia, the Czech Republic, Hungary, Italy, Poland, Slovakia, and Slovenia. Although its economic significance is far smaller than that of the EU,[163] it does undertake projects in transport, energy, science and technology, information, and cultural exchanges[164] and, therefore, could have contributed to the accomplishment of Ukraine's foreign economic goals. According to then prime minister Vilaly Masol, Ukraine was particularly interested in cooperating with the CEI in the spheres of power engineering and transport. In July 1994, it gained an associate (not a full) membership in the CEI because it had yet to undertake market reforms. In 1996, Ukraine, along with Albania, Belarus, Bulgaria, and Romania, finally became a member of the organization.[165]

Visegrad countries represented another arrangement to which Ukraine was attracted. The organization had a wide-ranging agenda combining both economic and security issues, and was composed of the four most stable and advanced of the post-Communist nations in their transition to capitalist democracy: Poland, Hungary, the Czech Republic, and Slovakia. As far as economic issues were concerned, the Visegrad Group coordinated their policies in migration and trade, as well as in preparations for admission to the then European Community. In particular, the group members established a regional customs union—the Central European Free Trade Area, or CEFTA.[166] Ukraine declared its interest in joining the Visegrad Group on many occasions. Here again, the voices of Ukraine's government and nationalist leaders sounded in unison. For example, in December 1991, Mykhaylo Horyn, vice chairman of Rukh and a member of Ukraine's parliament, said to Bronislaw Geremek, chairman of the foreign affairs committee on the Polish Sejm, that "Ukraine is very interested in joining the triangle Warsaw-Prague-Budapest." In February 1992, another Rukh leader Ivan Drach acted together with Ukrainian foreign ministry officials in urging their Polish counterparts to facilitate Ukraine's membership in Visegrad. Shortly thereafter, Ukraine's president and prime minister were announcing their country's interest in joining the group.[167]

Yet, the efforts to join the Visegrad arrangement or its free-trade association were unsuccessful to a significant extent because of Ukraine's lack of progress in serious economic reform.[168] One of the conditions for Ukraine's membership in Visegrad and CEFTA, as seen by the organization members, was its admittance to the World Trade Organization.[169] To facilitate the process of Ukraine's acquiring membership in the CEFTA, the Slovak Republic was determined to conclude a bilateral free-trade agreement with Ukraine.[170]

Other ideas of multilateral cooperation were also entertained by Ukraine's leaders. In 1993, for example, Ukraine signed an agreement to create the Eastern Carpathian Euroregion (ECER), composed of Ukraine's Zakarpattiya oblast, two *voivodships* in Poland, and some Hungarian jurisdictions. The undertaking's activities were supposed to include the construction of border-crossing points, the development of communication and tourism, and promoting small- and medium-sized businesses.[171] Another idea was to establish closer economic cooperation with Baltic nations. In a meeting between Leonid Kuchma and Latvian President

Guntis Ulmanis, the two sides expressed an interest in establishing a "common economic space" from the Baltic to the Black Sea, as well as in concluding a number of agreements on cooperation in trade and other issues.[172]

After 1996, Ukraine's policymakers continued pressing for the country's more pronounced European policy, while trying to secure its bilateral ties with the ex-hegemon. In words of first deputy foreign minister Anton Buteiko, "Without breaking off our relations with our former partners in the Soviet Union, the main thrust of our policy is toward integration with Europe and the Transatlantic powers."[173] In 1998, the partnership and cooperation agreement came into effect. Ukraine Prime Minister Valery Pustovoitenko, at a meeting of the Ukraine-EU cooperation council in Luxemburg in June 1998, said that Ukraine should become an associate member of the EU. Later, president Kuchma signed a decree confirming Ukraine's strategy of integration into the EU, and the Ukrainian cabinet ordered the Ministry of Justice to coordinate government activities in adapting Ukrainian legislature to the EU standards. The EU became Ukraine's second largest trade partner, after Russia. Ukraine also intensified its efforts to become a member of the WTO.[174]

Alternative Bilateral Ties

Bilateral ties are another vehicle for redirecting a country's economic activities from one region to another. During the first five years of its independence, Ukraine made considerable progress in establishing bilateral ties beyond Russia and the CIS. In Western Europe, Germany emerged as Ukraine's major partner. The two countries' interest in strengthening their economic ties was mutual.[175] Geographic proximity, tremendous economic power, and the potential for security cooperation made Germany particularly attractive as an economic partner.[176] Germany has also emerged as Ukraine's major partner in developing cooperation in energy, machinery, and communication issues.[177] By the end of 1996, the two countries had a number of trade agreements in effect.[178] At the time, Germany was Ukraine's largest trading partner in the European Union (EU); Ukrainian-German trade totaled $1.6 billion in 1995.[179]

Poland became another important partner for Ukraine. The start of successful bilateral relations was given by political steps that both nations had undertaken. Ukrainian nationalists began to establish contacts with leaders of the Polish *Solidarnost* as early as the end of the 1980s. In October 1990, Poland signed a declaration of friendship and cooperation with Ukraine, which was at the time a Soviet republic with no independent foreign policy. Finally, on December 2, 1991, Poland was the first nation to recognize Ukrainian independence. Economic relations also began to develop.[180] While the relationship between the two had not always been smooth, due to Poland's newly emerged economic and political interests in 1993, by 1995 the original impulses for partnership had gained the upper hand. Ever since, the two countries have referred to their bilateral cooperation as a "strategic partnership."[181] Further political cooperation helped to bolster bilateral economic relations. For the 1992-1996 period, Ukrainian-Polish trade increased five times, from $275.4 million to $1.39 billion.[182] Yet both sides acknowledged even larger potential for economic cooperation between "strategic partners."[183] For example, Poland is important to Ukraine because of its continued firm support of Ukraine's bid for the EU membership.[184]

In Asia and the Middle East, Ukraine was trying to develop trade cooperation with Turkey and Iran, especially for the import of energy products. Iran and some of the ex-Union republics, such as Turkmenistan and Azerbaijan, were seen by Ukraine's state as providing potentially strong alternatives to Russian energy supplies.[185] For example, in May 1993, an accord was concluded with Iran that included the sale of 4.5 million tons of oil to Ukraine and detailed a project to jointly construct a gas pipeline.[186] This potential, however, remained mostly untapped. Apart from various plans and a few actually implemented short-term agreements, little was accomplished, largely due to Ukraine's inability to find the necessary financial resources and to pay world-level prices for energy supplies.[187] By the end of 1993, it became clear to Ukraine that a "short-term solution to its vital fuel problem could not be found in Central Asia or the Middle East but only in Russia, and Ukraine had no choice but to accept and adapt to this painful reality."[188]

Turkey emerged as yet another partner of strategic significance. Along with Poland, it was one of the first nations to recognize Ukraine's independence in December 1991. Relations with Turkey were typically seen by Ukrainian observers as offering a chance to break away from the Russian embrace, because of Turkey's pivotal position in the Black Sea region (it controlled the Straits and, in the future, stood a good chance of gaining control over a lion's share of transport routes and oil pipelines leading to the Caspian area, Central Asia, and the Middle East).[189] As a result, a number of bilateral economic agreements were concluded, and in 1992 the volume of their trade increased dramatically, making Ankara one of Kiev's main trading partners. The rise of Ukraine's export volume was particularly impressive: after gaining the independence, it had always been six to ten times greater than that of its imports.[190] In 1994, the two countries signed a number of agreements, among them one on cooperation in the construction of the northern Turkish pipeline.[191] Turkey was thus increasingly becoming both an important trading partner and a territory through which alternative supplies of oil and gas could be delivered to Ukraine.

In the Third World, the Ukrainian government expressed a particularly strong interest in trade cooperation with China. China was quick to recognize the independent status of the former Soviet republics, hoping the newly independent nation would help counterbalance Russia's influence.[192] Partly as a result of increased political contacts, trade between the two ballooned.[193] According to Deputy Prime Minister Valerii Shmarov, trade between China and Ukraine for 1993 totaled $679 million, with Ukrainian exports to China accounting for $580 million.[194] By 1994, China was Ukraine's largest trading partner outside the CIS and its third-largest trading partner overall, after Russia and Turkmenistan.[195] There is strong potential for a further increase in their bilateral trade.[196]

Other bilateral economic partners of Ukraine include Hungary, the Czech Republic, Baltics, Moldova,[197] Belarus, and other ex-Soviet republics.[198] Overall, Ukraine's success in establishing relations with alternative partners may be evaluated as relatively modest when compared with that of Latvia. Such partners were identified, and some progress in getting closer to them was, indeed, made. Reorientation of export activities, as economists indicated, was particularly impressive.[199] Yet in terms of market access, not much has been accomplished as Ukraine has yet to become a member of Europe-based, free-trade associations and to develop bilateral relations with countries beyond the CIS area. As a result, it still remains strongly dependent on Russia's market, with all the negative implications of such dependency.

Notes

1. Torbakov 1996; personal interviews in Kiev, July 1998.

2. Wilson 1998, 6.

3. There is a debate among historians about whether the Treaty was intended to begin the process of integrating Ukraine into Russia or merely to establish a tactical alliance between equal sovereign nations. Those more nationalist-inclined historians typically emphasize the latter (for a discussion, see Basarab 1982; Rudnytsky 1987; Wilson 1998, 6-7). The subject reacquired political significance during the Ukrainian late-twentieth century transition to independence. (See, for example, Morrison 1993, 679; Kohut 1994, 132; Torbakov 1996.)

4. The enduring importance of the Pereyaslav myth can be seen from the fact that in 1992 a ceremony was organized in what is now the town of Pereyaslav-Khmelnytsky to renounce the agreement once and for all. As John Morrison said, "all Kiev's negotiations with Moscow take place in the long shadow cast by Khmelnytsky" (1993, 679).

5. Motyl and Krawchenko 1997, 240.

6. Western territories were composed of Galicia, Volhynia, northern Bukovina and southern Bessarabia. Two of these regions (Galicia and Volhynia) were previously under Poland, one (Bukovina) under Romania and one (Ruthenia) under Czechoslovakia (Szporluk 1979, 78).

7. With the exception of Volhynia, which was occupied by Poland in 1919.

8. Szporluk 1979, 78-80.

9. Motyl and Krawchenko 1997, 242.

10. Wilson 1998, 17.

11. It is no accident that this period gave rise to a full-fledged human rights movement in the republic and their *samizdat* publishing activities Solchanyk 1990, 177.

12. Motyl and Krawchenko 1997, 243.

13. Solchanyk 1990, 177.

14. Some scholars classify countries with dual political cultures as "cleft countries" (Huntington, 1996, 165). For other analyses of Ukraine emphasizing the country's cultural and political division between the "East" and the "West," see, for example, Rumer 1994, 132; Arel 1995; Burant 1995; Furman 1995, 72-74; Holdar 1995. In reality, Ukrainian territorial division is more complex and can be analyzed, for example, in terms of Northwest, Central, Western, Eastern, and Southern, or in other ways (see, for example, Subtelny 1995).

15. Khrushchev completed the process by transferring Crimea to the Ukrainian SSR in 1954 to mark the 300th anniversary of the Pereiaslav Treaty (Subtelny 1995; Wilson 1998, 17).

16. Scholars analyzed, for example, how Soviet federalism allowed local consolidation, undermining the stability of central power (Lapidus 1984; Roeder 1991).

17. Schroeder 1986, 300; Bradshaw 1993, 8.

18. Western Ukraine is Catholic, but the people of the eastern and more populous region practice an Orthodox religion which dates back as far as the Cossack movement and constitutes a crucial element of Ukraine's identity.

19. The authorities relied on the centralized Russian Orthodox Church to displace the Catholic Church and the revived (during the German occupation) the Ukrainian Autocephalous Orthodox Church, indoctrinating and absorbing their followers (Bociurkiw 1977).

20. Prazauskas 1994; Wilson 1998, 23. One striking fact of contemporary Ukrainian life, at least in the country's eastern and central regions, is what can be called an inter-linguistic communication style. During inter-linguistic conversations, two or more people engage in a talk while maintaining their own language preferences and not switching to either Russian or Ukrainian.

21. Burant 1995, 1127; Furman 1995, 73; Wilson 1998, 23.

22. The Ukrainian Helsinki Union, for example, laid the foundation for the emergence of the Ukrainian Republican Party (Prizel 1997, 339).

23. Martyniuk 1993, 40; Prizel 1997, 339-40.

24. Seventy-eight out of 450 seats.

25. Motyl and Krawchenko 1997, 249.

26. The vote inspired Ukrainian nationalists (*RFE/RL Daily Report*, "Chornovil Says West Ukraine Vote Exceeded Expectations," March 20, 1991).

27. *RFE/RL Daily Report*, "Republics and Successor States Final Referendum Results in Ukraine," 1991, December 5. Scholars continue to debate the "why" question, with some suggesting that the reasons for such overwhelming support for independence, particularly in the east, had to do with various misinterpretations of the meaning of "independence" (Glivakovski 1992; Laikov 1999).

28. For example, in January 1990, when various dissident movements formed a human chain of close to half a million Ukrainians and stretching from Lviv to Kiev, the action was accompanied by logistical support from what was then the communist government (Prizel 1997, 339).

29. In September 1992, for example, the Rukh and New Ukraine movements launched a campaign to force new legislative elections, but the drive failed to obtain the three million signatures required by law (Dawisha and Parrott 1994, 136).

30. During the 1994 elections, for example, both national-democrats and ultra-nationalists received only 13.8 percent of the total vote (Wilson 1998, 137).

31. One exception was Ihor Yukhnovsky, an opposition representative and one of the six vice premiers of Leonid Kuchma's first cabinet. The other was Viktor Pynzenyk, also vice premier and a member of Rukh. Both, however, did not keep their government jobs. In 1993, the former was replaced with Vasyl Yevtukhov, and the latter resigned in protest at the contra-reform policies (Prizel 1997, 346; *RFE/RL Daily Report*, "New Ukrainian Economic Appointments," March 29, 1993; *EIU Country Report*, 4th quarter 1993, p. 20-21).

32. Prizel 1997, 351.

33. The extent to which empire-saving forces were ready to sacrifice attributes of Ukraine's independence varied: socialists, for example, were not ready to denounce the Belovezhe agreements for the sake of restoring the pre-1991 status quo as proposed by communists (*Rosiia, iaku mi* 1997, 121).

34. Major parties of leftist (communist and socialist) orientation are the Socialist Party of Ukraine, Communist Party of Ukraine, and Peasant Party of Ukraine (Martyniuk 1993, 41).

35. Casanova 1998, 89.

36. The Communist Party of Ukraine was legalized in June 1993 (Martyniuk 1993, 39).

37. Prizel 1997, 361.

38. *Ibid.*, 360.

39. Casanova 1998, 99.

40. Yuri Luzhkov, Mayor of Moscow, and Konstantin Zatulin, at the time the Chairman of the State Duma Committee on the CIS Affairs, revealed themselves as particularly outspoken supporters of the pro-integration feelings (see, for example, *RFE/RL Daily Report*, "Ukraine's Foreign Ministry Protests Statement by Moscow Mayor," January 16, 1995; "Reaction Among Russian Officials to Crimean Events," March 20, 1995; "Soskovets, Duma on Ukraine," March 27, 1995).

41. Dawisha and Parrott 1994, 136.

42. Pogrebinsky 1993, 9; Prizel 1997, 346.

43. Even after the constitution had been adopted, the President's special power to issue decrees was extended for three years (Prizel 1997, 359).

44. *Ibid.*, 351.

45. While 46 percent of the media is directly owned by the state, the remaining 64 percent need the state for paper, access to printing presses, and financial support (*Ibid.*).

46. By contrast, in November 1990, when Kravchuk was associated with the party apparatus, his popularity among Kievans was so low that he did not even figure in the top twenty most popular politicians (Motyl and Krawchenko 1997, 252).

47. Morrison 1993, 685; Laikov 1999.

48. Motyl and Krawchenko 1997, 269.

49. For example, see his speech at the Rukh's congress in February 1992 (Kravchuk 1992, 205-208).

50. Dawisha and Parrott 1994, 137.

51. In a close race, Kuchma received about 52 percent of the votes cast while the incumbent president, Leonid Kravchuk, got 45.5 percent (*RFE/RL Daily Report*, "Kuchma Elected Ukrainian President," July 12, 1994).

52. *Nezavisimaia gazeta*, 15 June, 1994. In December 1991, 90 percent of Ukrainians voted for independence.

53. Morrison 1993, 685.

54. Methods of arriving to such conclusions were dubious, at best, and economically illiterate, at worst. For example, some of these calculations were based on the amount of coal and steel Ukraine was producing, without taking into consideration Ukraine's own energy needs or the world demand for coal. There was never a serious public discussion of issues of Ukraine's viability and potential of integration into the world economy. Quite often, people would learn about Ukraine's "competitiveness" and "richness" from propagandist materials (*listivki*) of nationalist groupings (personal interviews with a senior economist at the Institute of World Economy and International Relations and a chief of department at the National Institute of Strategic Studies, Kiev, July 1998).

55. Plushch 1993, 93. Similar remarks were widely circulated by many other politicians and policymakers. Hence, when Leonid Kravchuk emphasized the "necessity, by common efforts, to protect Ukraine from attempts to economically rob it" (1992, 207), he merely reflected an already existing and deeply shared belief.

56. Morrison 1993, 685; Babak 1995, 31-33; personal interviews.

57. Melnyk 1977, 172. More on this point in D'Anieri 1997, 16-17, and Wilson 1998, 168-69.

58. Dergachev 1996, 100-104.

59. In the study, Ukraine took first place with 83 points out of 100, followed fairly closely by the three Baltic republics and Russia (Corbet and Gummich 1990).The study was later criticized for not considering the extent of Ukraine's dependence on Russia for energy supplies as well as Ukraine's dependence on Russia and other republics for the final assembly of industrial products (Zviglyanich 1996, 125). Some scholars and policymakers denounced the study as having propagandist rather than scholarly intentions (personal interview with a former high-level government bureaucrat, National Bank of Ukraine, Kiev, July 1998). Others scholars offered more positive evaluations (Schroeder 1996, 23).

60. Motyl and Krawchenko 1997, 246; Plushch 1993, 68, 93.

61. This resistance is well documented in Solchanyk 1992, 1993.

62. *Izvestiia*, November 20, 1990.

63. *RFE/RL Daily Report*, "Ukraine Refuses to Sign Economic Accord," October 18, 1991; Nahaylo 1992a, 25.

64. *RFE/RL Daily Report*, "Other Republics Economic Treaty Criticized in Ukraine," November 13, 1991.

65. *RFE/RL Daily Report*, "Kravchuk on Foreign Visits, Independence, and New 'Union," October 8, 1991. Many similar statement were made by Kravchuk and others during the fall 1991 (see *RFE/RL Daily Report* September 30, 1991; "Gorbachev Cannot Imagine New 'Union' Without Ukraine," October 14, 1991; "Other Republics Economic Treaty Criticized in Ukraine," November 13, 1991).

66. Just a few weeks after the Belovezhie agreement, Kravchuk noted with pride in a public interview that Ukraine had been "the force" that had "destroyed the [Soviet] empire" (*RFE/RL Daily Report*, "Kravchuk on Ukrainian Independence and the Commonwealth," December 30, 1991).

67. *RFE/RL Daily Report*, "Ukrainian Presidential Aide Sees Commonwealth as Temporary," December 18, 1991; *EIU Country Report*, No. 1, 1992, 75.

68. *Moscow Programma Radio Odin Network*, "Rukh's Chornovil on CIS 'Imperial Momentum," in FBIS-SOV-92-068, April 8, 1992, 45-46; *Kiev Ukrayinske Radio First Program*, "Rukh Urges Suspension of CIS Membership," in FBIS-SOV-92-073, April 15, 1992, 44. At one point Vyacheslav Chornovil, a Rukh leader, went as far as to say: "Over a period of time we'll forget about the commonwealth" (*EIU Country Report*, 1st quarter 1992, 75). Addressing his followers later, in December 1992, he attacked the CIS as "one of the greatest moral and psychological blows against any newly attained independence" and described it as a "neo-imperial phantom" which existed to "pump resources out of Ukraine" (Morrison 1993, 689).

69. In 1993, annual inflation reached 10,200 percent (Aslund 1995, 127).

70. The country's 1992 foreign trade volume declined by 33.5 percent (Boss and Havlik 1994, 240).

71. Whitlock 1993; Smolansky 1995.

72. Gonchar 1995.

73. Martyniuk 1993, 39; Wilson 1993.

74. D'Anieri 1997, 21. According to Chairman of the Finance and Budget Committee of the Russian parliament Nikolai Gonchar, the "foreign economic relations of Ukrainian oblasts neighboring on Russia are almost entirely focused at Russian oblasts and regions." For example, this indicator for Kharkiv Oblast measures 80 percent, and for Luganks and Donetsk oblast, 90 and 85 percent, respectively. For their part, the foreign economic relations of a number of Russian oblasts that border Ukraine are also "tied" to neighboring Ukrainian regions. Above all, this is true of Belgorod, Rostov, and Bryansk oblasts (Gonchar 1995, 143).

75. *RFE/RL Daily Report*, "Ukraine Debates CIS Summit Participation," September 23, 1993; Kuzio 1994, 199; Garnett 1997, 64.

76. *RFE/RL Daily Report*, "Toward the Integration of Russian, Ukrainian, and Belarusian Economies," July 12, 1993; *Moscow ITAR-TASS*, "Sign Statement on Economic Integration," in FBIS-SOV-93-131, July 12, 1993, 1-2. The Economist responded to the development with the comment that "the growing recognition, particularly among Ukrainian managers, that post-independence optimism concerning an economic reorientation towards Europe was hopelessly misplaced" (*EIU Country Report*, 3d quarter 1993, 17).

77. *RFE/RL Daily Report*, "Nine CIS Prime Ministers Initial Agreement on Economic Union," September 24, 1993; *Kiev Ukrayinske Telebachennya Network*, "Ukraine Signs as 'Associate,'" in FBIS-SOV-93-185, September 27, 1993, 3; *Moscow ROSSIYSKIYE VESTI*, "Paper Reports on Signing of CIS Economic Union Treaty," in FBIS-SOV-93-187, September 29 1993, 1.

78. *Trade policy reform* 1994, 18; *EIU Country Report*. 2nd quarter 1994, 25. For full text of the treaty, see *Russia and Eurasia Documents Annual* 1995, 31-32.

79. *RFE/RL Daily Report*, "Ukrainian Leader Wary of Proposed New Economic Union," August 23, 1993; "Ukraine Debates CIS Summit Participation," September 23, 1993.

80. Morrison 1993, 691.

81. According to the treaty, associate status can be granted if a "state accepts only part of the commitments of this Treaty" and "with the EU countries consent." The treaty, however, left unspecified exactly what "part" can a state accept or reject (*Russia and Eurasia Documents Annual* 1995, 32.

82. *Kiev MOLOD UKRAYINY,* "Further on Kravchuk Comments on Return From CIS Summit," in FBIS-SOV-93-188, September 30, 1993, 28.

83. "We have signed all the economic documents which were put to the CIS Heads of State Council. Thus, I believe that in actual fact there is no difference between those classed as full members and as associate members of the Economic Union... We are playing and will continue to play the most full and active role in the Economic Union" (*Rossiyskiye Vesti,* "Kravchuk Denies Quarrel With Russia," in FBIS-SOV-94-082, April 28, 1994, 55).

84. Filipenko 1995, 54.

85. In a December 1995 government program, for example, the goal of establishing a free trade zone with Russia is listed among other measures intended to shore up Ukraine's foreign economic activities, such as stepping up exports of agricultural products and protecting domestic producers from foreign dumping (Yanevsky 1995, 57).

86. The Payment Union agreement was originally signed on November 21, 1994. Its participants pledged to create a Union-based payment system to deal with payments related to mutual trade and credit relations. Ukraine expressed its willingness to join the agreement after the introduction of the country's national currency (in September 1996), but never did so (*Trade Policy and the Transition Process* 1996, 197). The Customs Union further proclaimed a commitment to customs and payment regimes and eventual monetary union (*Kiev UNIAN,* "Belarusian Way of Integration with Russia Rejected," in FBIS-SOV-95-107, June 5 1995, 45; *Moscow INTERFAX,* "Kiev Not To Join CIS Customs, Payment Unions This Year," in FBIS-SOV-96-003, January 4, 1996, 42).

87. Ukraine's sensitivity toward these issues was clearly demonstrated in an exchange between the Russian president and Ukraine's foreign minister. In September 1995, Yeltsin issued an important decree outlining Russia's strategy in the CIS on the premise of reconstituting it as a great power (Mihalisko 1995). Responding to the decree, Ukraine's foreign minister wrote an extended memo for distribution in policy circles in which he argued that Ukraine did not view the CIS as a suprastate structure or a preferential arrangement; instead, Ukraine wanted to maintain "normal" and "equal" relations with Russia and other CIS members while remaining open for the larger integrative trends in the world (Garnett 1997, 63-64).

88. Even during his tenure as prime minister, Kuchma argued that "we are definitely being pushed toward this [closer integration with Russia] from below, and if we don't do it ourselves, others will do for us. I don't think there is any other way" (*Moscow Ostankino Television First Channel Network,* "Premiers Comment on Economic Integration," in FBIS-SOV-93-131, July 12, 1993, 3).

89. Solchanyk 1995, 50.

90. *RFE/RL Daily Report,* "Kuchma Denounces Campaign for New Political Union," January 17, 1995.

91. Ivan Plushch, for example, was of those who argued, in May 1991, before the Soviet disintegration, that Ukraine will eventually need to have its own currency (Plushch 1993, 69-70).

92. For such proposals, see, for example, Williamson and Havrylyshyn 1991.

93. Wilson 1998, 170-71.

94. Morrison 1993, 685.

95. *Komsomolskaya pravda*, "National Economic Policy Theses Detailed," in FBIS-SOV-92-060, March 27, 1992, 55. The program was only published later in *Holos Ukrainy* (May 1, 1992, 6-7).

96. *Ibid.* See also an interview with Yemelyanov published in *Uriadovii Kurier* (No. 13, March, 1992, 4).

97. During November and December, Ukraine printed 100 million coupons, which immediately spurred the inflation by 50 percent a month. Over 1992, prices increased 2500 percent (*Finansoviie izvestiia*, January, 21-27, 1993, VII).

98. When the governor of Ukraine's central bank, Vadim Hetman, expressed doubts over the wisdom of leaving the ruble zone, he was brusquely overruled by Kravchuk (Morrison 1993, 686).

99. Russia's isolationism was reflected, for example, in its unwillingness to coordinate its price liberalization with its CIS counterparts. Kravchuk was complaining at one point that "none of the policies, price, taxes or any other, is coordinated" (*Nezavisimaia gazeta,* January 13, 1993, p. 5). Another possible dimension of Russia's essentially isolationist policy stance had to do with its decision to stop issuing ruble credits to Ukraine (*RFE/RL Daily Report*, "Russia Suspends Credits to Ukraine," September 23, 1992). Russian intellectuals and policymakers generally believed that Russia would have been better positioned for further economic reforms if it had remained in the ruble zone alone (*Nezavisimaia Gazeta*, November 14, 1992, 1; Kliachko and Solovei 1995).

100. Other scholars arrived at similar conclusions (Morrison 1993, 685; Babak 1995, 33).

101. In other words, raw materials, energy products, and basic consumer goods to ensure production and supplies These agreements were signed by Ukraine with most republics during 1991 and 1992 (*Trade Policy Reform* 1994, 67).

102. *Uriadovii kurier*, No. 13, March 1992, 4; *Komsomolskaya pravda*, "National Economic Policy Theses Detailed," in FBIS-SOV-92-060, March 27, 1992, 55.

103. Personal interview with a deputy of Verhovna Rada who was present while the voting took place, Kiev, July 1998.

104. For example, in August 1991, Ukraine imposed a ban on the export of sixty scarce consumer goods. Prime Minister Vitold Fokin justified the measure on the grounds that large amounts of goods were taken out of the republic, goods that "we badly need ourselves." Farms were sending grain and other produce to the republics with higher than wholesale prices (*RFE/RL Daily Report*, "Temporary Ban on Exports from Ukraine," August 13, 1991). During 1992 and 1993, the government applied export quotas to a large list of raw materials, but also to certain capital and consumer goods, totaling about 180 products (*Pro perelik tovariv* 1992; *Trade Policy Reform* 1994, 66).

105. *Trade Policy Reform* 1994, 66.

106. Barter was first officially allowed in January, albeit with many bureaucratic complications (*Moscow News Fax Digest*, "Rules for Barter Operations Streamlined," in FBIS-SOV-92-114, June 12, 1992, 73-74). In early May, the government ruled that "all subjects of foreign economic activities of Ukraine have a right to conduct barter-based trade," and this was approved by the parliament (see *Pro poriadok provedeniia barternikh operatsii* 1992).

107. MacArthur 1997, 212.

108. Before the Soviet disintegration, Ukraine's trade with Russia accounted for up to 70 percent of its total trade (Bradshaw 1993, 27).

109. *Kyyivska pravda*, "Leaders Vow Political Offensive," in FBIS-SOV-92-247, December 23, 1992, 64-65; *Kiev UNIAR*, "Trade Union Congress Adopts Resolutions," in FBIS-SOV-93-166, August 30, 1993, 41.

110. D'Anieri 1997, 21.

111. *Uriadovii kurier*, June 26, 1992, 2; *RFE/RL Daily Report*, "Economic Agreements Signed Between Russia and Ukraine," October 23, 1992.

112. *RFE/RL Daily Report*, "Russian-Ukrainian Economic Relations," November 4, 1992; Smolansky 1995, 72.

113. *Izvestiia*, January 16, 1993; *RFE/RL Daily Report*, "Russian-Ukrainian Talks," January 15, 1993.

114. For example, in May, export quotas were eliminated for the following products: cement, iron ores, some petrochemicals, graphites, timber, paper, and ferrous metal manufactures (*Trade Policy Reform* 1994, 67). Quotas were reduced for many other products (*Pro Liberalizatsiiu* 1993).

115. D'Anieri 1997, 21.

116. Largely because the best bilateral intentions and promises remained on paper only.

117. *RFE/RL Daily Report*, "Ukraine, Russia Sign New Economic Accord," June 6, 1993. List of goods to be traded and prices were subject to repeated re-negotiations ("Annex" in *Trade Policy Reform* 1993).

118. Jung 1995, 51-52.

119. This dependency decreased after 1991, but was still significant. In 1994, Russia was Ukraine's most important trading partner, with Ukraine's exports to Russia accounting for about 40 percent and imports for 30 percent of total trade (*RFE/RL Daily Report*, "Ukrainian Foreign Trade in 1994," February 9, 1995).

120. Markus 1995e, 58; Kutsai 1995.

121. According to the calculations of Ukraine's Ministry of Foreign Economic Relations, a new agreement would have saved Ukraine about $1.15 billion annually. Ukraine placed blame on Russia for its failure to follow the agreement, arguing that Russia never eliminated or reduced the list of goods not subjected to the free-trade agreement. The list constituted 91.8 percent of all Russian goods that were exported to Ukraine (Kutsai 1995). A similar point was also made by other scholars (Samodurov 1997, 14; Sekarev 1997, 268).

122. Luzan and Luzan 1998, 99.

123. In general, the March program, in its main ideas, was influenced by the earlier-drafted program of the so-called democratic platform within the Communist Party of Ukraine. The latter was written in 1989, with close involvement of Rukh-affiliated nationalist-minded economists. Vladimir K. Cherniak was one of the program's principal authors responsible for the economic sections. One of the few, Cherniak was never a member of the Communist Party; instead he was a key participant in Rukh's activities and later was elected to parliament from Rukh (personal interview with a former Democratic platform activist and a Rukh's leader, Kiev, July 1998).

124. Nahaylo 1992a, 28.

125. *Den'*, July 15, 1998; *The Jamestown Monitor,* "Ukraine's Six No CIS," 1998, July 8; *Izvestia,* July 23, 1998.

126. Regarding the customs union, Kuchma insisted that "a free trade regime among the CIS states should be introduced first, and only then will it be possible to agree on a customs policy" (Varfolomeiev 1998). Kuchma also announced that he "categorically opposes" any Russian-Ukrainian-Belarusian union (*The Jamestown Monitor*, "Seleznev Calls Ukraine to Order" and "Ukrainian Reaction Reflects Internal Rifts," October 2, 1998; "Kuchma Sends Lukashenka Home Empty-Handed," March 16, 1999). Rather than entering Russia-dominant "unions," Ukraine attempted to counterbalance Russia's ambitions by joining Georgia, Moldova and Azerbaijan in the GUAM alliance. The organization united states with common security and economic concerns, especially in the transportation of oil from Caspian fields (Varfolomeiev 1998; *The Jamestown Monitor*, "GUAM Countries Speak with One Voice," October 7, 1998).

127. One striking example was Russia's introduction of value-added tax on Ukrainian goods in October 1996. The tax provoked the so called "sugar war" between the two countries. It contributed greatly to the decline of Russia-Ukrainian trade and was abolished only in February 1998 (*Nezavisimaia gazeta*, September 9, 1996; *Moskovskiie novosti*, November 16-23, 1997, 6; Sidenko 1998, 120; Tarasiuk 1998a).

128. *Rossiisko-Ukraiinskiye otnosheniia* 1998, 67-102; *Nezavisimaia gazeta*, February 26, 1998; February 28, 1998.

129. *Nezavisimaia gazeta*, February 26, 1998; February 28, 1998; *Sodruzhestvo NG*, March 3, 1998; Grinkevich and Kuz'menko 1998; *Nezavisimaia gazeta*, January 21, 1999; February 17, 1999.

130. *The Jamestown Monitor*, "Russia's Federation Council Conditionally Ratifies Treaty with Ukraine," February 18, 1999.

131. Rukh, the major nationalist movement, held 80 to 90 seats in the 450-seat parliament, whereas various leftist parties and movement controlled about half all seats. In September 1998, for example, half the parliament cheered Russia's parliamentary delegation and its chair, Gennady Seleznev, when he attacked Kyiv's leaders for limited participation in the CIS and called for the expansion of the Russia-Belarus Union. Seleznev was referring to the union as an economic and security bloc, a Slavic counterweight to the West. He also referred to Russians and Ukrainians as a "single people," thereby denying Ukrainian national identity (*The Jamestown Monitor*, "Seleznev Calls Ukraine to Order," March 4, 1998). In March 1999, the Ukrainian parliament decided in favor of joining the CIS Parliamentary Assembly, with 230 votes from those supporting the decision (*The Jamestown Monitor*, "Ukrainian Parliament Joins CIS Interparliamentary Assembly," March 4, 1999).

132. According to one poll, 61 percent of Ukrainians agree that "Ukraine must be independent despite the existence of many obstacles on the way to its statehood" (*Den'*, July 16, 1998).

133. Marples 1998, 15-16; *Nezavisimaia gazeta*, February 28, 1998.

134. At the end of 1992, for example, price controls were estimated to apply to about 30 to 40 percent of turnover, while administered prices applied to some 10 to 12 percent of turnover (*Trade Policy Reform*, 68).

135. *Ibid.*, 68.

136. Le Gall 1994, 67.

137. Lapychak 1995, 43.

138. *The Economist*, May 20, 1995, 47.

139. *RFE/RL Research Report*, "Ukraine Introduces National Currency," September 3, 1996.

140. Oleg Slepichev, the minister for foreign economic relations, declared in December 1993 that hard-currency exports to countries outside the CIS were down by 20 percent to $4.9bn in 1993, while trade within the CIS was in an even worse condition (*EIU Country Report* 1 Quarter 1994, 21). Within the CIS, the situation was particularly desperate due to the size of Ukraine's debt to Russia (mainly for fuel). At the end of the year, Ukraine owed Russia $2.5bn (*Ibid.*).

141. The foreign exchange tax introduced in February 1992 required the surrender of 20-75 percent of export proceeds (the share varying with the type of product), with no compensation. Since mid-1993 Ukrainian enterprises have been obliged to surrender 50 percent of all hard currency earnings (*EIU Country Profile* 1994-95, 28). In January 1993 Ukraine also imposed export tariffs on 103 commodities groups (*Ibid.*).

142. *EIU Country Report,* 2nd quarter 1994, 24.

143. Ukraine is considered to have a long-term comparative advantage in agricultural products (*EIU Country Report,* 4th quarter, 1995, 26), but may have needed time to develop its agricultural production to be competitive internationally.

144. In addition to its skepticism towards market economy, the Ukrainian elite was suspicious toward the West, typical of the Soviet-breed nomenklatura. In 1992, the exaggerated optimism was quickly replaced with an equally exaggerated resentment toward the West, which was accused of having eyes only for Russia and of trying to keep Ukraine as a backward colony, subservient to Moscow. As a result, state capacities were geared toward searching for a "third," supposedly less painful, way of reform, thereby lagging behind in terms of redirecting foreign economic activities toward Western countries (Morrison 1993, 692).

145. Ukraine's major nationalist movement Rukh, for example, has given only conditional support to Kravchuk and was divided between those who backed Kravchuk as chief spokesman for Ukrainian nationhood and those who pressed for speeding up domestic reform. In August 1992, this split in Rukh prompted an exodus of Kravchuk supporters who established a new political coalition called the Congress of National Democratic Forces. The remnants of Rukh created the New Ukraine movement that declared its political opposition to Kravchuk and called for accelerated domestic marketization, among other demands (Dawisha and Parrott 1994, 137).

146. *Kiev UNRINFORM*, "Kravchuk Meets Union Leaders To Discuss 'Crisis,'" in FBIS-SOV-93-113, June 15, 1993, 31; *Kiev Ukrayinske Telebachennya Network*, "Kravchuk Addresses Trade Union Federation," in FBIS-SOV-93-167, August 31, 1993, 42; *Kiev UNIAR*, "Union Committee Labels Price Hikes 'Genocide'" in FBIS-SOV-93-234, December 8, 1993, 52; *Kiev Ukrayinske Radio First Program Network*, "Trade Union Election Platform Advocates 'Civilized' Reform," in FBIS-SOV-94-004, January 6, 1994, 52.

147. *Moskovskiie novosti,* March 22, 1992; *Nezavisimaia gazeta*, April 9, 1993.

148. Whitlock 1993, 40.

149. Smolansky 1995a, 71, 79.

150. Markus 1995d, 19.

151. For example, Russia offered Ukraine to pay its debts by granting Russia 30 to 50 percent of the shares in Ukrainian energy enterprises or by trading its share of the Soviet Union's assets abroad. In the security domain, other proposals included that Ukraine give

up its post-Soviet share of the Black Sea fleet in exchange for forgiveness of its energy debt or to grant Moscow exclusive rights to Sevastopol, the headquarters of the fleet (Markus 1995d; Drezner 1997, 96-105).

152. In April 1994, for example, the Ukrainian leadership agreed to give up 30 percent of the shares in its gas facilities. At about the same time, it was also agreed that Ukraine would take only 20 percent of the fleet (164 ships) and sell the rest of its share (669 vessels) to Russia in exchange for forgiveness of its debt (Markus 1995e, 58).

153. *Nezavisimaia gazeta*, December 31, 1996; Drezner 1997, 103.

154. *Rosiia, iuku mi* 1995, 139.

155. *RFE/RL Daily Report*, "Kravchuk on Ukrainian Independence and the Commowealth," December 30, 1991; "More on Ukraine's Partnership Agreement with EU," March 24, 1994; "Zlenko on Ukraine and the EU," June 14, 1994; "Ukrainian Foreign Minister on EU," May 7, 1996.

156. Burant 1995, 1131; *EIU Country Report*, 3d quarter 1995, 27.

157. Sidenko 1997, 18; *RFE/RL Daily Report*, "More on Ukrainian Partnership Agreement with EU," March 24, 1994.

158. Burant 1995, 1131.

159. At the time of this writing, Ukraine is resuming its efforts to establish firmer cooperation with the organization. In June 1998, for example, Ukrainian Prime Minister Valery Pustovoytenko, at a meeting of the Ukraine-EU cooperation council in Luxembourg, again brought up the issue of Ukraine's possible associate membership in the nearest future (Varfolomeyev 1998).

160. As noted earlier, the real reform efforts came only in 1995.

161. Sidenko 1997, 19-20. A similar list was given in Budkin, et. al. 1995, 153-55.

162. *Kiev INTELNEWS*, "Foreign Trade Minister on Development," in FBIS-SOV-95-109, June 7, 1995, 58.

163. It mostly coordinates the economic and security activities of its members with those of other European countries. The CEI's major initial purpose was to facilitate membership to West European institutions, such as the EU (*RFE/RL Daily Report*, "Central European Initiative Agree on New Members," October 10, 1991).

164. Burant 1995, 1129.

165. *RFE/RL Daily Report*, "Central European Initiative Agree on New Members," October 10, 1996.

166. Cooperation among the group members began to decline after 1993, due to increasingly diverging interests (Bunce 1997, 244, 252-53; *Rossiia-Ukraiina-Vishegradskaia gruppa* 1997, 96-97).

167. Burant 1995, 1128-29; *RFE/RL Research Report*, "Ukraine Looks to Visegrad Triangle," May 26, 1992.

168. The other reason concerns security implications of Ukrainian membership in the organization. Such membership is hardly in Russia's geopolitical interests, and the Visegrad members cannot fail to take this into consideration (Burant 1995, 1129; *Rossiia-Ukraiina-Vishegradskaia gruppa* 1997, 96).

169. Joining the WTO was a key priority of Ukrainian leaders, but at the time their progress was relatively modest (*Kiev INTELNEWS*, "Progress in WTO, GATT Membership Talks," in FBIS-SOV-95-122, June 26, 1995, 71; *Kiev INTELNEWS*, "Deputy Primier on EU Free Trade Agreement Prospects," in FBIS-SOV-95-228, November 28, 1995, 55).

170. *Bratislava Rozhlosova Stanica Slovensko Network*, "Slovakia: Meciar on Ukraine's Efforts To Join CEFTA," in FBIS-EEU-96-017, January 25, 1996, 7.

171. Burant 1995, 1129.

172. The idea of establishing the Baltic-Black Sea League as an alternative to plans for integration within the CIS was proposed in July 1994 by representatives of Ukraine's Republican, Democratic, and Green Parties. The organizers envisaged the formation of a "Baltic-Black Sea bloc of free peoples" with participation of the three Baltic nations, Poland, Belarus, Moldova, Romania, and Bulgaria (*RFE/RL Daily Report*, "Baltic-Black Sea League Proposed," July 29, 1994). See more details in the Latvian chapter above.

173. *Financial Times Survey*, 1998, May 5, I; Tarasiuk 1998a.

174. Varfolomeiev 1998; Tarasiuk 1998a; *The Jamestown Monitor*, "Kyiv Sets Specific Goals for Relations with the European Union," October 15, 1998; "European Union-Ukraine Summit," October 19, 1998.

175. Along with the U.S., Germany is the biggest investor in Ukraine. By August 1995, German investment accounted for 20 percent of Ukraine's total investment, most of which went to the machine building industry, metals, domestic trade, the food industry, and light industry (*RFE/RL Daily Report*, "Foreign Investment in Ukraine," August 29, 1995).

176. *Ukraine, Russia, Germany* 1994, 167.

177. *Segodnia*, September 3, 1996, 5.

178. In September 1996, for example, German Chancellor Helmut Kohl and Ukrainian President Leonid Kuchma signed seven economic agreements, including a deal with a coal-mining enterprise and an agreement to modernize the Odessa airport (*RFE/RL Daily Report*, "German Chancellor Signs Agreements with Ukraine, September 4, 1996).

179. *Ibid.*

180. *RFE/RL Daily Report*, "Poland and Ukraine to Barter," July 19, 1991; "Ukraine and Poland Sign Economic Cooperation Agreement," October 7, 1991.

181. Burant 1997, 108-110; Geremek 1998, 76.

182. The real trade turnover is much higher, but the data do not capture the booming interborder "suitcase" trade.

183. The main difficulties were different level of economic development, low border access due to shortage of customs posts, and the lack of a payment mechanism (Burant 1997, 114).

184. *Jamestown Monitor*, "Ukrainian-Polish Informal Summit," September 29, 1998; Geremek 1998, 77; Pikhovchek 1998.

185. *Moskovskiie novosti*, March 22, 1992; Whitlock 1993, 40.

186. Whitlock 1993, 40; see also *RFE/RL Daily Report*, "Ukraine and Iran Cut $7 Billion Pipeline Deal," February 5, 1992; "Ukraine's Trade Ties with Turkmenistan, Iran," May 13, 1993; "Ukraine Signs Transport Agreement with Iran," July 12, 1993.

187. See, for example, *RFE/RL Daily Report*, "Ukraine-Turkmenistan Gas Dispute," March 5, 1992; "Turkmen-Ukrainian Gas Agreement Initialed," January 19, 1995; Smolansky 1995a, 71, 79; Smolansky 1995b, 18.

188. Smolansky 1995a, 84.

189. Smolansky 1995b, 22.

190. Turkey is in need of optical devices, automobiles, electrical appliances, ships, and airplanes, all of which are produced by Ukraine (Mhitaryan 1996, 9).

191. Smolansky 1995b, 33; Mhitaryan 1996, 9-11.

192. While the West grew increasingly critical of Kiev during debates in Ukraine's parliament over ratification of the START I and accession to the NPT in 1992 and 1993, Beijing restrained its criticism (see, Markus 1995d, 34).

193. In fact, a trade and economic cooperation agreement between Ukraine and China was signed a day before China officially recognized Ukraine's independence.

194. *RFE/RL Daily Report*, "Ukrainian-Chinese Trade Commission Meets," April 6, 1994.

195. *RFE/RL Daily Report*, "Jiang Zemin in Ukraine," September 7, 1994.

196. *RFE/RL Daily Report*, Li Peng in Ukraine, June 26, 1995.

197. For example, a free-trade agreement was signed with Estonia. It had been initialed in May 1995 and covered all products including agricultural ones, which led to a significant increase in Ukrainian-Estonian trade (*RFE/RL Daily Report*, "Estonia, Ukraine Initial Free Trade Treaty," May 19, 1995; "Estonian-Ukrainian Trade Increases Rapidly," July 2, 1996). In 1996-1997, Ukraine has also started to entertain the establishment of customs union with Moldova (*RFE/RL Daily Report*, "Moldova, Ukraine Strengthen Cooperation," January 11, 1996; "Moldova, Ukraine to Set up Customs Union," March 3, 1997; "Moldova, Ukraine Discuss Planned Customs Union," September 16, 1997).

198. Gaidukov and Chekalenko 1998.

199. Havrylyshin 1997.

Chapter 5
Belarus

Belarus pursued a much more pro-Russian foreign economic policy than did Ukraine and Latvia. It joined and became an active participant in the CIS and proposed to establish monetary and customs unions with the ex-metropole. In addition, Belarus has been the least persistent of the three nations in domestic liberalization and pursuing alternative economic relations. As a result, its trade with Russia has increased in importance since independence.[1]

National Identity

Belarus was the weakest of the three in its national identity dimension. Unlike Latvia, it had virtually no experience with independent nationhood and was always a part of various empires. Although some attempts to attain independence can be found in Belarus's history, particularly before its reincorporation into the Soviet empire, those attempts never led to any success, even for a short period of time. And, unlike Ukraine, the Soviet annexation of Belarus's western lands did not lead to the rise of nationalist feelings—for various reasons, Belarus's west was fundamentally different from Ukraine's. The crucial difference between Belarus, on the one hand, and Ukraine and the Baltic nations, on the other, is that the former was incorporated into the Soviet empire without having a clear sense of being different. Not surprisingly, Belarus has demonstrated a high degree of loyalty to the "Old Brother," and the policy of acculturation and assimilation by the Russians proved to be particularly successful.

The Experience with National Independence

The beginning of Gorbachev's perestroika caught Belarus by surprise, as the newly emerged nationalist movements had little to rely on in their nation-building efforts. Of course, Belarus, as with many other small nations, experienced various cultural influences, including those alternative to the influence of Russia,[2] but its people never actually had their own state. The country has always been a part of an empire—the Grand Duchy of Lithuania, then Poland, and after that, with the rise of Russian hegemony to the east, Belarus became a dependent of the Russian empire.[3] The only exception to this was a short period of independence in the immediate aftermath of the Russian disintegration in the early twentieth century. By that time, with Russia's defeat in war and the ensuing disorders throughout the empire, nationalism began to develop as Belarus was going through the *Adradzen'ne* (Revival) period.[4] During this period (1906-1917), the repressive policies of the Russian government were relaxed, the ban on the Belarusian language (as well as other non-Russian languages) was lifted, education was expanded and peasants began to attend school for the first time, and the publishing of Belarusian classic literature and Belarusian newspapers was allowed.[5] Belarus, however, did not manage to consolidate its independence. One reason was that the nationalist aspirations were almost always "a pawn in the larger schemes of the German military, Polish nationalists, and Russian revolutionaries."[6] Second, and no less important, national awareness in Belarus came late and as a purely intellectual phenomenon, with no roots among the peasants.[7] As a result, the Bolsheviks were more successful in imposing their control over Belarus than over Latvia and Ukraine, which only led to "the ten month period of symbolic independence,"[8] compared to about three years in Ukraine and twenty-two years in Latvia. When the Germans, who occupied Minsk, left in December 1918, the Russian army arrived and established the Belorussian SSR thereby terminating Belarus's independence period.

Nor could Belarus receive support for its national identity formation from its western lands after the manner of Ukraine. Like Ukraine, Belarus was united with the Soviet troops occupying and formally incorporating its western territories into the USSR in 1939, under the Ribbentrop-Molotov pact.[9] Yet Belarus's western lands were hardly comparable to those of Ukraine in terms of their ability to spur the process of identity formation. First, all these territories were under Russian control before 1914 and experienced heavy Russification,[10] whereas Ukraine's western lands were never part of Russian empire before their incorporation into the USSR and enjoyed a reasonable degree of linguistic autonomy while under different empires. Second and related to the previous, nationalist feelings were far less developed in west Belarus than in west Ukraine, in part the result of stronger influences from the Russian Orthodox church. Finally, Vilnius, west Belarus's traditional center of the intelligentsia's activities and a loose analogue of Ukraine's Lviv, was not included in Belarus's territory when the annexation took place.[11]

It should not come as a surprise then that, by the time of its incorporation into the USSR, Belarus was much less equipped to resist the influences of Sovietization and Russification than were Latvia and Ukraine. It possessed a much weaker sense of its historical or linguistic distinctiveness from the empire. Historically, Belarus had some opportunities for developing a stronger sense of national Self—Kastus Kalinowski's national uprising of 1863[12] and the "Revival" period of the early twentieth century were only two of them—but it has never been in a position to take advantage of those opportunities. Linguistically, too, Belarus was in a disadvantageous position. In the words of a historian comparing the two's linguistic situations,

> the west Belorussians found themselves in the USSR with little prior experience
> of using their language in social communication, while the Ukrainians of Gali-
> cia and Bukovina could look back at almost a century of such use of their lan-
> guage. Transcarpathia and Volhynia had also had their own schools and press
> during the inter-war period—something which west Belorussians had failed to
> achieve except for a brief period in the 1920s.[13]

In addition, Belarusians over the course of the eighteenth and nineteenth centuries were forced to change their religion: first, from Orthodoxy to the Uniate Church and then, in 1839, back to Orthodoxy, which further discouraged the development of their national distinctness.[14]

There is ample evidence backing the above conclusions about the relative weakness of Belarus's national identity. One indicator is the extent to which the policy of acculturation and assimilation by the Russians proved to be successful in Belarus, an inevitable price for a high degree of loyalty to the Old Brother[15] (see table 3.1 on page 48). By the mid-1970s, virtually all power in the republic was concentrated in the hands of non-Belarusians (mostly Russians), and all government record keeping was done in Russian. As a result, in 1984, for example, Belarusians were ranked in last place (15th) of the titular Soviet nationalities in the percentage of ethnic groups residing in their national republics and retaining the capacity to speak their native languages.[16]

Another indicator is the absence in the republic of historical attempts—comparable to those in Latvia and Ukraine—to encourage its national development. Latvians and Ukrainians tried to take advantage of the outbreak of World War II and to reassert their claims for independence from the Soviet regime. They also attempted to reassert their national rights in the 1950s and 1960s, in the aftermath of Stalin's death. Nothing of this kind took place in Belarus. While under occupation by Nazi Germany, Belarusians, by and large, choose against participating in anti-Russian military activities, having a deep mistrust and negative attitude toward the brutal German occupation regime.[17] Apart from emphasizing the heroic resistance to the German occupation,[18] little was done to forge Belarus's national feelings. As for the post-Stalin era, Belarus did not experience anything similar to Petro Shelest's attempts to "re-Ukrainize" the political apparatus by opposing the influx of non-Ukrainian cadres into the republic, or to Eduards Beklavs's attempts to reassert Latvian control over the republic.[19]

Other Factors Shaping Belarus's Identity

Short on the experience with either independent nationhood or national unification, something that would make it comparable with Latvia or Ukraine, Belarus's identity formation was very much affected by its experiences within the Soviet empire. Some of these experiences, such as the establishment of the republic's own territory and political institutions, might potentially have supported the growth of Belarus's national consciousness, as they did in Ukraine. In Belarus, however, the original Russification was too strong and the national idea too weak; Belarus's people were unable to take advantage of the Soviet institutional designs and to arrive at the time of the Soviet disintegration with a well-developed image of a national Self.

A Belarusian sense of nation could not be supported by the stability of its geopolitical borders: its very boundaries, legitimate ethno-territory, and the capital (Minsk) were established only in 1939, very late when compared to Latvia. When the Soviets expanded to the west and annexed the Baltics, they also annexed the western part of Belarus, which had previously been ceded to interwar Poland. Only then was the geographic denouement of Belarus as the BSSR (Belorussian Soviet Socialist Republic) completed and Belarus's nation, for the first time in its history, was united on its own legitimate territory.

In a similar manner, Belarus's acquiring of its own political institutions—Supreme Soviet, government, academy of science, etc.—came as an unsolicited gift from the existing Soviet regime. Unlike Latvia and Ukraine, Belarus did not have much of its own institutions, and so their establishment, with the shape and form designed by the Kremlin, did not face any significant resistance in the republic.

Economically, by the beginning of perestroika, Belarus was one of the most developed and urbanized Soviet republics and, therefore, should have acquired a nationwide, as opposed to local, sense of unity. This, however, was largely the result of late Soviet modernization efforts. Even as late as 1959, Belarus, compared to Latvia and Ukraine, was a less developed economy. For example, it had 46 percent of its total population living in cities, relative to 52 and 56 percent in Ukraine and Latvia, respectively.[20] The essentially rural basis of Belarus's society becomes even more obvious when one goes further back to the interwar and pre-Soviet periods.[21] The fact that Belarus caught up with most developed republics relatively late, during the 1960s and 1970s, suggests that Belarus's identity was also acquired late and, therefore, had little time to be consolidated.

Finally, Belarus's cultural experience with the Soviet empire was hardly encouraging for its national identity formation. By the time of the incorporation of its western region, most west Belarusians were Catholics possessing a somewhat better preserved linguistic identity. Yet, because of the particularly severe damage caused by World War II, intensive purges against the intelligentsia, and the Russification policy pursued by Stalin, the Belarusian west turned out to be much more assimilated to the Soviet culture. In the early 1990s, figures for the Catholic population in Belarus ranged from 8 to 20 percent.[22] As for language, despite the fact that Belarusians comprise up to 80 percent of total population, many preferred to speak Russian rather than Belarusian. In 1988, for example, 38.7 percent of titular Belarusians, who were urban residents, considered Russian their mother tongue, as opposed to 26 and 6.6 percent in Ukraine and Latvia, respectively[23] (see table 3.1 on page 48). All this suggests that Belarus might indeed "be compared to the Russified areas of Ukraine, but without complication of an opposing western nationalism."[24]

To summarize, by the beginning of perestroika, Belarus had little to use in its nation-building efforts. Its historical experience with independence was too brief (only ten months) to foster national memory. The Soviet annexation of Belarus's western lands, too, did not lead to the rise of nationalist feelings—Belarus was lacking a sense of its national distinctiveness. Soviet policies further discouraged the development of Belarus's national identity through practices of religious and linguistic Russification. In addition, Belarus, in terms of its economic development, caught up with Ukraine and Latvia relatively late and was still lacking a sense of nationwide unity. All these factors led some scholars to conclude that "Soviet nationalism superseded and served to eliminate Belarusian nationalism" and "there is evidence to suggest that the concept of New Soviet Man took on real meaning" in the republic.[25] This assessment overwhelmingly correlates with estimates of many Western as well as indigenous scholars.[26] If anything, taken together, the factors considered above can be helpful in explaining why nationalism never became a serious challenge to the empire savers' position in post-Soviet Belarus.

Domestic Structures

Belarus's society was far less mobilized and politicized than those of Latvia and Ukraine. As a result of Belarus's weak national identity, nationalist-oriented forces did not manage to win mass support in their struggle for strengthening the republic's independence. Over the five-year period of Belarus's postimperial existence, the nationalists became marginalized as a political force, whereas the empire savers gained an upper hand in the decision-making process.

Structure of the Society

Nationalists

The movements committed to national independence emerged in Belarus at about the same time as in the Baltic republics and Ukraine. Their emergence was stimulated mainly by concerns of the intelligentsia about status of the Belarusian language, as well as by more recent events: the discovery of 500 mass graves of Stalin's execution victims in the Kuropaty Forest by archeologist and future leader of most prominent nationalist movement, Zenon Poznyak, and the Chernobyl nuclear reactor accident.[27] In addition to the influences of Moscow's anti-Stalinist policies, Belarus's nationalists were very much influenced by the Baltic Popular Front movements.[28] The political agenda of Belarus's nationalists was closely modeled on those of the Baltic Fronts, and its "main goals" were specified as:

> achievement of independence for Belarus and transition to a commonwealth of independent states; establishment in Belarus of a democratic republican government without any party monopoly or dominance of any ideology; rebuilding of a market economy in the Republic closely linked with the economies of the neighboring countries; and renewal of the Belarusian nation and culture and rebuilding in Belarus of a civil society.[29]

The main nationalist movement in Belarus was the Belarus Popular Front (BPF) "Revival" established in October 1988; two other, less influential, organizations—the National-Democratic Party and the Social-Democratic Union (Hramada)—emerged in 1990 and 1991.[30]

Belarus's nationalists could never boast of wide support in society or among state officials. Nationalist forces were active mainly in Minsk and in some parts of the Hrodna and Brest regions.[31] In the words of both a Russian and a Belarusian analyst, "whereas in Baltic countries the Popular Fronts are truly nationwide movements ... Belarus's Popular Front's social basis is confined to intelligentsia in Minsk and other large urban centers."[32] Large sectors of the population were hardly aware of nationalists' efforts to attract wider attention to Belarus's national history and cultural situation. Symptomatically, a survey taken in 1992 showed that 32 percent of ethnic Belarusians considered the history of Russia and Belarus to be identical, 37.6 percent of ethnic Belarusians had no knowledge of Belarusian culture, and 55 percent denied that "nationalism" had any positive potential.[33] Nor were nationalists able to win the support of officials. On the contrary: in contrast to the Baltic republics and—to some extent—Ukraine, Belarus's movements for national revival were never tolerated, let alone supported, by the republic party and government officials.[34] From the time of its emergence, the BPF faced fierce resistance from the ruling establishment and even had to hold its founding congress in Vilnius because of harassment at home.[35] Media, too, was mainly controlled by the officials, and the Front's activists came to rely on *samizdat* (a network of self-circulated materials).[36]

As a result of social apathy and intolerance from the ruling establishment, nationally oriented forces stood little chance, and Belarus's national idea, in the words of independent and nationally minded observers, never took root on the Belarus soil.[37] The BPF and other nationalist movements never controlled a significant amount of seats in the national legislature. During the 1990 national elections, the BPF, as the main nationalist democratic opposition, secured only about 10 percent of the 360 deputy seats, mostly in the capital city of Minsk.[38] The 1995 parliamentary elections showed even poorer results.[39] Conservative politicians, whose mindset was formed during the Soviet era, dominated the parliament. All these factors made it impossible for Belarus nation builders to compete with the old political elite and its empire-oriented supporters.[40] With the rise of an increasingly dictatorial president, Aleksandr Lukashenka, nationalists' opportunities to challenge the empire savers were further reduced, as Lukashenka's intention appeared to be to eliminate the Belarusian Popular Front as a political force.[41]

Empire Savers

In contrast to nation builders, empire-saving forces found wide social support and were increasingly able to control the policy agenda. At least three organizations can be identified as pursuing the agenda of reintegration with Russia. The most powerful was the Party of Communists of Belarus established in 1992 as the successor party to the Soviet-era Communists. Two other organizations—the Slavic Union "Belaya Rus" and the Belarusian People's Movement—were more openly great power nationalistic and oriented toward cultural, and not just politico-economic union with Russia.[42]

That the empire-saving attitude was widely shared by Belarus's political class could be seen in its behavior regarding the republic's status of sovereignty. The process of Belarus's independence had been greatly retarded from the beginning. While the Declaration of State Sovereignty was adopted by the newly formed Supreme Soviet of the Belorussian Soviet Socialist Republic (June 1990),[43] no elaborate plans of independence existed prior to its adoption, and it was only in the aftermath of the failed coup that the republic's parliament mustered the majority required to give the declaration the status of constitutional law (August 25, 1991) prior to the adoption of the new constitution.[44]

The empire-saving views also found major support on the mass level, which was demonstrated by practically all elections and referendums held in Belarus from 1990 to 1996. In the first parliament that largely determined the policy agenda through the 1990-1994 period, 86 percent of seats belonged to Communists,[45] which eventually led to the ouster of Belarus's first moderately pro-independent leader, Stanislav Shushkevich. His followers—Viachelsav Kebich and, especially, Aleksandr Lukashenka—proved to be either ambivalent or openly hostile toward the republic's independence. During the 1995 presidential race, the two competed in the rhetoric of reintegrating the "While Rus'" (Belarus) into the "Great Rus'" (Russia), with no room left for the independence ideas.[46] Lukashenka, a staunch supporter of the empire-saving ideas, won 80 percent of the vote.[47] By successfully exploiting the low level of Belarusians' national identity, Lukashenka promoted Russian to a state language alongside Belarusian, restored a version of the old Communist flag, and gained popular approval of his wish to unite with Russia.[48]

Not surprisingly, all major channels of political influence—parliament, the presidency, media, and state apparatus—were monopolized by the empire-oriented forces, with little room for the nationalists' supporters.

State

The structure of Belarus's state was defined by the efforts of empire savers in policy circles and with support given to it by the empire-saving attitudes in society. The state went through two major stages in its formation. Until the election of Lukashenka a president, the state was relatively low-centralized and had low legitimacy in the sense that Belarus's first leader, Stanislav Shushkevich, was elected by the Supreme Soviet, not in nationwide elections. After Lukashenka's election, the state acquired more legitimacy and was transformed into a highly centralized institution.

Degree of Centralization

During the first two years of independence, the state was relatively low-centralized, with a dual-track policy symbolized by the Shushkevich-Kebich rivalry. Whereas the former was chairman of the Supreme Soviet and symbolized the supreme state power, the latter served as prime minister, in charge of day-to-day policies and with solid support in the parliament. The change came when the Constitution of 1994 declared Belarus a presidential republic and granted more power to the executive branch, although a balance between the executive and legislative branches was generally observed.[49] Lukashenka, however, was never satisfied with the amount of power granted to him and strove to eliminate checks and balances over his presidency. In 1996, he proposed his own draft Constitution for referendum, which received over 70 percent of the votes, with more than 84 percent of the Belarusian electorate participating.[50] Adopted with many violations,[51] Lukashenka's constitution gave him an awaited "legal" dictatorial power to veto legislative acts, with little chance for reconsideration, and to rule by decree without being vetoed by parliament.[52] As a result of Lukashenka's efforts, state power in the republic became highly centralized.

Legitimacy

Despite the dictatorial tendencies of the Lukashenka regime, Lukashenka's state-building policies enjoyed wider social support than the low-centralized state associated with his political predecessors. A poll taken in 1993, for example, showed that the then existing political system of pluralism and democracy was rejected by 48 percent,[53] whereas Lukashenka's regime and policies were repeatedly supported by 70 percent (and more) during nationwide referenda held on various issues from 1995 to 1997.[54]

Foreign Economic Policy

Russian Pole

Unlike its Latvian and Ukrainian counterparts, Belarus's political elite did not possess a belief in economic reorientation away from Russia. The collapse of Communist ideology and the party system in Moscow was not something that Belarus's nomenklatura had looked forward to, and it had a paralyzing effect on Minsk. Quite typically, Belarus's state sovereignty was proclaimed (in July 1990) only when the immediate neighbors—the Baltic republics, Russia, and Ukraine—had done so earlier in 1990. Pressured by the sovereignty proclamation made by neighboring republics, the Communist majority in the Supreme Council of the BSSR, at the urging of the Belarusian Popular Front, voted in favor of sovereignty. Even then, the Supreme Council's leadership did not see sovereignty as being in contradiction with the goal of preserving the Union, and so Article 11 of the declaration proposed "to immediately commence the elaboration of an agreement on a union of sovereign socialist states."[55]

The winds of change did bring to power some new people, such as the Supreme Soviet Chairman Stanislav Shushkevich and Foreign Minister Petr Kravchenko, but even those politicians were not imbued with the ideas of economic nationalism and, instead, believed in the necessity of new economic union in place of the old USSR. Despite the influences of more radical nationalist-oriented processes taking place in the neighboring Ukraine and Baltic countries, Belarus's new leaders were convinced that political sovereignty and economic union were not at odds with each other and should be pursued together, not one at the expense of the other. For instance, Petr Kravchenko, addressing the United Nations, listed achieving real independence and sovereignty for the nation and "creating a single economic space, a new union of sovereign states" as the first two foreign policy priorities.[56] This attitude helps to understand the direction taken in Belarus's new foreign economic policy.

The CIS Stance

Belarus's CIS stance was in many ways predetermined by its participation in Gorbachev's efforts to negotiate a new Union treaty among the Soviet republics from 1989-1991. Unlike the Baltic republics or Ukraine, Belarus's leadership had hardly any objections or reservations about the Gorbachev-proposed arrangements. They clearly did not see Belarus as a fully sovereign entity and were prepared for a limited form of sovereignty within a "renewed" federal union.[57] Some even went as far as to support the August 1991 anti-Gorbachev coup in Moscow, the initiators of which had pledged the introduction of a state of emergency for the purpose of restoring the USSR.[58] It was not until December 4, just a few days before Yeltsin and Kravchuk flew to Belarus to announce the establishment of the CIS, that Belarus's leadership started casting doubts on the republic's adherence to the Union treaty.[59] The leadership attitude in favor of a "renewed union" rested on wide social support. Polls indicated that about four out of five citizens of the BSSR were opposed to secession and condemned separatist efforts.[60]

Not surprisingly, Belarus's behavior in the immediate aftermath of the Soviet breakup was also at odds with those of Ukraine and the Baltics. Together with their Ukrainian counterparts, Belarus's leaders participated in the creation of the CIS, but their vision of the CIS diverged significantly from that of Kiev. Rather than viewing the CIS as a vehicle for a "civilized divorce," Minsk officials hoped that the CIS would become a viable construct, capable of preventing further disintegration and putting the union together.[61] Unlike their Ukrainian counterparts, they planned to develop multilateral cooperation within the CIS framework, rather than limit themselves to cultivating primarily bilateral ties with CIS members.

Committed to transforming the CIS into a viable arrangement, Belarus was a consistent signatory to all major economic and even some security agreements designed within the CIS framework. The CIS Economic Union agreement, for example, was signed in September 1993 and ratified in November of the same year.[62] Despite resistance from the national-democratic opposition,[63] even cornerstone documents rejected by some other CIS members,[64] such as the CIS Charter and the Security Pact, were embraced by Belarus officials. Obviously, even the CIS security agreements, let alone those on closer economic cooperation within the CIS framework, were not seen as threatening Belarus's national sovereignty. With Russia proclaiming a strategy of reintegrating the CIS area in 1993 and 1994,[65] not only was not Belarus's leadership pushed away from Russia and the CIS, it also became an ardent supporter of Russian efforts. Accompanied by Russia, Kazakhstan, and Kyrgyzstan, Belarus formed the CIS's newly emerged "inner core." In addition to previously signed agreements within the CIS framework, this continued the efforts to establish economic union with Russia and other "inner core" participants by signing new agreements on monetary union (1994) and customs union (1995).

Leadership's vision vis-à-vis the CIS and policies directed toward restoring a new Union were consistently opposed by Belarus's nationalists. The leaders of nationalist movements argued that the CIS would divert attention from the more important task—transforming Belarus into a sovereign nation. While the parlia-

ment was busy ratifying the CIS founding documents, the Belarusian Popular
Front called for the addition of seven provisos to the agreement for the sake of
bolstering Belarus's independence from Russia. When the CIS documents were
nonetheless ratified by a virtually unanimous vote, the Popular Front launched a
series of open-air meetings and started a campaign calling for new parliamentary
elections.[66] One of these meetings adopted a motion that asserted:

> The government and Supreme Soviet exhibited a disgraceful, slavish readiness
> to sign even Gorbachev's Novo-Ogarevo accord. Shushkevich was the only one
> who went to Belavezha [the scene of the Slavic summit] not knowing anything.
> The new commonwealth is a compromise between Russia, which wants to take
> over the role of the Soviet Union together with its property, and Ukraine, which
> is striving towards independence. Belarus remains an economic and political
> appendage of Russia... Minsk should not be a bureaucratic creature of the com-
> monwealth, the center of mafia structures, a place to dump worthless rubles and
> further Russify us. Our country should not be Russia's window on Europe but
> an independent [and equal] European state.[67]

Opposing all plans for restoring the Union and establishing the CIS, the BPF
instead advocated the creation of an East European Commonwealth with Belarus,
Ukraine, Lithuania, Latvia, and Estonia as participants.[68] The nationalists' pressures, however, hardly had any effects on the leadership attitude and policies.[69]

Currency Cooperation and Monetary Union with Russia

The first two years following Soviet disintegration brought severe economic
hardship to independent Belarus. Along with many other ex-Soviet republics, it
was badly hit by the disruption of old economic ties as well as Russia's institution of price liberalization. Plummeting trade volume, the doubling of the price
of fuel, a cumulative fall of more than 25 percent in GDP and real wages, and
very high inflation[70] (see table 3.2 on pages 60-61) were some of the consequences of the breakup of the USSR.

In the monetary realm, the republics faced a number of choices about how to
cope with rising economic problems. Latvia left the ruble zone and implemented
a program of rapid domestic marketization. Ukraine, albeit a slow reformer, also
decided in favor of leaving the ruble zone early and introduced a national currency. Belarus followed its own path. Neither reforms nor independent monetary
policy were put on the agenda. Instead, Belarus's leaders made an effort to secure
economic stability by avoiding inevitably painful reforms and staying within the
ruble area. In January 1992, Belarus followed Ukraine in introducing a coupon in
an attempt to protect local markets from invasion by outsiders with rubles.[71]
However, the goal of establishing the Belarus ruble as the sole legal tender was
never firmly set by Belarus's authorities. Subsequent actions confirmed that
Belarus itself was far from committed to currency reform.[72]

In October 1992, Belarus participated in an agreement "On a common market system and coordinated monetary and credit policies between states using the ruble as legal tender," along with seven other CIS republics. The agreement stipulated that the ruble would remain legal tender on the territory of those CIS states while permitting the issue of other forms of quasi-currency (coupons, etc.). It was also agreed that emissions would fall within an agreed total volume of ruble emission.[73] In September 1993, when the Russian Central Bank had announced a currency reform and unilaterally withdrew the old rubles from circulation,[74] Belarus was also among those asking Russia to form a new ruble zone. In so doing, it demonstrated its readiness to further subordinate parts of its monetary sovereignty to Russia's demands. An agreement was signed on September 7, 1993 in Moscow, with signatories pledging to accept not only the Central Bank of Russia as the sole emission center but also more tightly coordinated economic policies.[75] It was Russia, not Belarus, that yet again broke the agreement by setting unrealistic demands, thereby effectively ending the existence of the ruble zone.[76]

Although Belarus demonstrated its readiness to compromise its monetary sovereignty in hopes of overcoming its economic problems,[77] the leadership was, in fact, far from united as to monetary cooperation with Russia. Whereas the bona fide nationalists were too weak to play a major role in debates about Belarus's foreign economic policy, some mainstream policymakers with a political stance of centrism, or "moderate nationalism," did try to challenge the steps compromising the republic's national sovereignty. Belarus's chairman of the Supreme Soviet, Stanislav Shushkevich, for example, while not prepared to go as far as BPF's leaders in emphasizing Belarus's distinctiveness from Russia, did support the idea of Belarus's national independence and nation building and insisted on Russia's treatment of Belarus as a sovereign political entity. Several other policymakers shared Shushkevich's stance.[78]

Domestic struggle over the issues of monetary and economic independence was therefore represented by two major views. On the one hand, there were Shushkevich and his supporters arguing against trading national sovereignty and for economic and security cooperation with Moscow on equal terms.[79] On the other, there were those willing to push Belarus's attempts to establish close economic cooperation with Russia and other post-Soviet republics all the way to political unification, with Russia as a power holder. This temptation found its supporters on both sides. In Moscow, the empire savers seemed to be gaining momentum, while reformers such as Economics Minister Yegor Gaidar and Finance Minister Boris Fedorov resigned, in part due to their opposition to the negotiations over economic union with Belarus.[80] In Belarus, the conservative, empire-saving forces began to concentrate around Prime Minister Vyacheslau Kebich, who was more strongly oriented toward Russia than was Shushkevich and who was willing to accept economic union with Russia on terms that infringed on Belarus's sovereignty.

The following examples can illustrate the difference in views of the two politicians. In 1993, Shushkevich and the Belarusian banking authorities found unacceptable the monetary terms of the Russian Committee on Economic Relations, under which republics could remain in the ruble zone,[81] and began introducing a full-fledged national currency.[82] Kebich, however, favored remaining in the ruble zone, despite Russia's terms. In March, he proposed an economic "confederation" with Russia, having noted that Belarus "cannot exist without close cooperation with [Russia, Ukraine, and Kazakhstan]" and that "it is not Russia that needs Belarus ... it is we who need Russia."[83] Shushkevich responded to the idea of a confederation with Russia in the following way:

> The road to a confederation, if one is possible at all, is rather long and time is needed before other republics are ready to accept the idea. For the time being, it's Kazakhstan and Russia, which call for a confederation. They may have reasons for closer union but the idea of such a union is unacceptable to Belarus because it runs against the Belarusian constitution, which says we are seeking a neutral status.[84]

In their turn, empire savers also brought cultural arguments into the debate about Belarus's sovereignty. The question of Belarus's integration with Russia, Kebich and his supporters argued, was "not just a question of economic circumstances. We are linked by the closest spiritual bonds; we have a common history and similar cultures."[85]

Given the fact that Kebich had the support of the largest parliamentary faction, the conservative "Belarus" and the government under his control, he was increasingly capable of seizing initiative over Shushkevich and of conducting his own economic policies toward Russia. In September 1993, as a result of this policy, the prime ministers of Belarus and Russia signed an accord on monetary union within the CIS framework. In the summer of the same year, the parliament had first tried to remove Shushkevich through a no-confidence vote over the issue of his refusal to sign the CIS Collective Security Pact, one of the implicit Russian conditions for Russia-Belarus economic integration on Russia's side.[86] Finally, in January 1994, Shushkevich was ousted, with 209 voting against him and 36 for him, and he was replaced by one of Kebich's cronies, Mechyslau Hryb.[87] Unlike Shushkevich, Hryb was a proponent of the CIS Collective Security Pact and of economic integration with Russia, even at the cost of Belarus's sovereignty, and he had considerable support in the conservative parliament.[88] This attitude eventually triggered the policy of reintegration with the ex-metropole and was well summarized in an aphoristic expression of a plant director, in whose opinion it was "better to be in a defense union [with Russia] with a sound economy than impoverished but neutral in principle."[89]

With removal of Shushkevich, one of the few reform-minded individuals to hold a prominent government position, Belarus's efforts to reintegrate with Russia were bolstered considerably. In 1994, Belarus's parliament readily ratified the

CIS charter, including the section on collective security,[90] and in April a Belarus-Russia agreement on monetary union was concluded. According to the agreement, Russian troops were to use Belarusian military installations free of charge; the Russian Central Bank was to be the sole center for currency emission; Belarus was to cede control of its fiscal and monetary policy to Russia; and the country was to amend its legislation to bring it in line with that of Russia.[91]

The agreement came under fire from Belarusian nationalists for contravening the country's constitution and betraying its national sovereignty,[92] but it was signed under terms that were objected to by Shushkevich and the nationalists. Both nationalists and empire savers were hoping to find wide social support in Belarusian society. Shushkevich and the national-democratic opposition, for their part, demanded a new referendum and new parliamentary elections before the ratification of the treaty on economic union with Russia. They argued that the monetary union would turn Belarus into a "banana republic" in relation to Russia, if not another oblast of the Russian Federation, and they were hoping that people would vote against this kind of union.[93]

The reality proved nation builders wrong. The question of violations of the Constitution in connection with the signing of the monetary merger agreement was supported by only 63 votes in the 360-seat parliament.[94] The demands for referendum also did not go through. And if the 1994 presidential election, as well as the subsequent consolidation of the Lukashenka's regime was of any significance, Belarus's society was overwhelmingly predisposed toward union with the ex-metropole, so long as it provided the economic security sought. Ironically, it was again Russian, not Belarusian, opposition that prevented implementation of the accord.[95]

Trade Cooperation and Customs Union with Russia

The story of Belarus's search for trade cooperation with Russia runs parallel to its efforts to establish a monetary union with the ex-metropole. Immediately after the Soviet disintegration, Belarus's trade position was similar to those of Latvia and Ukraine, with all the three republics being heavily dependent on inter-republican trade.[96] Belarus, however, was the least psychologically prepared for conducting independent foreign policies and had chosen a path of normalizing and strengthening relations with Russia without investing too much effort in seeking out new trading partners. Its trade with Russia has increased in importance since independence.[97] As Russia began erecting trade barriers with the former Soviet republics, Belarus sought to preserve its economic links even at the cost of sovereignty and so pursued the creation of a customs union with Russia as a way of solving its economic problems.

In March 1992, after signing bilateral agreements with Russia, Kazakhstan, and the Kyrgyz Republic pledging not to impose tariffs or taxes, Belarus made the first effort to secure economic cooperation on the territory of the former USSR through a multilateral arrangement. Along with other CIS members (except Turk-menistan), it signed an agreement on principles of customs policy trying "to secure the free movement of goods across signatories' boundaries and a common customs policy with third countries."[98] Other economic agreements concluded by Belarus during 1992-1994, particularly those about entering the CIS Economic Union and Monetary Union with Russia, also intended to secure commercial ties with the republics.[99] In reality, however, largely due to Russia's unwillingness and restrained attitude, none of these agreements worked.[100] This did not deter Belarus from new attempts to reintegrate with Russia; on the contrary, with the election of Lukashenka as president, Belarus's efforts increased considerably.

In January 1995, deputy prime Minister Mikhail Myasnikovich—again at the initiative of the Belarus side—signed a series of agreements with Russian deputy prime minister Aleksandr Bolshakov, which made a number of conces-sions to Russia in return for a customs union.[101] In February 1995, building on these agreements, Belarus and Russia's presidents finally signed an agreement on a customs union. Like the monetary union agreement, the new accord allowed for the stationing of Russian troops in Belarus at two military bases in Hancavichy and Baranavichy free of charge. In exchange for cheap energy, Belarus also became a transit corridor for Russian energy exports to the West. Finally, the accord envisaged open borders and called for the two countries to align their tar-iff policies.[102] In May of the same year, the two presidents issued a separate decree "On canceling of the customs control on the border of Russian Federation with the Republic of Belarus," and in June their respective governments ruled to implement the decree.[103]

Belarus's trade policies stood in sharp contrast with those of Latvia and Ukraine, the countries that abstained from entering any preferential agreements with Russia. For example, Ukrainian policymakers argued that such agreements, the customs union in particular, would bring asymmetrical benefits to Russia and raised about forty different objections to Russian-designed customs arrange-ments.[104] Belarus's nationalists, too, were thinking in relative terms and launched a campaign against the customs union and Lukashenka's bid for economic reinte-gration with Russia. The Popular Front's "shadow cabinet" issued a statement indicating that the agreement signed would result in "the liquidation of the inde-pendence of the state, the complete poverty of the Belarusian nation, huge losses, and the irreversible desecration and destruction of national, material and cultural possessions."[105] It further argued that the "economic amalgamation of the states" promised by Point 2 of Article 1 of the agreement would only strengthen Russia at the expense of Belarus because the agreement was concluded on Russia's eco-nomic and security terms.[106] Another more centrist national-democratic party, the United Democratic Party of Belarus, added support to the BPF's efforts by argu-ing against the adoption of Russian tariffs by Belarus, one of the key points of the agreement. The step, in the view of the party, would hurt many dynamic and

promising sectors, such as electronics, instrument making, light, and food industries, because it would make them far less competitive on international markets.[107] Integration, if it had to occur, should be developed from below, proceed-
ing from the specific requirements of business rather than from politicians'
desires—this would be the only way to make it mutually advantageous.[108]

Nationalist efforts to stop Belarus's drive toward reintegration with Russia
interwove with efforts to fight the evolution of Lukashenka's regime in an
increasingly authoritarian direction. Faced with the opposition to his authoritarianism in the national parliament, Lukashenka advised the body to dissolve
itself[109] and called for a referendum with four questions, at least two of which
dealt with Belarus's further relations with Russia. The four questions were:
greater presidential power (including the right to dissolve the parliament), restoring Russian as the state language, developing closer links with Russia, and
restoring the old, Soviet-time red-green-white Belarusian national flag and
national coat of arms.[110] In desperation, opposition leader Paznyak asserted that
the reactionary Communist and authoritarian forces in Russia were using Belarus
as a political laboratory to try out methods for establishing Red-Brown (Communist and extreme imperial nationalist) authoritarianism within a traditional Slavic
framework (Russia-Ukraine-Belarus). He also asserted that Lukashenka's drive
would most likely lead to civil war and the loss of Belarus's independence.[111]
Pazniak and other opposition leaders of the parliament also went on a hunger
strike to protest Lukashenka's efforts.

These efforts accomplished little. By denying the national-democratic opposition—as well as the more progressive moderate politicians—access to the mass
media, Lukashenka won the referendum with an overwhelming 83.3 percent of
the vote in May 1995. The parliamentary election was held simultaneously, with
very few seats won by the opposition. Ironically, the support for Belarus's
nationalist efforts came from Moscow. Despite the referendum's results and
Lukashenka's victory, the Kremlin did not rush forward with integration. In July
1995, customs controls on Belarus-Russia trade were removed,[112] but some were
soon erected anew.[113] In addition, Belarus, despite the accord's terms, was not
bringing its legislature in line with Russia's.[114]

The customs union story was typical of Belarus's economic policy efforts
and represented a link in the entire chain of efforts to secure traditional ties with
the ex-metropole. Preceded by the monetary union drive, it was followed by
another integration agreement between the two countries, this one signed in Moscow on April 2, 1996. The Treaty on the Formation of a Community called on the
two sides to establish a politically and economically integrated community, so
they could pool their material and intellectual resources to improve living standards.[115] The treaty was easily ratified by Belarus's parliament,[116] but yet again
met with strong opposition in Russia,[117] and again remained largely a declaration
of intent. In the view of one commentator, the treaty contained a fundamental

contradiction because "Belarus expected an economic bailout, while Russia was unwilling to carry the costs of a union."[118]

After 1996, Belarus continued its attempts to reintegrate with Russia and, more broadly, the CIS at the expense of developing ties with European countries. Lukashenka's efforts to reinstall the command economy led to inflation, shortages of basic food staples, wage arrears, and a collapse of industrial production of alarming proportions[119]—the very outcome predicted by nongovernment economists.[120] His response to this was intensification of his Russia policy in hopes of obtaining additional resources to offset domestic social pressures. Along the lines of the 1996 treaty on Russia-Belarus union, a new agreement was signed in April 1997. The new agreement again provided for common citizenship, and called for coordinating security and economic policies and eventually the creation of a single currency.[121] And in December 1998, the two sides signed a political declaration "On further unification of Russia and Belarus" and promised to subject the unification treaty to the public discussion and referendum of their domestic constituencies. In Boris Yeltsin's opinion, this meant the beginning of a new nation.[122] Lukashenka, too, praised the accomplishments of the reunification process.[123] The two leaders, however, continued viewing the union in fundamentally different terms—something that had already become evident before 1996 and caused the union's failures. Lukashenka was thinking about preserving state sovereignty and was not about to give up Belarusian "accomplishments" (such as ownership of industry and collectivized agriculture) as the basis for the unification. Russia's policymakers, in turn, expected Belarus to amend its legislature in line with that of Russia and to be prepared for acting on the ex-metropole's other economic and political terms.[124] The difference of expectations again produced a number of obstacles to unification.[125]

Belarus's policy of reintegration with Russia would have not materialized without the considerable social support. Unlike their Latvian and Ukrainian counterparts, nationalists in Belarus had little chance to resist the influence of empire savers both inside and outside of parliament. The old elite firmly controlled power in the country and repressed all attempts to challenge it.[126] Having little support in parliament, the BPF tried to mobilize support for an early reelection and succeeded in collecting a sufficient numbers of signatures in favor of it.[127] This had little impact, however, mainly because of a lack of mass support for the nationalists' moves. The weakness of people's national sentiments greatly contributed to the failure of Shushkevich's efforts and to essentially the empire-saving orientation of Belarus's economic policy.[128] The predominant mood in the Belarus society appeared to be "it is better to be well fed and unfree than independent and starving."[129] Just as Latvia's society was considerably homogeneous in terms of sharing nationalist feelings, Belarus was united by its citizens' unwillingness to risk harming economic relations with the former metropole for the sake of illusory goals of national sovereignty.[130]

Lukashenka's unification drive generated fierce resistance from domestic nation builders, the forces committed to both Belarus's active participation in European institutions and gaining distance from Russia.[131] Despite the brutalities of Lukashenka's regime, there was evidence of increased support for the efforts of nationalist-oriented forces. In 1998, it was not only the Popular Front but a number of political and social movements united in protesting Lukashenka's authoritarianism and attempts to find the solution to Belarus's problems on the way to reunification with the ex-metropole.[132] The country's aggravated economic and political situation produced conditions for possible alliance between the working class and the nationally and reform-minded intelligentsia. Yet, up until the beginning 1999, Lukashenka maintained a tight grip on power.

Domestic Economic Institutions

Belarus's experience with establishing domestic market-oriented economic institutions went through two main stages. Until the end of 1994, the pattern of Belarus's domestic marketization was similar to that of Ukraine. With the election of Lukashenka as president, Belarus even made some efforts to reverse the processes of marketization, albeit with limited success. Motivated by the idea of reintegration with Russia, Belarus's leadership hoped that union with the ex-metropole would solve its economic problems.

Belarus was slow in deregulating prices, and it was not until the end of 1994 that economic decrees on price liberalization on important commodities such as dairy products, vodka, meat, and many services were signed. The new president, Aleksandr Lukashenka, made attempts to reverse the process of liberalization. For example, his decree of December 1994 lowered the liberalized prices of consumer goods.[133] Reversing the process proved extremely difficult, however, and the decree caused serious shortages of foodstuffs in January 1995.[134]

Government policy toward establishing Belarus's foreign exchange system illustrated the same point. In 1994 inflation averaged 30 to 40 percent per month, and the exchange rate depreciated further and ended the year at 10,600 Belarus rubles to the dollar.[135] However, instead of trying to reduce inflation by tightening its monetary policy (as it was done in Latvia and in post-1994 Ukraine), Belarus signed an agreement with its former metropole on monetary union and the reentry of Belarus into the ruble zone. Belarus continued this policy during 1995. In May of that year, in a national referendum, a majority (83.3 percent) of the population voted in favor of closer integration with Russia.[136] Clearly, Belarus did not see itself as independent and was not ready to take responsibility for its own economic problems. The country's leadership, in the words of *The Economist*, seemed "to look on economic integration with Russia as a substitute for reform."[137]

The same point can be illustrated with regard to Belarus's trade restriction policy. Despite the devastating impact of the disintegration of the command economy and the collapse of the Soviet Union on Belarus's trade volume and trade balance,[138] Belarus avoided measures to improve the situation by lifting quotas and surrender requirements until 1995.[139] Instead, the government activated the use of barter,[140] and its hopes of stopping the further fall of trade volumes relied on economic reintegration with Russia through monetary union. In April 1994, the government also introduced export tariffs in order to control the export of various commodities from Belarus.[141] Finally, aiming at reintegration, the Belarus government adopted separate tariff policies toward the countries of the former Soviet Union and those outside the area.[142] As a result of these measures, Belarus's trade with Russia was indeed increased, but so were its trade debts to the ex-metropole.[143]

Belarus's inconsistency and eventual failure with domestic economic reform can be attributed to its weak national identity and, hence, to the overwhelming predominance of empire-saving orientations in the society. Nationalist-oriented forces, with their belief in the virtue of Western marketization,[144] were in no position to influence the economic decision-making process. The lack of internal cultural motivation to become a genuinely independent actor in the world economy greatly contributed to Belarus's experience with establishing domestic market-oriented institutions. As two analysts aptly put it,

> Comparing Ukraine and Belarus, one notices the great importance of the independence factor. The strong presence of this factor in Ukraine finally mobilized the political elite to struggle with deep economic crisis that began in 1994 to threaten the unity and independence of the Ukrainian state. In contrast, Belarusian political leaders, Prime Minister Vyacheslau Kebich until July 1993 and President Lukashenka thereafter, have tried to realize the idea of monetary and economic union with Russia as a substitute for real economic transition.[145]

Yet, as in the case of Ukraine, this would be an incomplete explanation. As in Ukraine, Belarus's low commitment to domestic economic reform had to do in part with the leadership change. Also as in Ukraine, Belarus's early leaders probably could have begun more boldly and would have accomplished more than they did. But even more important, Lukashenka's antireform stance was hardly inevitable, and another president, should one have been elected, might not necessarily have pursued a Lukashenka-style dictatorship. Metaphorically speaking, given the social constraints it was unlikely that Belarus would have elected somebody like Ukraine's Kuchma to replace its own version of Leonid Kravchuk. But Belarus could have elected another Kravchuk (somebody like Viacheslau Kebich)—if there had not been a Lukashenka among the presidential candidates—and the economic reform, albeit as slow and inconsistent, as would have had a good chance of continuing.

Alternative Economic Ties

Absorbed with the efforts to transform the CIS into a Customs Union and reintegrate with Russia, Belarus did not express much interest in finding new trading partners and entering alternative economic arrangements outside of the former Soviet Union. Unlike Latvia and Ukraine, and although in a comparable trade situation, Belarus was much more passive in pursuing visible foreign economic activities before and after the Soviet disintegration. At least three alternatives to unilateral dependence on Russia were identified, but were never pursued by Belarus's leaders.

The most radical alternative was put forward by the Belarusian Popular Front as early as 1989 and may be termed the European alternative. The idea was to create a Baltic-Black Sea political-economic association that would unite Belarus, the three Baltic republics of Lithuania, Latvia, and Estonia, as well as Ukraine and Moldova. The association was supposed to help its members resist economic pressures from Moscow as well as gain gradual access to Western European markets. It would serve as a counterbalance to the huge Eurasian Russia and as a safeguard to sovereignty.[146] In the BPF's own words:

> The BPF comes out in favor of Belarus's entry into the European political, economic and defense structures, together with its Central-European neighbors: Baltic states, Poland, Ukraine. Alongside, we support all the initiatives aimed at the closer coordination of policies and economies of the Inter-Sea countries, those of Central and Eastern Europe... The BPF believes: the integration into Europe, our way back to our original and natural European home, is the only guarantee of the preservation and consolidation of the Belarusian independent statehood and of the Belarusian nation's survival. Historically, Belarus was formed as a typical Central-European country, its society has always shared the traditional Western values, and it was only first the Russian and later the Soviet occupations that tore the country away from its natural civilizational and cultural context. In the "Europe of Fatherlands" we can become ourselves, equal among equals.[147]

Another alternative was a compromise between complete separation from the CIS and subsequent membership in the Baltic-Black Sea Association. The Belarusian Social-Democratic Party ("Hramada") suggested that the best option for Belarus would be not to sign the CIS statute but, rather, to become an associate member and cooperate in the economic fields (without cooperating in military and defense affairs). Ideally, Belarus should initiate and create a new international organization, something like a smaller European Community, that could be joined by some of the ex-Soviet republics (Baltics, Ukraine, and Moldova) and by the former Community of Mutual Economic Assistance (CMEA) countries such as Poland, the Czech Republic, Slovakia, Romania, and Bulgaria.[148]

Finally, there was a more moderate idea favored by Shushkevich, according to which Belarus would not separate itself from the CIS and Russia, but would instead take full advantage of economic cooperation within the CIS under the following conditions: 1) such cooperation must be pursued for the purpose of strengthening, not weakening, Belarus's sovereignty, and 2) Belarus should not limit itself to the CIS, but search for other trading partners as well.[149]

None of these ideas was given serious consideration by Belarus's policy-makers. Even the latter, most moderate alternative did not have a chance to be fully implemented, mainly due to Shushkevich's resignation. Instead, President Lukashenka glorified an empire as an ideal means of coexistence for Belarus and Russia. Ironically, the idea of Baltic-Black Sea political-economic association advanced by Belarusian and Ukrainian nationalists was denounced by the president as conflicting with the goals of Belarus's sovereignty.[150]

Alternative Multilateral Arrangements

The first two years of Belarus's independence were marked by its interest in developing relations with European countries, particularly with members of the European Community. Although Belarus's leaders were never as explicit about their European orientation as their Ukraine counterparts, the interest in Europe seemed to persist. The idea of economic involvement in the "European process" had emerged in 1991, if not earlier. The head of the Supreme Soviet, Stanislav Shushkevich, and other officials traveled to European countries to investigate the opportunities for Belarus to obtain status as an associated member of the EC.[151] On the level of public statements, the idea was first articulated in September 1991 by Belarusian Foreign Minister Petr Kravchenko. While addressing the United Nations, he placed the involvment of Belarus in the European process next to other main directions in his country's foreign policy.[152] In 1992 and 1993, Shushkevich on a number of occasions expressed Belarus's willingness to join the European Community, emphasizing that entry into the EC should not be viewed as conflicting with Belarus's traditional close ties with Russia.[153]

In 1994, reflecting the leadership change, the country's drive toward Europe slowed considerably. In January 1995, after years of hesitation, Belarus finally initialized a partnership and cooperation agreement with the EU.[154] Symptomatically, Belarusian leaders neither looked at those relations as a priority over economic confederation with Russia nor anticipated that ties with Europe would go beyond bilateral relationships. Even while signing the accord in Brussels in early March 1995, President Lukashenka stressed that Belarus was interested in the agreement solely for the economic benefits it entailed; he did not see it as a step on the road to Belarus's integration with the EU.[155] After 1996 President Lukashenka became increasingly hostile toward the prospect of joining the EU, proclaiming at one point that "it is not Belarus that needs the European Union, but the European Union that needs Belarus."[156]

Europeans, in turn, expressed reservations about Belarus's entry into the EU. European Commission member Hans van de Broek said, for example, that Belarus was "on the farthest approaches from being admitted into the European Union" because of its lack of economic stability and democratic reform.[157] Another indication was the delay in signing the comprehensive trade accord between the EU and Belarus in 1996, also due to Belarus's lack of commitment to economic and political reform.[158] Later in the same year, the EU suspended enacting its provisional trade agreement with Belarus because of human rights abuses in the country, a result of the increasingly authoritarian policies of Lukashenka's regime.[159]

Beyond the European Union, Belarus, like Ukraine, tried to gain membership in the Central European Initiative and became an associate and, later, a full member of the organization.[160] Unlike Ukraine, however, Belarus expressed little desire to join the Visegrad Group. When asked whether Belarus was interested in the triangle, Chairman of the Parliament Shushkevich said in July 1992 that, although Belarus sought economic ties with Poland and other countries, "our country imports most of its raw materials, especially from Russia. We cannot in an artificial manner worsen relations with it."[161]

Bilateral Ties

A similar pattern was shown by Belarus's development of bilateral economic ties beyond Russia and the CIS countries. Most of these ties were developed during the country's first two years of independence and began to fade after 1994.

During the first years of independence, Belarus advanced bilateral ties with European and Third World countries, mainly via trade agreements granting MFN status.[162] In Western Europe, Germany became Belarus's most important neighbor and trading partner. In the words of Belarus's foreign minister, relations with Germany were more solid than with any other country in Western Europe.[163] During the 1992-1993 period, German exports to Belarus more than doubled.[164] In addition to developing trade ties, Belarus also had an interest in Germany as a potential creditor and as a supporter in its persistent drive toward EU membership.[165]

In Eastern Europe, Ukraine and Poland emerged as Belarus's two most important partners. Ukraine was the first among other nations to establish diplomatic relations with Belarus and remains its second most important trading partner after Russia.[166] Relations with Poland started to develop after the signing of a Declaration on Good-Neighborly Relations and Cooperation in October 1991. In 1991, Poland absorbed 19 percent of Belarus's exports and sold Belarus much-needed grain and sugar. Minsk also expressed interest in using the Polish port of Gdynia, which is closer and less expensive than Ukraine's Odessa, for the shipment of goods.[167] On one occasion, Belarus's foreign minister argued that the two sides should cooperate more closely because "the West was not ready to open its markets to either Polish or Belarusian goods."[168] At later stages, however, relations with Poland turned in a more problematic direction as a result of both domestic change in Belarus and Polish concerns about Belarus's excessive dependency on Russia.[169] From 1993-1994, Polish-Belarusian economic relations took even an greater turn for the worse with bilateral trade decreasing from $320 million in 1992 to $218 million in 1993. Economic agreements signed between Belarus and Poland were being implemented at an unsatisfactorily slow rate,[170] and disagreements over trade policies abounded.[171]

Belarus was slow to develop relations with developing countries, although this had more to do with indifference than with economic potential. The potential, as some analysts argued, was there: many Third World countries had been Soviet clients and relied on Soviet military equipment as well as other machinery, so Belarus, with its relatively large military-industrial complex, could have had a number of ready-made markets.[172] China was one example of neglected opportunity. The contrast with Ukraine is particularly instructive here: in 1995, bilateral trade stood at just $30 million annually, a mere fraction of Ukraine's $837 million.[173]

To summarize, Belarus's leadership did not take advantage of existing foreign economic options, having fallen behind Ukraine, the Baltic nations, and some other former republics. Belarus's successes in winning access to markets beyond the CIS area via signing free-trade agreements—bilateral or multilateral—or diversifying its economic activities in any other way should be recognized as modest, at best. With the ouster of Shushkevich and the rise of Lukashenka, the country practically ceased its search for new commercial partners outside Russia. As a result, trade dependence on Russia only increased in significance over the first five years of Belarus's political independence. "The focus on Russia," as one observer put it, "has led the country to neglect its relations with other countries, and Belarus is now widely perceived as a nonentity on the international scene."[174]

Notes

1. EIU, *Quarterly Economic Report 1998.*
2. Some Belarus intellectuals emphasize the cultural influences the nation went through while being a subject of the Grand Duchy of Lithuania, which in the early 1990s laid out the ground for the idea of establishing the Baltic—Black Sea federation (personal interview with a professor at Belarussian State University, Minsk, May 1999). Section three of this chapter returns to this point.
3. Clem 1996, 211.
4. The *Adradzen'ne* period is often referred to as "the formative years of Belorussian political nationalism" (Vakar 1956, 91).
5. Zaprudnik and Fedor 1995, 17-18.
6. Suny 1993, 35.

7. *Ibid.*; Zaprudnik and Urban 1997, 281.

8. Vakar 1956, 105.

9. The Soviet west Belorussia included the present oblasts of Brest and Grodno. It also included Bialystok, which was ceded to Poland in 1945 (Szporluk 1979, 79).

10. From 1859 to 1906, publication in Belorussian was prohibited in Russia, and it was only after 1906 that the first Belorussian-language periodicals were found (*Ibid.*).

11. Szporluk 1979, 80; Marples 1998, 14.

12. Zaprudnik 1993, 58.

13. Szporluk 1979, 80. Steven L. Guthier (1977) reached similar conclusions about Belarus's linguistic situation.

14. In this point, Belarus, too, is in unfavorable position if compared to Ukraine. One scholar wrote, for example, that the Uniate Church "could have become a foundation for the development of Belarussian national consciousness in the same way that it became a foundation for the growth of Ukrainian national consciousness in Galicia" (Burant 1995, 1132). Some of Belarus's intellectuals also emphasized this point (personal interviews with vice-rector of Belarusian State University and director of the Center for Studies of Gender and Nationalism at European Humanities University, Minsk, May 1999).

15. In the words of Jan Zaprudnik, the nomenklatura in Belarus was the most Russified part of this Russified republic (1993, 124).

16. Marples 1993, 262.

17. Belarus was occupied as early as June 1941 and remained under German occupation for almost the entire war period. Belarussians suffered enormously during the occupation, and this undoubtedly damaged their national character. More than two millions lives were lost and more than one million buildings destroyed. An American observer, after six months of travel across Belarus, called it "the most devastated territory in the world" (Zaprudnik and Fedor 1995, 22; Marples 1996, 120).

18. Zaprudnik and Urban 1997, 284.

19. This is not to say that Belarus did not have its own leaders interested in promoting national culture. Petr Masherov, who emerged as Belarus's leader in 1965, is sometimes referred to as one such leader. He often appeared in public in national costume and spoke the native language at some official functions (Marples 1996b, 3). It is not known, however, of Masherov having had on his agenda far-reaching reforms comparable with those designed by Shelest or Berklaus (personal interviews with journalists at *Belorusskaya gazeta*, Minsk, May 1999).

20. Schroeder 1986, 301.

21. Guthier 1977; Suny 1993, 33.

22. Zaprudnik and Fedor 1995, 36.

23. Prazauskas 1994, 152.

24. Chinn and Kaiser 1996, 158.

25. Marples 1996, 119.

26. One Belarus scholar concluded, for example, that "Belarussians have problems identifying themselves as a nation lacking a sense of shared origin, experience and culture" (Gapova 1998). Scholars, politicians, and policymakers across political spectrum generally share this view, although they are far from united regarding the implications of Belarus' identity weakness for practical policy (personal interviews, Minsk, May 1999).

27. Zaprudnik 1989, 37-45; Marples 1993, 261.

28. Not only did Belarus's nationalists follow many Baltic initiatives and programs, but they had joint activities, too. For a more detailed account of the Baltic-Belarus nationalist connection, see Mihalisko 1991; Muiznieks 1995.

29. Zaprudnik 1993, 151. For the political programs and views of Belarus's nationalists, see Poznyak 1989; Zaprudnik 1989; Mihalisko 1991; Marples 1993, 260-262; Zaprudnik 1993, 148-153; Andreev 1997.

30. Andreev 1997; Mihalisko 1997, 241-244.

31. Marples 1996, 122.

32. Furman and Bykhovets 1996, 63-64.

33. Marples 1993, 265.

34. Zaprudnik 1989, 50; Marples 1996, 116; Mihalisko 1997, 240.

35. In October 1988, for example, Minsk officials dispatched riot police to disperse a demonstration by the informal groups and Popular Front sympathizers. Tear gas, truncheons, and water hoses were turned on participants (Mihalisko 1991, 127; Andreiev 1997).

36. During the 1990 national elections, technically multiparty, the Communist Party had control over the media and its members headed most of the country's enterprises and institutions (Mihalisko 1991, 128; Markus 1995b, 75).

37. Personal interviews, Minsk, May 1999.

38. Markus 1995b, 75.

39. Marples 1995a, 10; Mihalisko 1997, 264-65.

40. The only exception appears to be the effect nationalist ideas had on adoption by the Belarus's parliament of the Declaration of Sovereignty in June 1990. By adopting the declaration, however, the Communist-dominated parliament was reacting to the rapidly shrinking center of the Soviet power, rather than to nationalist pressures at home. A nationalist-minded writer Vasil Bykau, recognized the "purely theoretical" significance of the declaration and ventured a rather pessimistic forecast: "There is not any real fulfillment of this sonorous declaration, and it is doubtful that with such an obvious, to put it mildly, conservatism of the CPB and the Soviets, sovereignty will be achievable in the near future" (Zaprudnik 1993, 153).

41. Marples 1996, 135. In 1996, Zyanon Paznyak and Sergei Naumchik, two prominent leaders of the BPF, were forced to seek political asylum at the United States in order to escape prison at home (*Segodnia*, August 2, 1996).

42. Andreev 1997; Mihalisko 1997, 245-46; Sergeiev and Fadeiev 1998.

43. Replaced by "Belarus" on September 19, 1991.

44. Paznyak 1995, 141.

45. Mihalisko 1997, 245.

46. Kotikov 1996. Those candidates opposing the integration—Paznyak and Shushkevich—garnered a total of 22.7 percent of the vote (Burant 1995, 1135).

47. Mihalisko 1997, 254.

48. Marples 1998, 14. Lukashenka, in his own way, expressed the generally widely shared desire of Belarussians to maintain close economic, political, and cultural ties with the ex-metropole (personal interview with Vice-Rector of Belarusian State University, Minsk, May 1999).

49. *Ibid.*, 254-55.

50. Markus 1997, 59.

51. Bykowski 1997.

52. Karmanov 1996; Shushkevich 1997.

53. Zaprudnik 1994, 135.

54. Kotikov 1996.

55. Zianon Paznyak, a leader of nationalist-democratic opposition, denounced such a union as a "noose around the neck of the Belarussian people" and proposed an alternative declaration of sovereignty. However, the opposition counterproposal garnered only 47 votes out of 345 (Zaprudnik 1993, 152-53).

56. "We stand for preserving, developing and giving new substance to traditional economic relations and on this basis—for participation in the process to form a community of sovereign states to replace the USSR" (*Moscow TASS*, "Kravchenko Addresses UN on Foreign Policy," in FBIS-SOV-91-189, September 30, 1991, 70). Very similar thoughts were expressed by Shushkevich (*Moscow Pravda*, "Shushkevich Previews Minsk Summit Meeting," in FBIS-SOV-91-251, December 31, 1991, 59).

57. Mihalisko 1992, 7-8.

58. Sanford 1996, 144; Mihalisko 1997, 242.

59. Mihalisko 1992, 8.

60. Zaprudnik and Urban 1997, 292.

61. *FBIS-SOV-91-251*, "Shushkevich Previews Minsk Summit Meeting," 1991, December 31, 59-60; Zalomai 1993, 10; Rozanov 1998, 69-70.

62. Boss and Havlik 1994, 243.

63. *RFE/RL Daily Report*, "Belarus Leader against Stronger CIS Integration," January 15, 1993; "Parliamentary Opposition in Belarus against Economic, Military Union with Russia," April 8, 1993; "Opposition to CIS Security Pact in Belarus," April 30, 1993.

64. Ukraine, Moldova and Turkmenistan abstained from signing both documents (Zagorski 1997, 12, 64).

65. Mihalisko 1995.

66. Mihalisko 1992, 8.

67. *Ibid.*, 8-9.

68. Zaprudnik and Urban 1997, 293; *Vecherniy Minsk*, "Popular Front Warns against Pro-Russia Orientation," in FBIS-SOV-93-249, December 30, 1993, 61.

69. On the first anniversary of Belarussia's Declaration of State Sovereignty on July 1991, the BPF's leader Zyanon Paznyak complained, for example, that nothing had changed in Belorussia in the year since sovereignty was declared. The republic, in his view, had the most reactionary leadership in the country (*RFE/RL Daily Report*, "Belorussian Sovereignty Day," 1991, July 29). In 1995, frustrated with the poor performance of nationalists in parliamentary elections, he said, "People's mentality has not changed. They still believe populist promises and will vote as the big promiser will tell them" (*Belorusskaya Delovaya Gazeta*, "Interview with Popular Front Leader Paznyak," in FBIS-SOV-95-186, September 26, 1995, 90).

70. Babosov 1993, 37; Boss and Havlik 194, 241.

71. Zaprudnik 1993, 197.

72. This was hardly surprising as the leadership view was that the introduction of national currency would mean "virtually a process of disintegration" (*Pravda*, "Shushkevich Previews Minks Summit Meeting," in FBIS-SOV-91-251, December 31, 1991, 60).

73. Boss and Havlik 1994, 245.

74. Russia was dissatisfied with the state of payments on the territory of the former USSR. By announcing a currency reform involving the withdrawal of old Soviet and Russian ruble notes from circulation on its territory, Russian leadership hoped to liberate itself from the 'burden' of the republics it believed it had been subsidizing. By so doing, it hoped to better position its economy for further reforms (see, for example, Lekant 1992).

75. Boss and Havlik 1994, 245; Sanford 1996, 140.

76. Shortly after, Russia demanded of its new partners the pooling of gold and hard currency reserves and oversight of their foreign trade operations. This proved too much and in November this new arrangement was terminated by the introduction of national currencies by many, including Belarus and Kazakhstan (Boss and Havlik 1994, 245; Webber 1997, 52).

77. Energy dependence was one aspect of this, and Minsk was hoping to continue to enjoy favorable prices for supplies of fuel from Russia (Markus 1995d; Sanford 1996, 140; Becker 1997, 124).

78. Chairman of the Belarusian National Bank Stanislav Bahdankevich was another high-profile policymaker committed to national independence in economic affairs. He was among few others who objected to Article 5 of the Russia-Belarus monetary treaty, whereby all Belarusian asserts and liabilities were to be transferred to the Central Bank of Russia and the National Bank of Belarus was to be abolished. Bahdankevich believed that questions of coordination in the issuing of money, the budget deficit, credit rates, and the rest could be decided through agreement between the two sovereign banks (*Rossiyskiye Vesti,* "National Bank Chairman of Currency Unification Treaty," in FBIS-S0V-94-079, April 25, 1994, 72; *Moscow Mayak Radio Network,* "National Bank Disagrees with Monetary Union Treaty," in FBIS-SOV-94-093, May 13, 1994, 54). Lukashenka removed Bahdankevich on September 15, 1995 (Marples 1995).

79. In this, Shushkevich was firmly supported by Belarus' bona fide nationalists, first and foremost the Belarus Popular Front, which argued—at least after 1992—in favor of the introduction of a national currency (*Moscow INTERFAX,* "Popular Front Releases Economic Reform Proposal," in FBIS-SOV-92-075, April 17, 1992, 54; *Radio Minsk Network,* "Popular Front Calls Russian Money Reform 'Treacherous,'" in FBIS-SOV-93-146, August 2, 1993, 65).

80. Markus 1997, 56.

81. Those included allowing the Russian Central Bank to regulate the amount of credit and cash issued by the National Bank of Belarus and bringing Belarus's legislation on banking into line with Russia's (*Rossiyskiye vesti,* "National Bank Chairman on Currency Unification Treaty," in FBIS-S0V-94-079, April 25, 1994, 72)

82. Markus 1995c, 64.

83. Dawisha and Perrott 1994, 183.

84. Zaprudnik 1994, 138.

85. Burant 1995, 1136. Similar remarks were made by Mechyslaw Hryb: "We do not conceal our vital interest in union with Russia. Our countries are very closely linked in all spheres, and our people regarded each other as brothers from time immemorial" (*Krasnaya Zvezda,* "Hryb Cited on Domestic Concerns, Russia Ties," in FBIS-SOV-94-072, April 14, 1994, 46).

86. Shushkevich had resisted the Pact for months, favoring Belarus's international status as a "neutral state," but he did not have much support in the pro-Communist parliament and therefore was severely constrained in conducting an independent foreign policy.

87. Markus 1995a, 47.

88. *Ibid.*

89. Mihalisko 1994, 114.

90. Burant 1995, 1135.

91. Markus 1995c, 64; Markus 1997, 56. For the text of the treaty, see *Nezavisimaia gazeta*, January 25, 1994 and *Minsk BELAPAN*, "Monetary Merger Treaty with Russia Detailed," in FBIS-SOV-94-072, April 14, 1994, 44. For various reactions to the treaty in the Russian press, see *Izvestia*, April 14, 1994; *Rossiiskaia gazeta*, April 19, 1994; *Vek*, April 15-21, 1994, 7; *Segodnia*, May 6, 1994.

92. A major charge was that the agreement violated those articles of the Constitutions guaranteeing that Belarus would conduct its domestic and foreign policy on an independent basis (*Minsk BELAPAN*, "Monetary Merger Violates 'Fundamentals' of Statehood," in FBIS-SOV-94-073, April 15, 1994, 56; *Minsk BTK Television Network*, "Paznyak on Relations with Russia, Merger," in FBIS-SOV-94-121, June 23, 1994, 46-47).

93. Mihalisko 1994, 115; Burant 1995, 1136.

94. *Radio Minsk Network*, "Deputies Uphold Constitutionality of Monetary Merger," in FBIS-SOV-94-082, April 28, 1994, 68.

95. Markus 1995a, 49; *Vek* April 15-21, 1994, 7.

96. See, for example, Watson 1994, 383; Bradshaw 1993, 29.

97. *EIU. Quarterly Economic Report 1994*, 4; Rozanov 1998, 71.

98. Barner-Barry and Hody 1995, 286.

99. The 1994 agreement, for example, promised to lift all trade customs duties and transit charges in the first stage (*Minsk BELAPAN*, "Monetary Merger Treaty with Russia Detailed," in FBIS-SOV-94-072, April 14, 1994, 44).

100. Markus 1997.

101. Markus 1995c, 64.

102. A list of some 200 goods that had different tariffs was drawn up (Markus 1997, 56-57; Drakokhrust 1997, 3). For a text of the agreement, see *Russia and Eurasia Documents Annual* 1995.

103. *On Canceling of the Customs Control* 1995; Feofilaktova 1996; Drakokhrust 1997, 3.

104. *Nezavisimaya Gazeta*, "Pinzenik Opposes CIS Customs Union," in FBIS-SOV-95-233, December 5, 1995, 45; *Uryadovyy Kuryer*, "Ukraine: Minister Explains Refusal to Join CIS Customs Union," in FBIS-SOV-96-019, January 29, 1996, 48.

105. *Minsk BELAPAN*, "Article Criticizes Customs Pact with Russia," in FBIS-SOV-95-018, January 27, 1995, 76.

106. *Ibid.*, 77.

107. *Kommersant-Daily*, "UDPB's Daneyko Cited on Customs Union," in FBIS-SOV-95-112, June 12, 1995, 66.

108. *Ibid.*, 67.

109. Under the old Constitution, the parliament's term was supposed to end by March 25, but the parliament claimed that, under the new 1994 Constitution, it could continue its work until a new parliament is elected (Turevich 1995, 11).

110. Sanford 1996, 146.

111. *Ibid.*

112. Becker 1996, 121; Feofilaktova 1996.

113. One of the reasons cited by Russia's side was rising illegal trade from other former Soviet republics, especially Ukraine, which was compromising Russian producers, especially those producing vodka, timber and strategic materials (Feofilaktova 1996; Markus 1997, 57). Belarus benefited significantly, however, from exploiting the customs union by taxing goods in transit to and from Russia via Belarus (*The Jamestown Monitor*, "Russian Subsidies to Belarus," October 9, 1997).

114. *Ibid.*

115. For the treaty's full text, see *Nezavisimaia gazeta*, April 1, 1997. For various analyses, see Marples 1996c; Turevich 1996.

116. Drakokhrust 1997, 4.

117. For contrasting views on the effects of the agreement, see *NG-Stsenarii*, May 5, 1997; Kozhokin 1996/97.

118. Markus 1997, 58; *The Jamestown Monitor*, "Belarus Economy in "Free Fall" – Will Moscow Bail It Out?" August 2, 1996. The treaty implementation was also complicated by the 1996 "Torg-Expo" scandal, which implicated a privileged company and the president's administration in the low-tariff import of alcohol into Belarus and its subsequent resale in Russia. As a result of operations such as Torg-Expo, nearly $1 billion was unaccounted for in Russia's customs budget (Feofilaktova 1996; Drakokhrust 1997, 4).

119. *The Jamestown Monitor*, "Lukashenka Frantic to Buy Social Peace," December 3, 1998.

120. Turevich 1998.

121. *RFE/RL Daily Report*, "Yeltsin Approves New Agreement with Belarus," April 3, 1997.

122. *Nezavisimaia gazeta*, December 26, 1998.

123. Lukashenka 1998. *The Jamestown Monitor*, "Primakov Keeps Rising in Lukashenka's Estimation," February 22, 1999.

124. *The Jamestown Monitor*, "High-Level Russia-Belarus Meeting Fails to Settle Differences," June 11, 1998; "Pan-Slavism Plus Collectivism Equals Empire," August 4, 1999; "Lukashenka Previews Treaty of Unification with Russia," April 8, 1999. For further clarification of Russia's preferences, see *NG-Stsenarii*, May 5, 1997; *Nezavisimaia gazeta*, December 26, 1998; *Nezavisimaia gazeta*, January 20, 1999; *The Jamestown Monitor*, "Liberal Imperialism and Belarus," January 21, 1999.

125. *Nezavisimaia gazeta*, January 20, 1999; *The Jamestown Monitor*, "Russia-Belarus Union: Saber-Rattling amid Economic and Political Failure," February 16, 1999.

126. In 1993, for example, the government banned public demonstrations, one of the few tools the BPF had at its disposal.

127. Zaprudnik and Urban 1997, 295.

128. Perhaps the best example is the Belarus June-July 1994 presidential elections where Russophone Alyaksandr Lukashenka was elected the country's first president with 80 percent of the vote, and the two major candidates were running on a platform of economic reintegration with Russia and competed in their pro-Russian rhetoric rather than supporting Belarus's national independence (*Nezavisimaya gazeta*, March 21, 1996; Burant 1995, 1135).

129. Plant director Mikalai Yarokhau told Belarusian Radio that "it is better to be in a defense union [with Russia] with a sound economy than impoverished but neutral in principle" (Mihalisko 1994, 114).

130. Interestingly enough, the argument about the effects of national culture on the economy and economic policy, similar to the one pursued in this study, was advanced in Belarus's academic press. For example, in his article "Russian Culture, Belarusian Character, and the Economy" published in the journal *Literatura i mastastsva*," Pavel Bich argued that Russian cultural stereotypes took root in Belarus' society and that "in order to build a normal statehood, economy, and policy, the Belarusians should liberate themselves from spiritual submission to Russia culture" (Zaprudnik 1994, 143-144).

131. *RFE/RL Daily Report*, "Demonstration in Minsk," April 2, 1997; *The Jamestown Monitor*, "Young Front Demonstrates in Minsk on Independence Anniversary," July 28, 1998; "International Support Sought against Re-Annexation of Belarus by Russia," January 4, 1999.

132. *The Jamestown Monitor*, "Belarusan Opposition Unveils Political Strategy," January 14, 1999; "Opposition Activity Picking up in Minsk," January 29, 1999; "Democratic Congress in Minsk," February 1, 1999.

133. Dabrowski and Antczak 1996, 49.

134. *Ibid.*

135. *WB* 1995, 40.

136. Markus 1995b, 78.

137. *The Economist*, May 20, 1995, 47.

138. In 1992, for the first time trade with the former Soviet Union went into deficit, and during 1993 trade continued to deteriorate.

139. Export licenses, for example, were required for seventy-five categories of products. Quotas were applied to mineral fertilizer, timber, and basic foodstuffs (*Trade Policy* 1994, 42).

140. *EIU. Quarterly Economic Report 1994*, no. 1, 32.

141. *OMRI Daily Report*, "Presidential Decree on Export Tariffs," February 9, 1996.

142. For example, in 1992 it imposed no tariffs or duties on trade with the former Soviet republics. Simultaneously, import duties on a wide range of goods from countries other than those of the former USSR were imposed with most rates in the 5 percent to 30 percent range (*Trade Policy* 1994, 41).

143. Belarus authorities claimed that Russia accounted for 61.4 percent of CIS trade in 1992, 71.3 percent in 1993, and 82.9 percent in the first eight months of 1994 (*EIU. Quarterly Economic Report 1994*, no. 4). In the meantime, by the end of May 1994, Belarus's trade debts to Russia rose to Rb681bn (US$395m) (*Ibid.*, no. 3, 42).

144. As was the case in Ukraine, Belarus's nationalists were not uniform in sharing the belief in the utmost significance of market reform. They were—at least implicitly— divided between those who placed the highest value on establishing the institutions of nationhood (national army, borders, currency, etc.) and those pressing for speeding up domestic reform. For example, the Popular Front's original proposals for economic reform can be seen as pro-nation rather than merely pro-market in their orientation. Similar to Ukraine's March 1992 program, these proposals seemed to overplay the significance of national currency and breaking away from Russia at the expense of other measures of economic stabilization, such as privatization and price decontrol (*Moscow INTERFAX*, "Pop-

ular Front Releases Economic Reform Proposal," in FBIS-SOV-92-075, April 17, 1992, 54). Some other democratic and nationally-oriented organizations, on the other hand, were more pro-market and less anti-Russian, emphasizing the necessity of price reform as a step in Belarus's economic recovery (*Kommersant-Daily*, "UDPB's Daneyko Cited on Customs Union," in FBIS-SOV-95-112, June 12, 1995, 66-67; Bogdankevich 1997). Overall, however, both groups were critical of governmental policies and appreciative, albeit to a different degree, of the importance of domestic economic reform.

145. Dabrowski and Antczak 1996, 77.

146. Paznyak 1995, 147; Andreev 1997; personal interviews, Minsk, May 1999.

147. *BELARUS: TO EUROPE* 1997. Belarus's nationalists, along with their Ukrainian and Latvian counterparts, perceived Russia as doomed to stay imperialistic and authoritarian and unable to become democratic and economically developed (*Moscow ITAR-TASS*, "BPF Leader Sees Russia as Enemy of Independence," in FBIS-SOV-94-112, June 10, 1994, 46; *London THE TIMES*, "Opposition Leader Promises to 'Sever Moscow Ties," in FBIS-SOV-95-025, February 7, 1995, 44).

148. Paznyak 1994, 148.

149. Similar ideas were developed in Antoniuk 1997; Davidenko and Matiushevski 1998.

150. Lukashenka 1997b.

151. *Moscow INTERFAX*, "Idea of becoming EC Associate Member Explored," in FBIS-SOV-91-193, October 4, 1991, 64.

152. *Moscow TASS*, "Kravchenko Addresses UN on Foreign Policy," in FBIS-SOV-91-189, September 30, 1991, 70; Paznyak 1994, 142.

153. *RFE/RL Daily Report*, "Shushkevich on the Belarusian Ruble," May 20, 1992; "Lalumiere in Belarus," May 5, 1993; Zaprudnik 1993, 212.

154. According to the agreement, Belarus was to obtain MFN status and removal of restrictions on its exports (*RFE/RL Daily Report*, "European Agreements with Belarus," March 8, 1995).

155. Burant 1995, 1134.

156. Maisenia 1996.

157. *RFE/RL Daily Report*, "EU Official on Belarus," November 3, 1995.

158. *RFE/RL Daily Report*, "European Commission Urges Trade Accord with Belarus," November 3, 1995; "Belarus Signs Interim Trade Agreement with EU," March 26, 1996.

159. *RFE/RL Daily Report*, "Belarusian Reaction to EU Trade Ban," June 17, 1996; "EU Issues Warning," December 16, 1996; *Violation of Human Rights in Belarus* 1997; *European Union Declaration on Belarus* 1997.

160. Burant 1995, 1134; *RFE/RL Daily Report*, "Central European Initiative Agree on New Members," October 10, 1996.

161. Burant 1995, 1133.

162. During 1992-1993, such agreements were signed with Poland, the Czech Republic, the Slovak Republic, Romania, Finland, Austria, China, Vietnam, Mongolia, the U.S., Kuwait, and Cuba. During the same period, similar agreements were initiated with India, Turkey, and Switzerland.

163. *RFE/RL Daily Report*, "Belarusian Foreign Minister in Bonn," March 4, 1994.

164. Markus 1995c, 65.

165. *RFE/RL Daily Report*, "German Credits for Belarus," June 29, 1992; "Belarusian Foreign Minister in Germany," August 29, 1994.

166. Zaprudnik 1993, 217; Lukashenka 1997a.

167. Zaprudnik 1993, 216; *Moscow INTERFAX*, "Trade, Cooperation Agreement with Poland," in FBIS-SOV-91-200, October 16, 1991, 73.

168. *RFE/RL Daily Report*, "Walesa in Belarus," June 29, 1993.

169. *RFE/RL Daily Report*, "Polish-Belarus Relations," November 23, 1992; "Polish, Ukrainians, Belarusian Foreign Ministers Meet," July 22, 1996.

170. *RFE/RL Daily Report*, "Poland, Belarus Reach Economic Agreements," June 9, 1993; "Walesa in Belarus," June 29, 1993.

171. *RFE/RL Daily Report*, "Polish Foreign Minister in Belarus," October 26, 1994. In 1995, a high ranking Belarusian official was complaining that Polish tariffs on Belarusian goods were 15 percent higher than those of the European Union countries (*RFE/RL Daily Report*, "Belarus Official on Trade with Poland," June 23, 1995).

172. Markus 1995c, 65. See also Zaprudnik 1993, 211.

173. Markus 1995c.

174. *Ibid*. For similar observations see Tsegolnikov 1994; Maimenia 1996; *Belarusian Review*, 1995/96, Winter, 12.

Chapter 6
Evidence from Other Ex-Soviet Republics

The purpose of this chapter is to explore whether the main argument of this thesis holds among other ex-Soviet republics. I propose a means of comparing the foreign economic orientations and assessing the merits of competing explanations for their differences, such as market conditions, relative power, political institutions, and national identities. The evaluation is based on bivariate regressions of various independent variables to the foreign economic policy score. The analysis also suggests several deviant cases, and I offer a qualitative analysis of two of these cases.

Foreign Economic Orientations of the Post-Soviet Republics

In order to capture the variation in the NIS's foreign economic policies, I emphasize the significance of preferential agreements that were concluded by the ex-Soviet republics with Russia, on the one hand, and countries beyond Russia, on the other. For the purpose of consistency, throughout all the fourteen cases, I apply only one criterion for determining the variation in the republics' economic policies. Specifically, I focus on multilateral agreements, assuming that this criterion is sufficient for capturing the variation in the republics' behaviors and that, in one way or another, these behaviors will reflect their bilateral and unilateral policy inclination, as well.[1] On this basis, a way of ranking of the post-Soviet republics' foreign economic orientations is proposed, and three major types of policy behavior are identified. In particular, the post-Soviet nations are classified as those favoring economic integration with Russia (the "inner core"), those interested in active reorientation away from the former hegemon (the "spoiler"), and those whose policy stances situate them between the two poles (the "outer core").

Preferential Agreements and Foreign Economic Orientations: The Dependent Variable

The newly emerged post-Soviet nations faced important policy choices vis-à-vis Russia and the Commonwealth of Independent States,[2] as well as countries beyond the former Soviet area. This section considers the policies they pursued toward these two poles. Specifically, I investigate the extent to which the ex-Soviet republics went into two major agreements within the CIS framework—the CIS Economic Union and the Customs Union. Should these agreement have been implemented in full, the CIS would have become an area of economic integration, with policies discriminatory toward non-CIS members.[3] Having constituted the economic body of the Russia-initiated CIS, these agreements should therefore serve as a reasonable base for making judgments about the new nations' economic policies toward the Russian pole.

I also look at the ex-Soviet republics' policy stances vis-à-vis the introduction of national currencies. The ex-Soviet nations varied with regard to their willingness to participate in Russia-initiated monetary arrangements. Prior to Russia's unilateral decision to end the existence of the ruble zone, some of the republics had already made a decision to introduce national currencies and, therefore, to leave the ruble zone for the sake of pursuing more independent external policies. Others republics, Belarus and Kazakhstan among them, remained committed to the idea of currency union and signed a September 1993 framework agreement with Russia that envisaged a "ruble zone of a new type." In the end, it was only Russia's unilateralism that eventually forced these nations to embark on the path of adopting their own national currencies.[4]

In addition to the ex-Soviet nations' policy choices vis-à-vis their traditional economic partners, I consider preferential economic (primarily trade-related) agreements adopted by the new republics beyond the former Soviet area. For example, Baltic nations, in an effort to diversify their trade away from Russia, expressed interest in joining the European Union and initialed a free-trade accord with the organization. Another example is the behavior of Central Asian republics that decided to join the Economic Cooperation Organization (ECO), a preferential arrangement launched in 1992 with the participation of Turkey, Iran, Pakistan, Afghanistan, and Azerbaijan.[5]

Table 6.1 summarizes the ex-Soviet nations' foreign economic orientations toward Russia and countries other than Russia. The summary offered was derived from four sources—three for the republics' orientations vis-à-vis Russia, and one for orientations toward countries beyond the former USSR.

Table 6.1. Foreign Economic Orientations of the Ex-Soviet Republics, 1991-1996

	Components				Score
	CIS Economic Union	CIS Currency Union*	CIS Customs Union	Preferential agreements with countries beyond the former USSR	
Armenia	-1	-1	0	0	-2
Azerbaijan	-1	0	0	+1**	0
Belarus	-1	-1	-1	0	-3
Estonia	0	0	0	+1***	+1
Georgia	-1	0	0	0	-1
Kazakhstan	-1	-1	-1	+1**	-2
Kyrgyzstan	-1	0	-1	+1**	-1
Latvia	0	0	0	+1***	+1
Lithuania	0	0	0	+1***	+1
Moldova	-1	0	0	0	-1
Tajikistan	-1	-1	0	+1**	-1
Turkmenistan	-1	0	0	+1**	0
Ukraine	-0.5 (associate member)	0	0	0	-0.5
Uzbekistan	-1	-1	0	+1**	-1

Sources: Zagorskii 1997, 64; *Trade Policy* 1996, 189-93; *The European Free Trade Association* 1996; Webber 1996, 291.

*   A decision to introduce or abstain from introducing independent currency in 1993 in reaction to Russia's announcement about taking rubles out of circulation

**   ECO (Economic Cooperation Organization)

*** Two free trade treaties: with EC (European Community) and EFTA (European Free Trade Association)

The republics' orientations can be described by observing their decisions whether to participate in multilateral preferential economic agreements within and beyond the former Soviet area. Let us assign a score of +1 when a nation becomes a member of an organization outside the area, and a score of -1 when it joins an organization limited to former Soviet republics. In a similar manner, let us assign a score of +0.5 for an associate membership or a bilateral free-trade agreement with an organization outside the former Soviet area and a score of -0.5 for the same arrangements within the area. If consistent, the exercise should provide us with an objective foreign economic orientation score of the republics. As a result Georgia, for example, can be assigned a score of "-1" since it signed one economic agreement with Russia within the CIS framework and no agreements beyond the ex-USSR area. Azerbaijan would score higher ("0"), since it entered one agreement within the CIS ("-1") and one beyond the CIS ("+1"). Associate memberships and bilateral free-trade agreements with regional organizations were coded as 50 percent significant relative to gaining a full membership (100%) in an organization, on the one hand, and not participating in it, on the other. Ukraine's behavior, then, should be evaluated as "-0.5," and that of three Baltic nations as "+1" (the summation of two bilateral treaties, each with a score of 0.5). A full record of the republics' dependent variable scores is also presented in table 6.1.

The derived classification is imperfect in terms of capturing the foreign economic orientations of the republics, as it mainly focuses on one dimension of foreign economic policy (preferential agreements, primarily multilateral). It can, therefore, be criticized as insufficiently robust. Yet, since no systematic data on the republics' unilateral policies, as well as on bilateral arrangements they might have entered, are available, I choose to rely on the previously-described means of capturing the ex-Soviet republics' foreign economic policies. In so doing, I was reassured by the reasoning that no classification or typology is perfect and that the sources I relied on, despite their possible deficiencies, were objective in sense that I, as the author of this project, was in no way responsible for their creation.[6]

"Inner Core," "Outer Core," and "Spoilers": The Three Types of Policy Behavior

The previously proposed score assignment yields at least three types of economic policy behavior in the former USSR. The "inner core" group includes republics that chose to keep loyalty to traditional economic partners and showed relatively little interest in finding new partners. Armenia and Kazakhstan signed two of the three main CIS economic agreements, and Belarus became a signatory to all of them. None of them entered into preferential agreements beyond the former Soviet area.

The "outer core" republics, while maintaining an interest in economic ties with their traditional partners, were less committed to it. In addition, some nations within the group made visible efforts to diversify their economic relations. This group is diverse and unites three distinct subgroups. Azerbaijan and Turkmenistan signed one of the key CIS agreements (on Economic Union), but also entered the Economic Cooperation Organization, a preferential arrangement with Turkey, Iran, Pakistan, Afghanistan, Kyrgyzstan, and Tajikistan as participants. Ukraine became an associate member in the CIS Economic Union and did not enter into any preferential arrangements beyond the former USSR. Georgia and Moldova signed the CIS Economic Union agreement, but likewise nothing beyond the former Soviet area. Finally, Kyrgyzstan, Tajikistan, and Uzbekistan each signed two CIS agreements, and also entered the Economic Cooperation Organization.

The final group, the "spoilers," were the most determined to become full-fledged members of the world economy and to find new, primarily Western, trading partners. The Baltic nations, as members of this group, decided against any affiliation with the CIS, instead committing themselves to gaining membership in Western political and economic organizations. The three types of policy behavior are summarized in figure 6.1.

The Determinants of Post-Soviet Foreign Economic Strategies: Hypotheses and Evidence

I consider three groups of possible explanations for the republics' foreign economic orientations—economic, political/policy, and national identity. Their evaluation is based on bivariate regressions of the foreign economic policy score on independent variables and visual inspections of their relations. Such evaluation can only be tentative, especially given that the number of cases (fourteen) is limited.[7] For this reason, a multivariate technique would not be meaningful.

Economic Explanations

Economic explanations are a logical place to start in an analysis of economic policy. Three explanatory variables were identified as potentially significant for understanding the causes of foreign economic orientations. Other indicators might be employed, but these three were assumed to be sufficient for obtaining a general picture of the importance of economic variables.

Figure 6.1. The Ex-Republics: The Three Types of Policy Behavior

Low degree of deviation from the traditional pattern			High degree of deviation from the traditional pattern
"Inner core" (-3;-2)	*"Outer core" (-1;0)*		*"Spoilers"(+1)*
Armenia	**Georgia**	**Azerbaijan**	**Estonia**
Belarus	**Kyrgyzstan**	**Turkmenistan**	**Latvia**
Kazakhstan	**Moldova**	**Ukraine**	**Lithuania**
	Tajikistan		
	Uzbekistan		

Hypotheses

GEOGRAPHIC PROXIMITY. Geographic proximity is a variable commonly used for explaining patterns of trade[8] and one that is potentially important for explaining foreign economic orientations. The rationale here is that the closer a country is to an alternative center of economic activity, the more likely it is to entertain the option of diversifying or even completely switching its economic activities away from traditional partners. Again, the fact that the ex-Soviet republics were emerging from command economies, with no or little market incentives for development, makes the case even stronger. The collapse of socialism, for the first time in more than fifty years, allowed the republics to attempt to find their places in the world economy as defined by their own analyses of comparative advantages, and not determined by Moscow's state planners.

Geographic proximity is usually captured by calculating the distance between trading countries. The ex-Soviet republics had a diverse geographic location—from Central European to Central Asia and Caucasus—and different large potential markets in close proximity. In the case of Turkmenistan, for example, it would make more sense to calculate the distance from Iran, its closest neighbor, than with European countries. To obtain a measurement of geographic proximity, the distance in miles (as the crow flies) was calculated between the ex-Soviet nations' capitals and the capitals of neighboring countries—the large markets closest to them. In the case of the Western post-Soviet republics, the target countries were Germany and Sweden, while the Central Asian and Caucasian republics were assumed to be interested in developing ties with Iran, Turkey, and China.

GRAVITY. In addition to geographic distance, it may also be argued that what is important in determining foreign economic reorientation is a country's access to alternative markets and the relative size of those markets. For example, the gravity model designed for predicting patterns of trade normally supplements the geographic distance measure with variables designed to capture the size of the closest alternative markets.[9] In order to supplement the distance with the size of the alternative markets, I obtained data measuring the extent of the former Soviet republics' trade with countries others than Russia. After learning about the republics' largest potential markets, I constructed a gravity variable in which the economic size of the republics' largest trading partners outside Russia (measured as the size of their GDP in U.S. dollars) was weighted by the geographic distance between a particular republic and its largest alternative trading partner. For instance, in the case of Estonia, the absolute size of Finland's GDP was weighted by the distance between Helsinki and Tallin, the capitals of the two countries.

NATURAL RESOURCE ENDOWMENT. Resource endowment is a variable widely used by trade theorists for explaining patterns of commercial activities and distribution of gains from trade. If the point of departure for formulation of foreign economic policy is a country's comparative advantages in resource endowment (natural resources, labor, technology, etc.), then in a newly independent nation we should see shifts in economic policy and in the direction of trade to the extent that former trade departed from what would be expected under comparative advantage alone. Those nations that are resource rich should be able to gain more from international market exchange and, therefore, should tend to be more interested in diversifying their economic activities away from the old, politically organized economic area.

A measurement of natural resource endowment (oil and gas in particular) is one very rough way of capturing variations in the republics' comparative advantages. Some scholars have argued that for the postsocialist nations, a reorientation of trade is easier in resource-based goods, such as mineral fuels, wood, metals, leather, and vegetables, because quality is more uniform and less important to sales than in the case of machinery and equipment.[10] One can hypothesize then that the greater a country's resource-extraction capabilities, the more likely a country is to pursue a policy of economic diversification/reorientation away from its traditional markets. Exports of primary commodities expressed as a share of total exports might be an appropriate way to measure a country's natural resource endowment.

Various economic, political, and national identity determinants and their measurements are summarized in table 6.2.

Evidence

Table 6.3 shows the results of bivariate regressions of the foreign economic orientation score on each of the independent variables. In particular, it indicates that the regression coefficients for gravity and natural resource endowment are positive and that the one for geographic distance is negative, as was expected. However, none of the variables is statistically significant, suggesting that there are no significant relationships between the republics' geographic proximity, gravity, and natural resource endowment[11] and their policies of foreign economic orientations. The coefficients of determination (R^2) are too low to capture a significant portion of the variance.

The low explanatory power of the economic variables can at least partially be attributed to the fact that we are dealing with former Communist economies. Isolated for a long period of time from the world market-based incentives, these economies were not build around their comparative advantages in resource endowment. Instead, they were heavily integrated into what used to be called the "unified economic complex," built from above and primarily dependent on the decisions of Moscow planners, thus suggesting a need to employ variables that are of a political nature.

Table 6.2. Possible Economic, Political, and National Identity Determinants of the Ex-Republics' Foreign Economic Policies

	Economic Determinants			Political Determinants		National Identity Determinants			
	1	2	3	4	5	6	7	8	9
Armenia	489	0.006	34	1	29	1	1	1	9.3
Azerbaijan	601	0.007	89	2	18	1	1	2	2.1
Belarus	598	3.44	61	2	28	0	0	1	25.8
Estonia	238	1.88	59	0	8	2	1	2	4.7
Georgia	634	0.006	95	0	20	1	1	1	1.7
Kazakhstan	2037	0.27	57	1	31	0	0	2	2.5
Kyrgyzstan	2158	0.25	24	0	33	0	0	2	2.1
Latvia	450	3.88	69	0	14	2	1	2	5
Lithuania	426	3.99	77	0	16	2	1	2	2.1
Moldova	790	0.37	61	1	27	0	0	1	6.8
Tajikistan	2523	0.11	98	0	29	0	0	2	2.2
Turkmenistan	410	0.87	92	1	29	0	0	2	1.3
Ukraine	750	0.003	70	2	28	1	0	1	17.2
Uzbekistan	1033	0.22	96	2	27	0	0	2	1.5

1. Geographic proximity, as distance to the nearest largest market, in miles
2. Gravity, ratio of the economic size of the republics' largest trading partners outside Russia (measured as the size of their GDP in U.S. dollars) and the geographic distance between a particular republic and its largest alternative trading partner (measured in miles as the crow flies), the data about the republics' largest trading partners outside Russia were for 1994
3. Endowment with natural resources, as exports of primary commodities, % of total exports, 1992
4. Military power, as estimate of ability to resist an attack from Russia (2 = over 40,000 of armed forces, 1 = 10,000 to 40,000, and 0 = less than 10,000)
5. Sovereignty, time elapsed, in months, between March 1988 as a starting point and declaration of republican formal sovereignty or the equivalent
6. Independence experience, an estimate of number of years of independent statehood in the twentieth century (0 = no experience; 1 = some experience; 2 = significant experience)
7. Territorial unity, an estimate of stability of geopolitical borders (0 = relatively unstable; 1 = relatively stable)
8. Cultural distinctness, similarity or difference with/from Russia in language and religion (2 = different on both dimensions; 1 = different on one dimension)
9. Cultural resistance, percent switching native language to Russian, 1979

Sources: www.indo.com/cgi-bin/dist/; *World Development Indicators 1999*; *EIU*, various; Kaminski 1994, 241; Spruyt 1997, 327; Evangelista 1996, 183; the author's estimates; *RFE/RL RR*, 1993-95; Laitin 1998, 46

Table 6.3. Bivariate Regressions of the Ex-Republics' Foreign Economic Policies on Hypothesized Economic, Political, and National Identity Determinants

	Coefficient	R^2
Economic Determinants		
Distance	-0.0006	.14
Gravity	0.2704	.12
Natural Resources	0.0165	.10
Political Determinants		
Military Power	-0.0603	.19
Sovereignty	-0.1201**	.56
National Identity Determinants		
Independence Experience	1.0484**	.52
Territoriality	1.1875*	.26
Distinctness	1.2778**	.28
Resistance	-0.0826*	.24

Note: Number of Cases is 14. Entries are unstandardized regression coefficients.

* $p < 0.05$

** $p < 0.025$

Political Explanations

The next step is to consider the merits of political explanations relative to economic ones.

Hypotheses

MILITARY POWER. Relative military power explanations, commonly used in analyses of nations' military strategies and alliances options have also been applied in some studies of economic policy. The underlying logic has been that economic viability is an important dimension of a nation's power, in addition to its military capabilities. A nation's economic policy choices, then, may be viewed as a reflection of relative power maximization drives.[12] If the hypothesis applies, some of the former Soviet republics may, for example, have pursued policies of economic restructuring away from the ex-hegemon and entered an economic arrangement with a potentially powerful actor in order to extract marginal power benefits (such as balancing against Russian military threat) from it. Therefore, the nations that are weaker in terms of power might be expected to pursue more aggressive policies of foreign economic diversification.[13]

Military power was estimated as each republic's ability to resist an attack from Russia, the most likely hegemon. Size of armed forces is one common measurement of a country's military capabilities. Republics were divided into three groups in terms of their abilities to resist a possible Russian attack: relatively powerful (assigned a score of 2 for armed forces over 40,000 troops), possessing limited power (1 = 10,000 to 40,000 troops), and incapable of significant military resistance (0 = less than 10,000 troops).

EAGERNESS FOR SOVEREIGNTY. My final measurement has to do with the Soviet republics elites' struggle for sovereignty within the USSR. It is introduced here as a political measurement serving to express peripheral elites' power maximization drive.[14] The underlying logic is that the peripheral elites' dissatisfaction and frustration with distribution of political authority within the system may at later stages find its reflection in secessionist economic policies. One might hypothesize that, when given a chance at attaining independence, those who are dissatisfied and frustrated with the system to a larger degree are likely to pursue a more aggressive policy of economic reorientation than those who are relatively satisfied.

An available measurement of each republic's drive for sovereignty is time elapsed (in months) from Estonia proclaiming its formal sovereignty in November 1988 to Kyrgyzstan following suit in December 1990.[15] During this time interval, all the republics declared formal sovereignty or the equivalent (e.g., in Georgia, constitutional amendments gave the republic legislative sovereignty and the right to its natural resources; in Armenia, parliament passed a declaration of independence).

Evidence

As table 6.3 indicates, political variables in general may be seen as more promising tools for explaining the ex-Soviet republics' policy outcomes. The regression coefficients for the military power and the eagerness for sovereignty variables are negative, as expected. Eagerness for sovereignty turned out to be a particularly promising variable: it is significant at the .0025 level and explains 56 percent of the variance.

The fact that the elites' drive for sovereignty proved to be the strongest predictor (R^2 = .56) may suggest the existence of a complex causal chain linking national identity and policy outcomes, as theorized earlier in this study (see chapter 2). It may well be that the sovereignty variable captures the domestic structures variable that was employed for spelling out the effects of strength of national identity on the ex-Soviet republics' foreign economic policies. It may simply correlate with the strength of national identity, a suggestion that seems reasonable, since the sovereignty effort may very well be tied to the republics' structural and historical national identity characteristics. To clarify the issue, one needs to explore more fully the merits of the national identity hypothesis, to which we now turn. The domestic political reform variable seems to point in the same direction: if all of the newly independent nations, having emerged out of the same empire, inherited domestic institutions that were essentially an imperial product and, therefore, did not vary enough, then it seems only logical to look at the republics' underlying set of longitudinal historical orientations, typically captured with the words "culture" and "national identity."

The National Identity Explanation

In this section, I tentatively evaluate the merits of explanations from the strength of national identity. As with economic and political explanations, national identity is very rich in content and cannot be captured completely through a single indicator. Consistently with the theoretical framework offered in this study (chapter 2), I identify and test in a preliminary fashion four variables. They may be seen as being responsible for creating necessary ideational and institutional conditions for a political nation's emergence and development as a unit. These four shape a nation's identity by establishing its cohesiveness and differentiating it from the outside world. For postimperial nations, national identities would vary depending on how strongly people in those nations identify themselves with the nation as a nonimperial entity and view the ex-metropole as threatening their independent existences. One can then hypothesize that a new nation endowed with a relatively stronger national identity should be able to challenge the institutional legacies of the former empire in a relatively more efficient way and so assume control over its policies including foreign economic policies. Other things being equal, the stronger a country's national identity, the more likely the country will be to perceive economic cooperation with the former hegemon as a threat to its security and the more likely that its policy will run counter to the old, empire-initiated economic pattern.

Hypotheses

EXPERIENCE WITH INDEPENDENCE. One appealing way to operationalize national identity effects on policy making is to look at the republics' experiences with independent nationhood before their incorporation into the empire. Those with longer experience with independence should be able to preserve a stronger memory of this experience through the period as part of the empire and to reactivate this memory in the nation-building process once the opportunity arises.

The fourteen republics fall into three distinct groups in terms of their experiences with national independence.[16] Baltic nations exemplify nations with relatively strong identities. All enjoyed a quarter-century period of independent statehood before they were incorporated into the Soviet empire in 1939, thus allowing them to maintain a sense of independent identity even during the Soviet occupation and despite Soviet efforts to incorporate them culturally as well as politico-economically. These republics are coded 2 (significant experience with independence). At the other extreme are Belarus, Kazakhstan, Moldova, and the four Central Asian nations. While different in many dimensions, these nations are similar in not having experience with independent statehood before their incorporation into the Soviet empire (coded 0). Finally, Armenia, Azerbaijan, Georgia, and Ukraine would fall somewhere between those two poles. As compared to the Baltics, the experience with national independence was rather short-lived and fragmented for these nations, but it proved sufficient to develop and retain—even through the period of Soviet empire—a set of historical myths glorifying the idea of national independence. For these reasons, these nations, along with the Baltics, are sometimes referred to as "historic nations." They were coded as 1 (some experience with independence).[17]

TERRITORIALITY. Another way to capture some aspects of national identity strength is to look at the stability of nations' geopolitical borders. Territoriality, or relative stability of geopolitical borders, is often seen as fostering people's emotional attachment and sense of unity relevant to national identity formation. It can be measured by tracing whether, over a 100-year period, a nation lived within essentially the same geopolitical borders or whether those borders were relatively fluid. In the latter case, the borders might have been established anew as a result of imperial policies or imperial expansion. As a result of these rearrangements, a new combination of ethnic groups would emerge, thereby delaying the process of (sub)political identity formation. In the USSR, this happened with Central Asian republics, which were essentially created "from above" in the 1930s, as well as Ukraine, Moldova, and Belarus (which were reunited as subpolitical entities within Soviet territory under the Molotov-Ribbentrop pact). Relative stability of political borders, or territorial unity, was coded as 1 and border change for the size of one-third or more was coded as 0.[18]

CULTURAL DISTINCTNESS. Nations' primordial characteristics may also be relevant for making comparisons in terms of national identity strength. Political elites may choose to emphasize their nation's distinctness in cultural features such as religion, language, customs, and racial appearance, particularly if these nations are relatively homogeneous on these dimensions. Therefore, while cultural features alone do not constitute the sense of a nation's identity, they can play an important consolidating role in the nation-building process.[19] Relatively strong cultural distinctness and homogeneity can reinforce peripheral nationalism and contribute to the process of economic reorientation away from the metropole.

This study proposes two ways of measuring nations' distinctness from the metropole on primordial culture dimensions. One measurement has to do with ethnicity, capturing the republics' linguistic differences from the ex-metropole. The other has to do with religion, capturing whether or not a republic is different from the ex-metropole on this dimension. Those newly emerged nations that differ from Russia in its mainstream religious denomination (that is, non-Orthodox) can be coded as 1, and those not differing from Russia (Orthodox) can be coded as 0. As a result of summing up the republics' linguistic and religious distinctness from the metropole, one can identify two groups of nations: those differing from Russia on both dimensions (coded as 2) and those differing on one of the two dimensions (coded as 1).

CULTURAL RESISTANCE. Our final measurement captures the degree to which a nation was capable of resisting assimilation pressures from the metropole, or the degree of cultural resistance. Presumably, a nation with a stronger sense of identity should have been more successful in preserving its religious and linguistic authenticity. Various figures on the ex-Soviet republics' linguistic Russification may be a reasonable way of capturing their degrees of cultural resistance. For the purpose of this analysis, I look at the percentage of indigenous population switching from their native languages to Russian during the Soviet period.

Evidence

The results of the tests (as reported in table 6.3) suggest that national identity variables have strong explanatory power. The regression coefficients for all variables other than cultural resistance are positive as expected. All of the variables are statistically significant at the .05 or .0025 level, with national independence experience having the greatest explanatory power ($R^2 = .52$). Although each of the selected measurements, when taken separately, can be perceived as insufficient in capturing the strength of national identity,[20] as a group they do imply that the national identity dimension should not be ignored by those interested in explaining the republics' international policies.

The results may also be interpreted as indicating the difficulty of separating national identity variables from political variables. In the previous subsection discussing the impact of political variables, I identified eagerness for sovereignty as the variable with the strongest explanatory power and speculated that this may have been due to this variable's relation to national identity. The sovereignty variable correlates with the strength of national identity, particularly when operationalized as a republic's length of historical experience with independence (coefficient of correlation is .87), and the two variables account for a similar percent of the variance (56 and 52 percent, respectively).

It thus appears that the reason why sovereignty, a political variable, turned out to be such a strong predictor has to do with its being tied to national identity, which is a variable cultural in nature. This further strengthens the previous suggestion that the sovereignty variable seems helpful in spelling out the causal effects of national identity by loosely capturing the domestic structures variable. This conclusion is consistent with the causal chain identified previously (see chapter 2) and suggests that the foreign economic policies of the postimperial nations may indeed be caused by the strength of national identity reflected in domestic political struggle, among other factors.

The Limitations of the National Identity Explanation

National identity is not the only dimension that shapes foreign economic orientations, and the behavior of some of the ex-Soviet republics cannot be satisfactorily explained on the basis of national identity strength and must be studied separately. In this section, I discuss the limitations of this explanation by constructing the composite index of national identity strength. Armenia and Turkmenistan illustrate other influences that can override national identity.

The Composite Index of National Identity Strength

To a certain degree, constructing a composite index is always an arbitrary process, first, because there is a variety of techniques, each with its own limitations, and second, because a scholar makes choices from a wealth of available measurements. For all these reasons, it is important to make explicit rules for constructing the index of national identity strength. In constructing the index, I take the following steps: first, I select different dimensions of national identity strength; second, I rank these using the same technique consistently; third, I prioritize these selected dimensions and so assign higher scores to some and lower to others; and fourth, I sum the ranks of all dimensions.

For constructing the index, I selected five different indicators (dimensions), each representing historical, geographic, economic, and cultural aspects of national identity formation. These five are already familiar: a nation's historical experience with independence before its incorporation into the empire, the presence or absence of stable geopolitical borders (territoriality), the degree of economic integration, cultural distinctness, and cultural resistance to assimilation pressures. The measurements of most of these are available and were summarized in table 6.2.

To rank these five, I propose a simple technique. All five will be estimated on a scale "low-medium-significant" and coded as 0, 1, and 2, respectively. Each indicator yields itself to this kind of ranking. National independence experience of the republics can be classified as "no experience," "some experience," and "significant experience." The territoriality dimension has two values: relatively stable geopolitical borders (coded as 1) and relatively unstable geopolitical borders over a 100-year period (coded as 0). The degree of economic integration[21] can be coded as 2 ("significant") and as 1 ("medium"). No "low" ranking will be used here, as even the less integrated republics, such as Tajikistan and Kyrgyzstan, could boast 32 and 38 percent levels of urbanization, respectively. With regard to cultural distinctness, the ex-Soviet nations can be coded as 2 when they are different from the metropole on both language and religious dimensions, and coded as 1 when they differ on only one of these dimensions (typically, language). Finally, the degree of cultural resistance to assimilation can be operationalized as relatively high (coded as 2) and relatively low (coded as 1). The fact that

Ukraine and Belarus display particularly large proportions of natives switching to the Russian language may be seen as susceptible to the relatively high degree of assimilation relative to the rest of the republics. The results of the ranking are summarized in table 6.4.

The selected five indicators are not, however, equal in terms of their effects on national identity strength and must therefore be prioritized. In so doing, I follow the previously developed points about the logic of identity formation (see chapter 2) and assume the primary significance of historical practices in establishing national identity of the postimperial nations. It is through historical practices that the new meaning of sovereign statehood emerged and eventually became a part of domestic political discourse capable of challenging the traditional imperial practices and authority structures. Institutions, however significant, are assumed to have secondary importance—they provide a space for meaning distribution, but they do not produce meanings on their own. History and historical practices do.[22]

Table 6.4. The Ex-Soviet Republics: Selected National Identity Strength Indicators, Their Ranking and Score

	Indicators					Score
	1	2	3	4	5	
Armenia	4	1	2	1	1	9
Azerbaijan	4	1	1	2	1	9
Belarus	0	0	2	1	0	3
Estonia	8	1	2	2	1	14
Georgia	4	1	2	1	1	9
Kazakhstan	0	0	2	2	1	5
Kyrgyzstan	0	0	1	2	1	4
Latvia	8	1	2	2	1	14
Lithuania	8	1	2	2	1	14
Moldova	0	0	1	1	1	3
Tajikistan	0	0	1	2	1	4
Turkmenistan	0	0	1	2	1	4
Ukraine	4	0	2	1	0	7
Uzbekistan	0	0	2	2	1	5

1. Independence experience
2. Territoriality
3. National economic integration*
4. Cultural distinctness
5. Cultural resistance

*   As level of country's urbanization (%), 1989 (Bradshaw 1990, 8)

This assumption suggests that national independence experience should be at least as important in defining the strength of national identity as the other four institutional characteristics taken together. This yields ranking the national independence dimension as 0, 4, and 8, instead of the previously suggested 0, 1, and 2 for "low," "medium," and "significant," respectively. Ranking the five indicators in terms of their relative significance allows us to preserve the previously identified explanatory power of a nation's historical experience with independence.

A summary of the previously suggested rankings of national identity dimensions yields the composite score of each republic's national identity strength (table 6.4).

How Much Is Explained? How Much Is Left Out?

The constructed composite index of national identity strength also suggests the importance of the variable for explaining the ex-Soviet republics' foreign economic orientations. As is summarized in table 6.5, the variable turned out to be highly statistically significant, and its overall explanatory power (judging by the percentage of explained variance) is relatively high ($R^2 = 0.53$). Yet almost half of the variance is left unexplained, indicating that the explanation from national identity strength should in no way be considered sufficient and needs to be supplemented by other explanations if we are to understand the foreign economic policies of the ex-Soviet republics in their full complexity.

As tentative and approximate as a single measurement of national identity strength can be, it does allow us to visually inspect the relations between the ex-Soviet republics' national identities and their foreign economic orientations. This can be accomplished by simply plotting the scores of foreign economic orientations and national identity strengths against each other, as presented in tables 6.1 and 6.4. Figure 6.2 emerges as a result of the exercise.

A visual inspection of the relations between the ex-republics' national identity strengths and their foreign economic policies further suggests the possibility of existing causal relations between the variables. What figure 6.2 demonstrates can be deemed a modestly good fit, as Moldova, Tajikistan, Kazakhstan, Kyrgyzstan, Uzbekistan, Ukraine, Azerbaijan, Georgia, and the Baltics fell relatively

Table 6.5. Bivariate Regression of the Ex-Republics' Foreign Economic Policies on Hypothesized National Identity Determinant (as measured by national identity strength score)

	Coefficient	R^2
National Identity Strength	0.2107*	.53

Note: Number of Cases is 14. Entries are unstandardized regression coefficients.
* p < 0.001

Figure 6.2. The Ex-Soviet States: Foreign Economic Orientations versus National Identity Strength

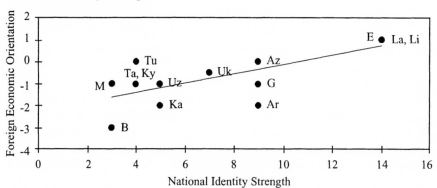

close to the trendline, or the line of best fit.[23] Yet the figure also clearly demonstrates the outliers, the presence of which did not allow us to go beyond explaining 50 percent of the variance. A separate account of the outliers' behavior is needed to make the analysis more complete.

Outliers and Possible Explanations of Their Behavior

The most extreme outliers are Turkmenistan, Armenia, and Belarus. Their deviation from the line of best fit is too significant to be attributed to any type of measurement error and left with no further attention.

It is clear from figure 6.2 that the outliers can be divided into two main groups, those that fell above the trendline and those below it. The former—judging strictly by the hypothesized relations between national identity and foreign economic policy—are deviant in the sense that they should have been less aggressive in their foreign economic reorientation efforts. Turkmenistan is the strongest representative of this group. Despite its relatively weak national identity status, Turkmenistan's foreign economic policy score is higher than that of Ukraine and similar to that of Azerbaijan, with both being countries with stronger national identities.

Turkmenistan's relatively aggressive foreign economic policy stance vis-à-vis Russia can in part be explained by its close geographic location to an alternative trading partner (Iran) and a rich endowment of mineral resources, particularly oil and gas. As table 6.3 indicates, Turkmenistan has the strongest energy potential in the region (with the exception of Russia), which put it in a relatively favorable position of succeeding in reorienting its economic activities away from Russia and the CIS and toward countries capable of paying hard currency for Turkmenistan's oil and gas exports. Due to these comparative advantages, one can speculate that Turkmenistan chose to be more aggressive in its policy of economic reorientation than the strength of its national identity would allow.

Below the line of best fit are Belarus and Armenia. Judging on the basis of their national identity strengths, these two should have been more aggressive in their foreign economic reorientation policies.[24]

Belarus, while fairly weak on the national identity dimension, does possess some attributes of it, such as (sub)political institutions, a relatively high degree of economic integration, and relative ethnic homogeneity. After the disintegration of the USSR, Belarus, like many other newly emerged nations, expressed an interest in finding new economic partners beyond the former Soviet region, as well as in building state institutions appropriate for joining the world community of sovereign nations. Admittedly, societal support for these policies was weaker than in Ukraine or the Baltics. Yet the chances are that it would have stayed on the track of continued nation building and strengthening relations with the outside world if not for the election of Lukashenka as Belarus's first president in 1995. Arguably, it was the "Lukashenka factor" that greatly contributed to Belarus's losing interest in anything other than economic and political reintegration with Russia. And, quite symptomatically, Lukashenka demanded that Minsk be Moscow's equal in any union, something that might eventually have elevated his position to leader of a superstate.[25]

One possible reason for Armenia's deviant behavior is its close proximity to Turkey and Azerbaijan, both of which are often viewed by Armenia as potential threats to its freedom and independence. Historically, Armenia relied on Russian security protection from a culturally alien Turkey. The notion of a threat from Turkey goes back to at least 1915, when some one million Armenians were executed or died during forced marches across Turkey to the deserts of present-day Syria.[26]

A Closer Look at Two Deviant Cases

The national identity explanation is not very helpful in explaining the foreign economic policies of Armenia and Turkmenistan. Other variables, mainly geopolitical and economic in nature, are better suited to the task. To demonstrate it, I turn to a somewhat more detailed qualitative analysis of two of the deviant cases as they were identified in the statistical analysis conducted above.

Armenia

Armenia pursued a significantly less aggressive foreign economic policy than might have been expected on the basis of its national identity strength. Its deviant behavior can be better explained by its historically rooted perception that neighboring Muslim countries (specifically, Turkey and Azerbaijan) represent a threat to Armenian security and that Russia, on the contrary, can be seen as an ally in neutralizing this threat.

Foreign Economic Policy

Armenia represents an intermediate case in terms of its national identity strength. If this argument and conceptualization have any merits, we should expect Armenian foreign economic policy to follow a pattern of medium deviation from its traditional partners in the former Soviet area. Specifically, Armenian economic orientation should be similar to those of other republics with moderately strong national identities, such as Azerbaijan, Georgia, and Ukraine—restrained cooperation with the CIS and Russia and a relatively active search for external economic partners.

Yet this is hardly an accurate description of Armenian foreign economic policy. Table 6.6 summarizes the discrepancy between the expected and *actual* international economic policies of Armenia.

Despite the expectations, Armenia appeared to do little to restructure its trade away from Russia and the CIS area. It emerged as a relatively active participant in CIS economic affairs by signing most major agreements, of which the Economic Union and Payment Union agreements were most prominent. This was in accord with the attitudes of Armenia's key policymakers vis-à-vis the CIS. Prime Minister Hrant Bagratian, for example, was cited as viewing CIS economic integration as a means of repairing economic ties severed with the break-up of the Soviet internal market.[27] The exception was the Customs Union agreement, which Armenian leadership considered joining, but upon reflection decided it would be "neither wise nor advantageous" for Armenia to do at that moment.[28]

In its currency policy, Armenia tried hard to stay in the ruble zone. Even after the Russian Central Bank announced the withdrawal of old rubles from circulation, Armenia did not follow the route of introducing independent currencies, as Azerbaijan, Georgia, and Turkmenistan opted. Instead, it joined Belarus, Kazakhstan, Tajikistan, and Uzbekistan in asking Russia to create a "ruble zone

Table 6.6. Armenia's Expected and Actual Foreign Economic Policies

Expected Policy	Actual Policy
Moderately aggressive reorientation	*Moderately passive reorientation*
restrained participation in the CIS	relatively active participation in the CIS
restrained cooperation with Russia	active cooperation with Russia
relatively active search for external partners	relatively active search for external partners

of a new type" and only introduced its currency in November 1994, when the new ruble zone had also collapsed.[29]

Armenian trade policy toward Russia also demonstrated its willingness to preserve old economic ties. While not entering into the Customs Union, Armenia secured its relations with the ex-hegemon by signing a free-trade treaty (September 1992) and a number of deal-specific agreements.[30] As a result, it retained a relatively high degree of trade dependence on Russia after the Soviet disintegration.[31]

Beyond the former USSR, Armenian economic policy appeared to be more dynamic. This indicates that Armenia did want to find alternative economic partners, even given its limited options. In 1992, it joined the Black Sea Economic Cooperation project, although the actual benefits of this were rather low.[32] It also demonstrated its willingness to develop relations with European countries by trying to gain membership in the Council of Europe and the World Trade Organization, as well as holding regular consultations with the European Union. Armenian leaders also developed dynamic trade relations with Iran, which helped Armenia to survive the economic blockade that Azerbaijan and Turkey imposed on it as a consequence of the decade-long conflict over Nagorno-Karabakh.[33]

Explaining Armenian Policy

Armenian foreign economic policy cannot be adequately explained on the basis of a national identity perspective; Armenia behaves more like republics with weak national identities while its own identity can hardly fit such classification. In our own classification (see chapter 2), Armenia should be placed somewhere in between republics with strong national identities represented by Baltic states and those with weak identities, such as Belarus, Moldova, and the Central Asian nations.[34] There is ample evidence indicating that Armenian identity is stronger than that of a nation with the said economic policy outcomes. First, Armenia as a nation did have, albeit briefly, an experience with national independence in the aftermath of the Bolshevik revolution (1917-1921). Second, it had a preserved memory of relative cultural and territorial autonomy as early as the fifth and sixth centuries, before it had been divided between the Ottoman and Persian empires and, later, became a Russian protectorate.[35] Third, it has been consistently well developed economically (in relative terms), both before and after the Socialist revolution. Finally, Armenia has been a remarkably culturally homogeneous nation, with up to 95 percent of its population composed of ethnic Armenians.

All these factors helped to create a persistent sense of distinct national Self in Armenia, and this was preserved during the Soviet period and became evident with the imperial decline. The Armenian National Movement was created relatively early and began to press for a more pronounced independence within the USSR.[36] In 1990, in a relatively free and fair election, Armenian nationalists won a majority of seats in the national legislature, thereby ending the long-term dominance of the Communist Party. Although the support given to them was not as strong as in the Baltic nations,[37] the mood was essentially anti-Communist and pro-nationalist. Levon Ter-Petrossyan, chairman of the Armenian National Movement and a former dissident, was soon elected president.[38] This is the picture of national identity development that reminds us—if a parallel may be drawn—of the Baltic republics rather than of Belarus and Central Asia.

Nor can Armenian foreign economic policy be satisfactory explained on the basis of its economic resource endowment. It is true that Armenia, relative to republics like Azerbaijan, Kazakhstan, Turkmenistan, and Uzbekistan, is rather poor in natural resources[39] and therefore might have been expected to be passive in its reorientation away from resource-rich Russia. Yet the Armenian resource situation is generally similar to that of the Baltic nations and Ukraine, with these latter nations having pursued much more aggressive policies of economic reorientation. Something else must have determined Armenian foreign economic choice.

One particularly prominent factor makes Armenia special in the list of all other ex-colonial nations of the former Soviet area and may, therefore, be helpful in explaining its deviant economic policy behavior. In particular, Armenia was the only one of these nations with a relatively pronounced national identity that perceived its historically close relations with Russia, the ex-metropole, as beneficial rather than threatening to its national well-being. This perception of Russia as an ally is intimately related with perceiving another powerful neighbor, Turkey, as a threat to Armenia's security and very existence—a fear that can be traced at least to the 1915 Turkish genocide of Armenians. For decades following the genocide in Ottoman Turkey and the loss what were considered historically Armenian territories in eastern Anatolia, Armenians looked to Russia and/or the Soviet Union as the guarantor of their security. Armenia is a small country sandwiched between Russia, on the one hand, and Turkey and Iran, on the other, and it had little choice but to rely on one of its powerful neighbors for aid and geopolitical protection. With the end of the USSR, the perception of Turkey as a threat to Armenian interests was reinforced by Armenia's conflict with Azerbaijan over Nagorno-Karabakh, in which Turkey on number of occasions demonstrated its support for Azerbaijan.[40] In the words of a scholar of Armenian foreign policy, "History has shown that Russia, with all its vacillation, remains a vital factor in Armenia's security and future."[41]

The threat perception factor helps to explain the choices Armenia made in its foreign economic orientations. Armenian leadership viewed foreign economic relations through a broader security lens and made a deliberate decision to cooperate with Russia. Such a decision did not mean Armenia's readiness to abandon its ties with external partners and reintegrate with Russia, as happened to be the case with Belarus. With their relatively developed sense of national Self, Armenians were willing to compromise their sovereignty in order to protect it, but not to abandon it entirely. Such a strategy included a selective approach to joining

Russia-initiated economic initiatives. For instance, Armenian leadership saw Armenia as forming—along with Russia, Kazakhstan, and Belarus—the "nucleus of the Commonwealth" and fully intended to maintain its active participation in the organization.[42] On the other hand, both President Ter-Petrossyan and Prime Minister Hrant Bagratyan specified on several occasions that such participation would not involve joining the CIS Customs Union, let alone the Russia-Belarus reintegration process.[43]

Yet the choice of such a strategy did contain the seeds of potential reabsorption into Russia, particularly in the light of Armenia's chosen commitments to tight security relations with the ex-metropole.[44] Unsurprisingly, the economic policy choice did not come easy to Armenian leadership. From 1989-1991, Armenians were quite critical of Gorbachev's attempts to revive the Union and even viewed—if erroneously—the Soviet leadership as siding with Azerbaijan over Nagorno-Karabakh.[45] Accordingly, Armenia's primary foreign policy objective was defined as rapid integration into the world community. Russia and other former Soviet republics were included, but only as second-tier priority nations; the first tier originally included Armenia's immediate neighbors (Azerbaijan, Georgia, Iran, and Turkey).[46] With the Soviet disintegration, however, the original foreign policy design underwent a dramatic transformation—economic and security dependence on the ex-metropole made Armenian leaders reconsider their views and rely on ties with Russia significantly more than had been planned. With a formal declaration of independence adopted, the Armenian president drew a clear distinction, however, between political and economic independence,[47] and Armenia pursued the policy of close cooperation with Russia and the CIS. Characteristically, one observer described this transformation as a "180-degree turn."[48]

The foreign economic policy eventually chosen was basically supported by Armenian society. Whereas many other post-Soviet, nationalist-oriented movements demonstrated high degrees of animosity toward Russia, Armenian nationalists were different. From the beginning of their activities, their main goal was to settle the Nagorno-Karabakh issue and neutralize the threat from Turkey, not to establish independence from Russia.[49] Not surprisingly, most opposition parties and the population at large shared the Armenian leadership's perception of Russia. As the Reverend Husik Lazaryan, chairman of the Armenian National Movement, put it, "Russia was and remains our number one partner in all spheres."[50]

Turkmenistan

Foreign Economic Policy

Turkmenistan's foreign economic policy also cannot be satisfactorily explained on the basis of a national identity perspective as developed in this study. On this basis, Turkmenistan falls within the group of postimperial republics with weak national identities[51] and, therefore, it should have pursued the policy of passive reorientation away from its traditional partners. More specifically, it should have been an active participant in CIS economic initiatives; it should have cooperated closely with Russia at a bilateral level; and it should have been relatively passive in its search for external economic partners. These expectations are misplaced and not matched with reality to an even higher degree than in the case of Armenia (see table 6.7). The actual policy of Turkmenistan can be better described as a moderately aggressive reorientation.

In CIS affairs, Turkmenistan's participation can be fairly characterized as passive. The closest analogy that comes to mind is Ukraine. Like Ukraine, Turkmenistan opted in favor of becoming a CIS member, but abstained from signing the major CIS agreements. It did not sign the CIS charter in Minsk in January 1993,[52] nor was it originally willing to participate in the CIS Economic and Payment Union arrangements,[53] let alone the Customs Union and the integration agreement between Russia and Belarus. Such a detached policy toward the CIS firmly rested on Turkmenistan's attitude that the CIS should be nothing more than a consultative body, while concrete agreements should be bilateral. Very much in line with Ukraine's leadership, Turkmenistan's leaders felt that the purpose of the CIS should have been to divide up the former USSR among its successors in a civilized way, not to rebuild the old relationship or integrate their economies.[54]

Turkmenistan's bilateral cooperation with Russia was likewise more restrained than might have been expected, although Turkmenistan's president, Saparmurat Niyzov, declared a preference for building foreign economic relations on a bilateral basis. In the monetary realm, Turkmenistan was not among those republics asking Russia to create a new ruble zone after Russia's Central Bank announced in July 1993 its decision to withdraw the old rubles from circulation. Instead, it accelerated its plans to introduce its own currency, the *manat,* hoping to survive outside the ruble zone.[55] In other aspects of economic relations with Russia, Turkmenistan has been more cooperative, often being pressured with the tough realities of survival. For example, it was dependent on Russia for its gas export needs—because the pipeline to Europe traversed Russia's terri-

Table 6.7. Turmenistan's Expected and Actual Foreign Economic Policies

Expected Policy	Actual Policy
Passive reorientation	*Moderately aggressive reorientation*
active participation in the CIS	passive participation in the CIS
active cooperation with Russia	restrained cooperation with Russia
relatively passive search for external partners	relatively active search for external partners

tory—and, therefore, had to cooperate with the ex-hegemon in the area of transport and communication. Responding to various economic dependencies, Turkmenistan signed a number of cooperation agreements with Russia.[56] Unlike some
republics, however, Turkmenistan did not sign a free-trade agreement with Russia, fearing a drain of commodities from domestic markets. Instead, export
restrictions and state orders were imposed.[57] As a result of these policies, the
share of Turkmenistan's trade with Russia decreased from about 45 percent in
1990 to only 6.6 percent in 1996.[58]

Finally, Turkmenistan has been notably active in developing economic ties
with external partners. Iran and Turkey emerged as the most important partners
of Turkmenistan, particularly in the area of transport and gas pipelines, which is
one of the surest ways to lessen dependence on Russia.[59] Turkmenistan possesses
natural gas reserves that are over 30 percent of the world stock, and its leader
proclaimed the country soon to become a "second Kuwait." [60] Turkmenistan
signed a number of deal-specific bilateral agreements with Iran and Turkey and
even joined the multilateral Economic Cooperation Organization (ECO), which
is a preferential arrangement launched in 1992 with Iran, Turkey, and other countries as participants.[61] The interest was mutual. Turkey was by far the biggest and
most important provider of technical and financial support to Turkmenistan,[62]
and Iran proved to be particularly interested in developing a pipeline link with
the country. From the outset, behind Turkmenistan's efforts to cooperate with the
two countries was the idea of constructing a transcontinental pipeline to Europe
from Turkmenistan, via Iran and Turkey.[63] One of the first results of Turkmenistan's cooperation with its southern neighbors was the opening of the 125-mile
pipeline to Iran, with the capacity to transport some 12 billion cubic feet of natural gas per year.[64]

Explaining Turkmenistan's Policy

For pursuing such a policy, Turkmenistan should have possessed a relatively
developed sense of national identity, but this is not in accord with reality. While
differing from the ex-metropole culturally—that is, linguistically and religiously—Turkmenistan does not qualify as having a developed sense of national
Self in all other dimensions: it does not have any historical experience with independence prior to 1991; its territoriality was only established with its incorporation into the Soviet Union; and it remained an underdeveloped and primarily
agrarian society, with predominantly tribal and clan-based identities.

Unsurprisingly, no overarching sense of nation has been built in Turkmenistan, which helps to explain why "the nationalist, democratic groups that arose in
the late 1980s in Turkmenistan, unlike other former Soviet republics, never
became mass movements, never came close to taking or even influencing power,
and are today isolated and marginalized or exiled."[65] The lack of nationalist pressures led to the absence of resistance to the new Union treaties before the Soviet

disintegration. For Turkmenistan's leadership, as well as for the leaders of other Central Asian republics, the fall of the USSR was a tragic event, something for which it was not prepared psychologically, politically, or economically.[66]

An economic resources perspective alone cannot satisfactorily explain Turkmenistan's policy. Certainly, Turkmenistan possesses more than enough natural resources to survive on its own, and it would only be logical to expect that it would pursue an active export policy. Yet there is hardly anything predetermined about such policy being directed away from Russia and other CIS members and toward partners like Iran and Turkey. Kazakhstan, for example, is another resource-rich country south of Russia, which nevertheless opted in favor of maintaining much closer ties with Russia and the CIS. Thus, an economic resources explanation, while useful, must be complemented by other explanations to obtain a more adequate picture.

Our understanding of Turkmenistan's foreign economic policy will be more complete if we add another structural factor—geographic location—into consideration. One look at the map will immediately tell us that geography is indispensable for explaining the Turkmenistan's policy. Turkmenistan has no common borders with Russia, but it does have a long common border with Iran and sits in close proximity to Turkey.[67] The two structural factors (natural resources and geography), combined with the strategic calculations of Turkmenistan's leader, Saparmurat Niyazov, should help us to obtain a more complete picture of the driving forces behind the country's economic policy.

In 1991, when the push and pull between the Kremlin and the republics was about to reach its peak, Turkmenistan was rediscovering that it was a respected member of the international community in its own right. Despite the country's structural incompleteness, infrastructural deficiencies, and the lack of qualified labor,[68] Western economic experts considered Turkmenistan to be the Central Asian country with the greatest chance of economic success (with the possible exception of Kazakhstan).[69] Apparently, this potential spurred Niyazov's own calculations and expectations. In 1992, for example, being carried away with the image of a new era of prosperity coming and a "new Kuwait" emerging, the government abolished heating and electricity fees, only to reinstate them at the end of 1993 when the propaganda wave came to an end.[70] Realizing the need for foreign investment to develop Turkmenistan's advantages in gas, oil, and natural resources, Niyazov proclaimed an "open door" policy.[71] In order to offset the influences from Russia and other CIS states on its foreign economic course, Niyazov also formulated the concept of "positive neutrality." The concept emphasized bilateral relations and the necessity of avoiding alliances with more powerful neighbors that could threaten Turkmenistan's independence, while still maintaining the maximum freedom of policy maneuverability.[72] Clearly, Turkmenistan's leadership was determined to take advantage of the country's geoeconomic position.

Turkmenistan, however, was not hostile toward Russia so long as the latter did not interfere with the defined foreign economic course. In addition to the aforementioned dependence on the Russian-owned pipeline to Europe, Turkmenistan was pressed by a lack of qualified labor and, for that reason, wanted to keep the more educated Russian minority within the country.[73] Finally, military defense considerations also played a role in the country's relations with Russia. In 1992, the Turkmen foreign minister granted, for example, that "if it weren't for Russia, we would have confronted great problems in our defense policy. It's become a geographic reality that we are defending Russia's southern borders."[74] All these considerations help to explain Turkmenistan's careful relations with Russia, relatively close bilateral ties, and its gradual reorientation toward countries beyond the ex-USSR.

The country's weak national identity was no obstacle to Niyazov's plans of economic reorientation. Whereas in Belarus and, to a certain extent, in eastern Ukraine the leadership was confronted with strong empire-saving pressures, Turkmenistan's moderately aggressive reorientation did not face any social resistance. In the words of one scholar, "Niyazov, the former First Secretary of Turkmenistan's Communist Party, does seem to enjoy full backing from almost the entire population. Calling himself Turkmenbashi, 'Leader of the Turkmens,' he has the strongest support in the country, all ethnic and tribal difference notwithstanding."[75] There appear to be two major reasons for this. The first has to do with Turkmens' peculiar identity. Turkmens are culturally much more distinct than Russia's "Slav brothers" in Ukraine and Belarus.[76] They could not have been Russified in such a high proportion and did not identify themselves with the ex-metropole to the extent that Belarus and eastern Ukraine did. A second reason is the authoritarianism of the Turkmenistan leader, who eliminated opposition by banning political parties and practiced extremely tight control on the country's political life.[77]

The exercise undertaken in this chapter generally confirms the merits of the previously derived hypothesis that, in postimperial nations, the strength of national identity may be causally related to international economic policies. A bivariate statistical technique indicated that the strength of national identities, especially when combined with the analysis of domestic structures, was indeed the strongest predictor of the postimperial nations' foreign economic behavior. It thus cannot be ignored by IPE scholars of the post-Soviet region.

This is not to say that the strength of national identity is some sort of a single explanation, the application of which should provide us with all the sought answers about the post-Soviet nations' behavior. The chapter's results should be treated with caution, in part because, by its nature, any statistical analysis, especially a bivariate one, is far from precise and complete. Also, even the strongest national identity indicator, historical experience with independent statehood, was able to capture only about half of the variance. A whole range of other factors—including the economic and political characteristics of the NIS, and their leaders' personal agendas and skills—need to be considered in obtaining an adequate picture of the shape of things to come in this and other postimperial, postcolonial parts of the world.

Notes

1. Multilateral preferential agreements are good indicators of governmental intentions. Potentially, they can lead to high degree of economic reorientation and generally require relatively strong commitments on the part of those willing to join an economic arrangement. By going into such arrangements, nations voluntarily place restrictions on their unilateral policies, thereby limiting their policy flexibility.

2. I assume here that, for the ex-Soviet republics, Russia and the CIS constitute parts of the same orientation given Russia's leadership in initiating and preserving the CIS, as well as the large size of Russia's economy and resources (On asymmetric position of Russia's economy in its size, degree of diversification, and endowment with natural resources relative to other republics, see Krivogorsky and Eichenseher 1996, 34-5; Shishkov et al. 1997, 83-4).

3. The CIS Economic Union treaty envisaged the creation of a market-based common economic space by such means as free trade (involving a unified customs regime), a multilateral payment mechanism involving national currencies (followed at later stage by possible monetary union), and transnational ventures in investment, finance, and production. The Customs Union further proclaimed a commitment to customs and payment regimes and eventual monetary union, and its signatories agreed to "coordinate their customs policies and create a single customs space regulated by common acts" (Webber 1997, 50, 55).

4. Shortly after, Russia demanded of its new partners the pooling of gold and hard currency reserves and oversight of their foreign trade operations. This proved too much and in November this new arrangement was terminated by the introduction of national currencies by many, including Belarus and Kazakhstan (Webber 1997, 52; Markus 1995).

5. See more in *Trade Policy* 1996, 189-93.

6. Another possible objection might be that each of membership with a multilateral organization is an indicator of this organization policy as much as a nation policy toward it. My answer to it is that I trace nation behavior vis-à-vis several organizations, not just one, which allows me to identify at least some continuity and consistency in nation policy.

7. Just as correlation does not prove causality, bivariate regression cannot establish causal relationships.

8. Hewett 1976; Van Selm 1997, 60.

9. Van Selm 1997, 60.

10. Sorsa 1994, 146.

11. In addition to measuring the republics' endowment with natural resources by exports of their primary commodities, I tried to measure it by exports of oil and gas (as a percentage of the republics' exports), but this effort did not improve the results ($R^2 = 0.01$).

12. Hircshman 1945; Knorr 1975.

13. Or, alternatively, they might choose to bandwagon with Russia. The neorealist explanation is indetermined vis-à-vis balancing/bandwagoning choices, but it does assume an equally uniform foreign policy response among equally vulnerable economic actors.

14. The eagerness for sovereignty itself may be caused by a country's sense of national identity, but may also be affected by other factors, such as degree of economic development, integration, territorial and population size, ties with international associations, etc., as it is documented in literature on secessionism (see, for example, Emizet and Hesli 1995).

15. Measuring the sovereignty drive by the republics' behavior during the period of 1988-1990 allows us to eliminate the possibility that the drive itself might have been caused by the republics' foreign economic policies. Empirically this is not the case, as the sovereignty drive predates the republics' economic reorientation during the period of 1991-1996.

16. See chapter 2 for elaboration on criteria of this classification.

17. The "0 to 2" scale was chosen instead of years of independence because there is no agreement among scholars regarding the exact length of experience with independence among the former Soviet republics during the twentieth century, let alone during the entire period of several centuries since the emergence of modern concepts of the sovereign nation and nationhood as proclaimed by the Peace of Westphalia. Some consensus seems to have been established, however, that the Baltic nations represent a separate group due to their interwar independence and that Central Asian republics, along with Moldova and Belarus, had minimal or no experience with independence at least since the seventeenth century (Dawisha and Parrott 1994; Prazauskas 1994; Chinn and Kaiser 1996). Most scholars also seem to agree that Georgia, Armenia, Ukraine, and, to an extent, Azerbaijan had some experience with independence before and after the 1917 Russian revolution (Brzezinski 1990; Dawisha and Parrott 1994; *RFE/RL Research Report* 1994-1995; Chinn and Kaiser 1996).

18. Again, this measurement was selected in an attempt to avoid involvement in a more nuanced discussion about the nature and the amount of territorial changes among the republics. What we need to consider is whether or not such changes existed in principle. The chosen "0 to 1" scale seems satisfactory in serving this purpose.

19. For the argument about importance of ethnicity and cultural unity for understanding the consequences of the Ottoman, Habsburg, Russian, and Soviet empires and imperial break-up, see Barkey 1997.

20. For example, the republics can be coded differently with regard to their experience with independent statehood. Those with some experience can be coded 1, while those without it as 0. Or degree of primordial distinctness can be measured in a different way, producing different results in terms of relationships between national identity and foreign economic policies.

21. The economic integration dimension is relevant for national identity formation as it was discussed in chapter 2. A more developed economy fosters a nationwide sense of unity and "belongingness," and undercuts purely local or ethnic ties (Gurr and Harff 1994, 91; Coleman 1995, 12), and a nation's identity may gain strength in the process of a country's economic modernization and integration. A variety of more and less aggregated variables can be used for measuring the level of nations' economic development. For the purposes of this chapter, level of urbanization, an aggregate indicator of economic

development, is proposed as a way to capture variation in the republics' degrees of economic integration.

22. See chapter 2 for elaboration on this reasoning.

23. By dropping the main outliers—Turkmenistan, Armenia, and Belarus—from the data set, an R^2 as high as 0.81 can be obtained.

24. Georgia and Kazakhstan also fall within the group although to lesser extent. One possible cause of Kazakhstan's deviant behavior is that, in addition to having a weak sense of national identity, the republic has a large number of ethnic Russians residing on its territory (which is about equal to the amount of indigenous people)and, is therefore, severely limited in its foreign policy options. Georgia's deviant behavior can be attributed to Russian geopolitical interests requiring a stronger dependence of Georgia on Russia than might have been otherwise. At earlier stages of its post-Soviet development, Georgia was indeed far less interested in preserving close economic and security ties with Russia than it was in the later period. For example, it did not join the Russia-initiated Commonwealth of Independent States until the Spring of 1994. The reason why it eventually did was believed by many to be the decision of Shevardnadze to strike a Faustian bargain with Russia, one that would require Georgian membership in the CIS and Russian troops to remain in Georgia in exchange for Russia's help in settling the military conflict with Abkhazia (*The Washington Post*, June 6, 1994, A13).

25. Markus 1997, 56.

26. See Dudwick 1997, 473, 475.

27. Webber 1997, 21.

28. *RFE/RL Daily Report*, "Armenian President Snubs Seleznev," May 9, 1996. Under the influence of the process of Russo-Belarusian integration, even the idea of joining the Russia-Belarus union was entertained and found considerable support in Armenian society, although it was never seriously considered by policymakers (Danielyan 1998).

29. Webber 1997, 52-53.

30. Moyiseiev 1997, 87.

31. Its exports to and imports from Russia comprised 52.7 and 48.8 percent, respectively (Menon 1998).

32. *RFE/RL Daily Report*, "Turkey Hosts Black Sea Regional Conference," February 4, 1992; Webber 1996, 312.

33. Danielyan 1998.

34. Scholars are generally in agreement that Armenian identity cannot be accurately classified as weak and, conversely, often characterize it as "strong" or relatively well developed (Diuk and Karatnycky 1993, 157; Webber 1997, 19).

35. Hovannisian 1994, 239; Dudwick 1997a, 472.

36. Armenia was one of the first to initiate the process of secession and claim independence from Moscow (Barner-Barry and Hody 1995, 209). While interested in economic ties to the Soviet Union, Armenia also resisted the Gorbachev-initiated new union treaty as coming too late (Brown 1992, 104).

37. In the Baltic republics' 1990 elections, communists were effectively marginalized and gained only a handful of votes, whereas in Armenia communists received about 25 percent of the vote and remained one of two the largest parties (Dudwick 1997b, 81, 87).

38. Dudwick 1997a, 489.

39. Before the war with Azerbaijan, Armenia was receiving most of its energy, 80 percent of gas in particular, from this Azerbaijan (Dawisha and Parrott 1994, 190; Barner-Barry and Hody 1995, 222).

40. Hovannisian 1994, 254; Adalian 1995, 332.

41. *Ibid.*, 266.

42. *FBIS-SOV-93-093*, "Ter-Petrosyan Comments on Conflicts," May 17, 1993, 1.

43. *RFE/RL Daily Report*, "Armenian President Snubs Seleznev," May 9, 1996; Fuller 1996, 30; Danielyan 1998.

44. Adalian 1995, 319-320; Fuller 1996, 29-30.

45. Fuller 1996, 29.

46. Adalian 1995, 312, 315; Danielyan 1998.

47. Fuller 1992, 47.

48. Adalian 1995, 319.

49. Brown 1992, 102; Dudwick 1997b, 82.

50. Fuller 1996, 29.

51. For other scholastic evaluations of Turkmenistan's national identity as weak, see Szporluk 1992, 110; Webber 1997, 25.

52. *RFE/RL Daily Report*, "Seven States Sign CIS Charter," January 25, 1993.

53. *RFE/RL Daily Report*, "Economic Union Treaty Signed," September 27, 1993; Brown 1994, 59; Zagorskii 1997, 64. Some sources indicate, however, that Turkmenistan did join the Economic Union (Moiseyev 1997, 28; Zagorskii 1997, 64) and even the Payment Union treaty at a later stage (Webber 1997, 70).

54. Niyazov 1995, 1998a; Freitag-Wirminghaus 1997, 75.

55. Maillet 1995, 45-47; *RFE/RL Daily Report*, "Turkmenistan to Introduce Its Own Currency in October," July 28, 1993; "Turkmenistan Introduces Its Own Currency," November 2, 1993; *FBIS-SOV-93-222*, "Niyazov Discusses Ties with Russia, New Currency," November 19, 1993, 58.

56. Moiseyev 1997, 216-17; *FBIS-SOV-95*, "Trade, Cooperation Agreements Signed with Russia," May 11, 1995, 92; "Economics Minister on Trade Pact with Russia," August 9, 1995, 70.

57. Webber 1997, 54. At a later stage, a free-trade agreement with Russia was signed, but with a list of goods-exceptions subjected to tariffs (El'anov and Ushakova 1997, 95).

58. Bradshaw 1993, 27; El'anov and Ushakova 1997, 90.

59. These two were usually listed by the president as the country's most important external partners, whereas their presidents were referred to as "brothers" (Rotar' 1995).

60. Niyazov 1995, 41; *FBIS-USR*, "Turkmenistan's Dream of Becoming 'Second Kuwait,'" June 2, 1994, 71.

61. *Trade Policy* 1996, 189-93; Webber 1997, 59.

62. Freitag-Wirminghaus 1997, 77.

63. The expected maximum capacity of the pipeline is thirty-one billion cubic meters per year (Mesbahi 1994, 222; Freitag-Wirminghaus 1997, 78). Other ideas of Turkmenistan's leaders included a 8,000 kilometer pipeline from Turkmenistan through Uzbekistan, Kyrgyzstan, and China to Japan and a 1,700 kilometer route through Afghanistan to Pakistan's Arabian Sea ports (Menon 1998).

64. The opening of the pipeline was characterized by a Western expert as a victory for Turkmenistan, "because it's the first to get its reserves to market through a non-Russian pipeline" (*Washington Post*, December 30, 1997, A5).

65. Oschs 1997, 313. See similar observations in Szporluk 1992, 110; Dawisha and Parrott 1994, 51; Freitag-Wirminghaus 1997, 67, 69. One observer even has suggested that Turkmenistan, due to the durability of its tribal ties, was "the least nationalistic of all the Central Asian republics" (Rezun 1992, 128).

66. Brown 1992, 25.

67. Nissman 1995.

68. Hunter 1996, 66-71; Freitag-Wirminghaus 1997, 72.

69. Brown 1992, 34-35.

70. In the words of one observer, the slogan "ten years of prosperity" was changed to "ten years of stability" (Freitag-Wirminghaus 1997, 71).

71. Islam 1994, 169.

72. Ochs 1997, 313-14; Niyazov 1995.

73. This was, in part, the reason why only Turkmenistan chose to sign a dual citizenship treaty for ethnic Russians, who make up 7 percent of its population (Pannier and Rutland 1996, 28).

74. Dawisha and Parrott 1994, 220. In July 1992, Turkmenistan signed a bilateral agreement with Russia that established a joint military command between the two countries (Clark 1994, 193).

75. Freitag-Wirminghaus 1997, 68.

76. As a Russian prominent expert of Central Asia put it, "Russia and Central Asia belong to different civilizations" (Malashenko 1998, 162).

77. Ochs 1997.

Chapter 7
Conclusions and Implications

In this final chapter, I summarize the overall findings and address objections likely to be raised to the argument pursued. I also draw the implications of my analysis for theory and policy making.

The Main Results

The main purpose of this study was to formulate and test in a preliminary way an additional national identity hypothesis for studying foreign economic policy. I do not mean to suggest that other factors, such as market and power considerations, do not figure in understanding the ex-Soviet republics' foreign economic policies. Rather, by selecting for analysis the region where cultural influences on state policy making are very palpable and explicit, I sought to demonstrate the limits of more conventional accounts and illustrate the possible explanatory opportunities of bringing cultural variables into international political economy. Unlike industrially developed Western societies, in which culture and identity have been formed and articulated through the process of nation building during the nineteenth century and the first quarter of the twentieth century, the ex-Soviet nations are at the beginning of a long and painful road toward shaping their future institutions. These nations are emerging out of empire and entering the world community with a very different set of ideas about this community and their own place in it. Their policies cannot be adequately understood without paying close attention to these ideas, to the new nations' varying historical memories and perceptions of the metropole, and the outside world.

A combination of qualitative and statistical (bivariate regression) comparisons has been undertaken in the present study. The national identity hypothesis was formulated and refined through a detailed analysis of Latvian, Ukrainian, and Belarusian foreign economic strategies. The three matched case studies provided an illustration of how the causal process takes place and how national identity is transformed into economic policy making.

Varying Policy Outcomes

Immediately after the Soviet breakup, the three republics in question pursued distinctive policies of restructuring their respective economic patterns.

Latvia decided against joining the CIS, despite the invitations of the new Russian regime led by Boris Yeltsin. After nationalists had won the 1990 elections and became the predominant force in both parliament and government, the fear of Moscow began to manifest itself in the policy of minimizing links with the CIS. At least since August 1989, Latvian leaders entertained the idea of achieving economic independence from the USSR and after the Soviet disintegration, they chose to deal with CIS members on a strictly bilateral basis, specifically via signing bilateral most favored nation treaties and barter agreements. The idea of signing preferential economic agreements within the CIS framework, such as Economic Union or Customs Union, never had any appeal to Latvian policymakers. The relations with Russia, too, remained relatively undeveloped. The Baltic policymakers kept viewing the economic relations with Russia in terms of relative gains and security risks involved. The attitude was best summarized by Latvia's foreign minister Valdis Birkavs: "Let the volume of trade with Russia increase, but let the relative share of Russia in our total trade decrease."[1]

To compensate for the lack of cooperation with the traditional partners, Latvia was preparing itself for diversifying its economic activities away from Russia and the CIS states. Along with other Baltic states, it became one of the fastest reformers of the former Soviet region. Price liberalization, for example, was concluded by the mid-1992. All the Soviet-era trade restrictions, such as state orders, export quotas and licenses, were abolished and replaced with export taxes and tariffs. And by the end-1993, Latvia finally established a coherent foreign exchange system and introduced an independent currency unit. In addition to these domestic economic changes, it was actively searching for new economic partners beyond Russia and the former Soviet region. In terms of finding alternative multilateral arrangements, its major accomplishment was getting closer to eventually joining the European Union (EU), which was overwhelmingly considered as the number one priority on Latvia's policy agenda. In 1996, after concluding a free-trade accord and gaining an associate membership status in the organization, Latvia became the first in the post-Soviet region to apply for full membership in the EU. In addition to the EU, it joined the European Free Trade

Association as an associate member. It also established a free-trade area with each other and concluded a series of bilateral free-trade agreements, mostly with European states.

Ukraine has chosen an intermediate course and pursued a dualistic foreign economic policy. Compared to Latvia, Ukraine entered the CIS, even participated in its establishment, but it has never been supportive of the CIS initiatives. Despite some domestic pressures, Ukrainian leaders refused to join the customs union of Russia, Belarus, Kazakhstan, and Kyrgyzstan or the Russia-Belarus union. Instead, they viewed the newly created organization as an "instrument for civilized divorce" and forum for consultations. Until approximately the mid-1993, Ukrainian leadership even advocated a commercial break from Russia, its major trading partner. However, as soon became evident, most of the government-outlined measures aiming at restricting trade with Russia could not work because of Ukraine's heavy dependence on the ex-metropole. The country's leadership had a little choice but to adopt a much more cooperative economic stance towards Russia and, with the election of Leonid Kuchma Ukraine's second president, Ukraine became a consistent advocate of a free-trade zone with Russia. For example, in February 1995, the two countries signed an agreement "On the mechanism of realization of the free trade agreement," and in 1997, the Treaty on friendship and economic cooperation between the two sides was concluded. The treaty included, among other documents, the Program of Russia-Ukrainian cooperation until the 2007 and promised to facilitate the development of trade and economic relations.

Like Latvia and other Baltic states, Ukraine was determined to diversify its economic activities away from Russia and the CIS and toward Western partners. However, Ukraine has been much less successful in doing so than its Baltic neighbors. In part, this can be attributed to Ukraine's slow and inconsistent domestic reform. Despite many government announcements about intentions to accelerate economic reform, the actual reform was not started until late 1994—early 1995. Prices were being regulated, and there were no consistent policies as far as monetary and trade regulations were concerned. Again, the situation has only changed with Kuchma's arrival. It should not, therefore, come as a surprise that Ukraine, while declaring its commitment to finding alternative economic partners, accomplished relatively little compared to Latvia. Like Latvia, Ukraine expressed a strong interest in eventually gaining EU membership, but never became an associate, let alone a full, member in the organization. Ukraine also failed to gain a membership in the Visegrad Group, another organization of European states it was interested in joining. In terms of relations with multilateral partners, it only became a member of the Central European Initiative, a far less significant organization in terms of market access than the EU. Bilaterally, Ukraine developed trade relations with many European, Asian and Middle East countries relying mainly on barter and deal-specific agreements, not on free-trade agreements.

Finally, Belarus pursued the effort to reintegrate with Russia and, broader, the CIS at the expense of developing ties with European countries. From the very birth of the CIS, Belarus was the most willing participant and consistent signatory to the CIS major economic initiatives. Moreover, it became an ardent advocate of forming the CIS "inner core" via establishing monetary and customs unions with the ex-hegemon. As Russia began erecting trade barriers with the former Soviet republics, Belarus sought to preserve its economic links even at the cost of sovereignty. These efforts were further followed up by attempts to create an even tighter union with the ex-metropole. For example, in 1997, an agreement was signed providing for common citizenship and called for coordinating security and economic policies and eventually creating a single currency. While Russia was generally unwilling to carry the costs of the union and had a different perception of it, Belarus did accomplish some of its goals insofar as its trade with Russia has increased in importance since independence.

As far as the efforts to reach out beyond Russia and the CIS area, Belarus's economic policy was similar to that of the pre-1995 Ukraine. Prices were not liberalized until the end of 1994, exchange rate was kept depreciated, inflation was rising, and the old Soviet trade instruments (such as quotas and surrender requirements) were widely practiced. With the election of Alexandr Lukashenka, Belarus's first president, the country's leadership even tried counter-reform and accelerated the establishment of customs and monetary union with Russia as a substitute for domestic reform. Not surprisingly, Belarus has been the least persistent of all of the three states in pursuing alternative economic relations.

The foreign economic policies of Latvia, Ukraine, and Belarus after the Soviet breakup are summarized in table 7.1.

Explaining Policy Outcomes

These policies are poorly explained by conventional international political economy perspectives. According to the power perspective, these nations should have taken advantage of a period of relative international calm to pursue similarly aggressive policies of switching their trade away from Russia and the CIS. In fact, this is not in accord with reality. The market perspective would also predict a similarity in the three republics' economic behaviors and thus is inadequate for understanding stark variations in policy. According to this perspective, the republics should have adopted similar economic policies because they are similar in size, natural resource endowment, economic structure, and geographic location—as is widely recognized by experts on the former Soviet economy. Additional alternatives will be later considered in this chapter and are also insufficient for explaining the observed policy variation.

The study indicates that the main reason for Latvia's, Ukraine's, and Belarus's varying behavior has to do with different perceptions of external threats

Table 7.1. Latvia's, Ukraine's, and Belarus's Foreign Economic Policies

	Latvia	Ukraine	Belarus
The Russian Pole			
The CIS stance	no participation	no participation	active participant
Monetary policy	independent currency (1993)	independent currency (1996)	monetary union with Russia
Trade policy	promotion of MFN agreement	promotion of free-trade area	customs union with Russia
Domestic Preparations	fast reformer	slow reformer	slow reformer until 1995; counter-reformer after 1995
The Western Pole	EU—associate membership	EU—partnership/ cooperation accord	EU—partnership/ cooperation accord, with the emphasis on its strictly bilateral basis
	EFTA—associate membership	CEI—membership	CEI—membership
	inter-Baltic free-trade area		
	a number of bilateral free-trade agreements	many bilateral barter and deal-specific agreements	limited number of bilateral barter and deal-specific agreements

to their security and national autonomies. These perceptions were predominantly cultural in nature and grew out of the nations' historical experiences with their immediate neighbors, especially Russia. Depending on such experience, the ex-Soviet republics developed different national identities, or images of themselves and of the external environment and therefore behaved differently vis-à-vis Russia (the metropole) after the empire fell apart.

The Baltic republics had a significant experience with national independence before they were incorporated into the empire and "joined" the USSR with a clear sense of being different. A historical sense of national distinctness was reinforced by established geopolitical borders, cultural differences, the presence of (sub)political institutions, and economic modernization. As a result, with the end of USSR, nationalists figured most prominently in national debates in the Baltic republics and managed to mobilize society around their demands. In 1989, determined to reduce what they perceived as threat from Russia, the leaders of Popular Front stated the goal of total economic independence. Anticipating the difficulties of negotiations with Moscow and sensing the possibility of Moscow ordering an economic blockade against them, they nonetheless urged a continuation of the independence drive as a way to eventual salvation. Apart from Moscow, the empire savers' voices were weak, and the republic stood by the chosen path of gaining distance from Moscow. It was these nationalist beliefs that found their reflection in the Baltic nations' economic policies of reorientation away from Russia and the Russia-initiated CIS.

Ukraine serves as an example of a country with a moderate degree of national identity strength. Although it had some historical experience of independence and some memory of it, particularly in its western lands, such experience never had a chance to be consolidated. This made it difficult to create a strong, overarching sense of "Ukrainian" overcoming the sense of relatively pro-Russian east and relatively anti-Russian west of Ukraine and, as a result, Ukrainian nationalism could not provide Ukrainian leadership with firm social support for implementing its policies. It briefly gained prominence when the old communist ideas were discredited in the course of Gorbachev's reforms and the so-called party of power decided to abandon them. The triumph of the nationalists, however, proved to be rather short-lived. After 1992, with economic recession and a decline of living standards, the ruling elite became less receptive to nationalist ideas and somewhat more sympathetic to the empire savers' demands. This duality of national identity and domestic political debate found its reflection in Ukraine's dualistic foreign economic policy.

Finally, Belarus had relatively weak national identity and did not feel threatened by the ex-metropole, which led to its essentially pro-Russian policies. Unlike Baltics and some other ex-Soviet republics, Belarus's people did not have their own state for almost their entire history and have long suffered under the domination of neighboring powers. Its very boundaries and legitimate ethno-territory and the capital (Minsk) were established only in 1939, and the crucial difference between Belarus and the two other cases was that it alone was incorporated into the Soviet empire without possessing a clear sense of being different. As a result of this weak identity, Belarus's nationalists could not command the support of wide sectors of the population and proved to be incapable of competing with the empire savers or the old political elite. The parliament was dominated by conservative politicians whose mindset was formed during the Soviet era, and the empire savers thus remained in control of the policy-making process. This argument is summarized in table 7.2.

The study confirmed and extended to IPE a key finding that has already been established in other subfields of international studies according to which national

Table 7.2. National Identity/Threat and Foreign Economic Policy Outcomes in Latvia, Ukraine, and Belarus: The Causal Process

Identity/Threat ➤ **Domestic Structures** ➤ **State Economic Behavior**
(Causal variable)   (Intervening variable)   (Dependent variable)

Identity/Threat	Domestic Structure	Economic Policy Outcomes
Strong (Latvia)	Society mobilized around nationalists (empire savers are weak). *Nationalists* control policy-making process.	*High* degree of deviation from the old pattern (active participation in multi-lateral agreements with countries other than Russia, but not with those having Russia as a participant).
Moderate (Ukraine)	Society is heterogeneous. Nationalists are strong, but so are empire savers. *State* controls policy-making process.	*Medium* degree of deviation from the old pattern (passive participation in multilateral agreements with Russia as a participant and beyond).
Weak (Belarus)	Society mobilized around empire savers (nationalists are weak). *Empire savers* control policy-making process.	*Low* degree of deviation from the old pattern (active participation in multilateral agreements with Russia as a participant, but not in those without Russia).

identity, as a cultural norm, exerts both constitutive and regulative effects on state actors.[2] The constitutive effect revealed itself in the fact that in Latvia, Ukraine, and Belarus the economic considerations and security dilemmas were framed in culturally different, sometimes mutually exclusive terms. The degree of national identity development in the nations that emerged from the empire helps us to understand the cultural context in which the decision-making process of these nations was taking place. To Latvian policymakers, getting away from the ex-metropole and "going West" for new economic relations made perfect sense, as their minds were preoccupied with the idea of strengthening national independence at the expence of Russia's dominance. The same idea, although not as firmly socially established, dominated the minds of Ukrainian politicians. Of the three republics, escaping the ex-imperial area made the least sense to Belarus. Unlike Latvian and Ukrainian leaders, Belarus's policymakers did not seem overly concerned with consolidating their acquired sovereignty. Whereas both Latvia and Ukraine kept viewing the ex-metropole as a security threat and were prepared to suffer if necessary in order to firmly establish their independence, in Belarus national independence was overwhelmingly viewed as an abstract concept worthy of sacrificing for the sake of achieving economic survival.

This argument about national identity influences does not imply that the post-Soviet nations neglected economic considerations in their external policies. Rather it suggests that these nations' economic considerations turned out to be embedded in varying cultural contexts and it is only in these cultural contexts that economic interests could be formed and meaningfully function. The three countries' policymakers all faced comparable economic dilemmas and yet made sharply different economic policy choices operating in different cultural universes. In their economic decisions, these policymakers were motivated by both economic and national identity concerns, but it is the latter concerns that turned out to have had the decisive impact. The structure of economic interests was undergoing change following the process of establishing cultural meanings, not vice versa. It follows then that economic rationality should not be seen as entirely separated from its cultural context and that the latter that determines the former, not the other way around. Once the cultural identity is established, economic interests, too, start taking root.

The second phase of this project aimed to confirm the existence of regulative effects of national identity on state behavior and included a statistical test of the national identity hypothesis, as refined during the first phase. Compensating for the relative shortcomings of small-n analysis, this phase employed additional empirical evidence and helped to strengthen the causal inferences of the research. A bivariate statistical technique allowed us to explore the relative significance of various economic, political, and cultural explanations and suggested that national identity strength based especially on the NIS's historical experience with independent statehood is the most prominent variable in further investigations of their international economic policies. A systematic analysis of all fourteen ex-republics added support to the originally formulated hypothesis and demonstrated that not only does culture matter in explaining varieties of economic policies, it seems to be the single strongest predictor of the newly emerged nations' economic behavior, relative to explanations of an economic and/or political nature. The analysis suggests a high probability that the ex-Soviet republics' foreign economic orientations may indeed be causally determined by the strength of their national identities and perception of threat from the ex-metropole.

This is not to say that the strength of national identity is some sort of a universal explanation application that should provide us with all the desired answers about the post-Soviet nations' behavior. The study's conclusions should, of course, be treated with caution. Even a composite index of national identity strength managed to capture only about half of the variance, suggesting that while national identity strength cannot be ignored by IPE scholars, it should not be viewed as an universal explanation. As argued in chapter 6, there are a number of cases of deviant behavior that should be explained with the help of variables other than those advanced in this paper. Economic and political characteristics of the NIS, their leaders personal agendas and skills—all of these factors need to be considered when seeking a sufficient picture of the shape of things to come in this and other postimperial, postcolonial parts of the world. But at least in these parts of the world, as this study has argued, culture and identity should become prominent explanatory variables.

To summarize, the study's results imply that culture remains an important motivation in nation economic decision-making and that cultural, idea-based influences should be treated as significant in their own right, and not merely subsumed as interest-based phenomena.[3] By selecting for examination a region where cultural influences on state policy making are explicit, this study reminds IPE scholars of the relevance of those influences worldwide and opens itself to further empirical investigations beyond the former Soviet region. The conceptual universe of cases is potentially rich and includes, in addition to the former USSR, eastern European countries—former members of the Soviet block—and postimperial nations in general.

Possible Objections

Five types of possible objections may be raised to the argument pursued in the study: the behavior of external actors other than Russia; the behavior of Russia itself; the republics' political institutions; leadership and policy commitment to domestic economic reform; and ethnic identity.

The Behavior of External Actors Other Than Russia

First, one might argue that the ex-Soviet republics could have benefited from economic cooperation with external actors in varying degrees, and the republics' foreign policies might therefore be seen as a reflection of such cooperation. The strongest way to make the argument is to consider the importance of the republics' varying access to international markets. Various analyses indicated, for example, that Latvia and other Baltic republics were treated separately from the rest of the former Soviet republics. For example, they obtained Most Favored Nation and Generalized System of Preferences statuses from Organization for Economic Cooperation and Development (OECD) countries earlier than the other republics.[4] Presumably, this separate treatment should have put Latvia in a better position to reorient its commercial activities toward the Western countries and, thus, should have encouraged Latvian policymakers to "go west."

The market access argument, however, is only partially applicable to explaining the policy differences described above. Even based on the core of the argument, one cannot explain the policy differences of Ukraine and Belarus, as these two were granted the market access privileges by OECD countries at approximately the same time.[5] The main problem with the argument has to do with the fact that, as this study has argued, the formation of Latvia's, Ukraine's, and Belarus's foreign trade policies had begun before they received formal independence and were granted preferential access to Western markets. For example, their various decisions vis-à-vis participation in the Commonwealth of Independent States were predetermined by the events of 1990-1991—Gorbachev's new Union treaty initiatives, the August 1991 coup, and the post-coup rise of Russia—and made before the end of 1991.[6] Latvia's trade policy was predicated on beliefs in the virtues of economic nationalism that had been formulated back in the late-1980s. Being granted market access has, at best, reinforced its policy choice, but has virtually no independent causal effects.

The Behavior of Russia

The other side of the "equation" is the behavior of Russia, the ex-metropole of the Soviet empire. One might argue that the ex-Soviet republics' reorientation policies were the reflection of various Russian pressures, rather than of various strengths in their national identities. Both political and economic behavior of Russia might have contributed to the republics' policies.

Military and Political Threats to Security

One might assert, for example, that Latvia and Ukraine experienced more threats to their security and independence from Russia than Belarus, and it was these external threats that pushed Latvia and Ukraine away from the ex-metropole. For example, in January 1991 Latvia experienced a direct invasion, with Soviet Army troops seizing the main newspaper publishing plant and attacking the Interior Ministry. Russia's post-1991 intentions can also be viewed as threatening the republics' security. As monitored via Russia's public statements, particularly those about status of ethnic Russians, Russian military presence, and the strategy of "reintegrating the Near Abroad," the newly independent nations could well have perceived those intentions as disturbing.[7]

The argument is flawed, however, as it does not spell out the sources of the republics' various perceptions of Russia. Having suggested the reasons for Latvian and Ukrainian concerns with Russia's behavior, it does not tell us why Belarus was not nearly as worried, despite the fact that Russia maintained military bases for its strategic forces on Belarusian territory. In the realist spirit, the argument assumes national independent military and security posture and, therefore, cannot explain why Belarus made significant steps to weaken its military status relative to Russia[8] at the cost of improving its economic relations. The national identity argument pursued in this study does not "black box" domestic sources of various security perceptions and so can do a better job in explaining the Belarus "anomaly." It suggests that Latvia's and Belarus's varying perceptions of Russia were cultural, rather than merely political, in nature.

Economic Coercion

The supporters of economic sanctions[9] argument might suspect that Russia was hardly a passive player and was probably using its available economic levers when possible. The Russian economic statecraft then might have been responsible for the observed policy outcomes in the three republics. There are indeed plentiful examples of Russia applying or threatening to apply economic pressures on the republics to achieve its foreign policy goals. Daniel Drezner documented, for example, how Russia applied various economic pressures on Kazakhstan, Latvia, Turkmenistan, and Ukraine to extract various concessions from them.[10] He showed, in particular, how Russia and Russian companies manipulated its energy prices in dealing with energy-dependent Latvia and Ukraine.[11] This should have and did prompt the two nations to search for alternative energy sources so as to avoid similar Russian pressures in the future. It should then have contributed to their foreign economic reorientation policies.

The economic coercion argument should therefore expect the republics to pursue policies of economic reorientation away from the source of potential economic dependency. This expectation, however, is not met once applied to Latvia, Ukraine, and Belarus. All three were heavily dependent on Russian energy supplies and experienced similar pressures from Russia to pay their energy debts. Therefore, all three, objectively speaking, should have been interested in breaking away from such dependence. Nonetheless, the republics' responses to their dependence were remarkably distinct. Latvia decided against joining the CIS economic initiatives and backed the decision with rapid domestic marketization preparing for eventual breakthrough in relationships with the West. Ukraine, on the other hand, chose in favor of participating in the CIS and kept delaying its domestic economic reform up until 1995, negatively affecting its ability to pay energy debts. Finally, Belarus, instead of activating its search for alternative economic partners and marketizing the domestic economy, tried to solve the problem by paying off the arrears with foreign credits and political concessions to the ex-metropole.[12]

Russian Protectionism

One might also assert that Latvian, Ukrainian, and Belarusian policy outcomes resulted from Russia's protectionist pressures, rather than from the nation's own cultural identities. The policy of preferential economic agreements is always a two-way process and, in conducting their policies, the two could not disregard Russia's own preferences with regard to tariff and nontariff restrictions. Russia began erecting trade barriers as soon as the Soviet Union fell apart and maintained them—contrary to its own outcry for the necessity of "reintegrating" the ex-Soviet space—at relatively high levels even after MFN and free-trade agreements with the republics were concluded.[13] Russian protectionism might have caused the republics to pursue reorientation more actively than did the policy of economic openness.

Although the three did indeed have to pay attention to Russia's trade policy, they were not ultimately dependent on it in their responses. There are at least two categories of evidence indicating that the republics were conducting their trade policies relatively independently of Russia. First, the design of these three's policies began before the Soviet breakup and Russia's emerging protectionism, a fact observable via the three countries' attitudes toward the new Union treaty during 1990-1991. Second, the actual variation in Russia's treatment of Latvia, Ukraine, and Belarus had not emerged until 1995. Only then did Russia sign a customs union agreement with Belarus and, in May of the same year, eliminate its trade restrictions on the border with Belarus.[14] In the same year, Russia also signed an agreement with Ukraine ("On the mechanism of realization of the free-trade agreement"), which was supposed to give Ukraine considerable advantages in its trade with Russia relative to Latvia and others not bound with the ex-metropole by free-trade treaties. As far as the period before 1995 is concerned, Latvia, Ukraine, and Belarus were hurt by Russia's discriminatory barriers to a relatively similar degree, and yet they pursued quite different economic policies.

National Political Institutions

Those favoring the national political argument[15] might assert the relevance of domestic arrangements in understanding the three republics' policies.

This study does not argue that domestic structures are unimportant—they are merely insufficient for explaining the observed policy variation. The domestic structures' shapes, by themselves, do not adequately explain the variation in Latvia's, Ukraine's, and Belarus's policies. For example, the "homogeneous society—low centralized state" combination does tend to produce the society dominated type of policy network, but it does not tell us yet what kind of social groups are likely to mobilize society around their demands. Those groups may be entirely different in their policy preferences: they might be nationalist, as in case of Latvia, or empire-oriented, as in Belarus. The national identity dimension, once employed, tells us which of these groups is likely to be dominant and which is likely to be marginal, and so helps to determine why one society is more nationalistic than another. As the study indicates, domestic structures are important in spelling out the national identity effects on policy making, but it is national identity strength—and not the domestic structures—that triggers the causality process. It is national identity that comes first, thereby determining the shape of domestic structures and defining foreign economic policy outcomes.

Leadership and Policy Commitments

Next, one might argue that the republics' behaviors cannot be adequately understood without exploring qualities of political leaders and their personal commitments to economic reorientation policies. For example, a frequently heard comment about Belarusian President Alexandr Lukashenka is that his dictatorial style is something that drives the republic away from developing economic relations with the West. The comment implies that Belarus, had it had another, more democratic leader, might have had different foreign trade policy as well.[16]

While not without truth, the argument is only partially helpful in explaining the republic's policies during the five years of its independence. The problem lies in the argument's narrow focus on individual policymakers and their perceptions of what might be an optimal foreign economic strategy for their countries. The individually tailored argument may be helpful in explaining policy differences across various governments associated with individual state leaders, but it is less useful when applied to state policies as continuously outliving various governments and cutting across them. The argument made in this study is of the latter nature: it has been built by observing the policies of Latvia, Ukraine, and Belarus from 1990 to 1996, a period during which a number of governments and policy leaders were changed. For example, in 1995 Belarus elected Lukashenka as its first president, but was previously ruled by Stanislau Shushkevish and, more briefly, by Viacheslau Kebich. And Ukraine went through a significant change from Kravchuk's to Kuchma's leadership. What matters in explaining this kind of overarching policy change is not so much an individual perception of a beneficial policy, but a perception expressed by nation as a whole and monitored via various nationwide reactions to policy choices by individual national leaders. This national perception cannot be separated from a nation's previously formed image of itself, or its national identity.

Ethnic Identity

Finally, one might admit that national identity does make a difference in the republics' foreign economic policies, but suggest that national identity should be conceptualized in a different way. For example, one might argue that national identity does not need to be understood in constructivist terms, as something formed out of the republics' historical experiences before and during the empire. The supporters of a primordialist account may suggest that the ethnic components of national identity, such as language and religion, should account for countries' economic orientations. For example, one might assert that Ukraine and Belarus were religiously and, to a lesser extent, linguistically closer to Russia and therefore could not break away from it to the extent Latvia did.

This study does not argue that ethnicity is irrelevant-under some circumstances it may figure quite prominently. What it does argue, however, is that language and religious compositions of the republics' population should be viewed as a historical phenomenon, and not something given or waiting to be discovered. Primordial factors might in fact matter, but not when removed from their social and historical contexts. For instance, what do we make of the fact that the Latvian population, as compared with that of Belarus, is much more heterogeneous in terms of the proportion of ethnic Russians residing in the country?[17] A purely primordialist account might mistakenly assume that it is Latvia which should be more pro-Russian in its foreign policy orientation, and that it is Belarus which should reorient itself away from Russia, not vice versa. The linguistic data, however, will begin to make sense after we place them in the relevant sociohistorical context. It is sociohistorical factors, such as the degree of linguistic Russification and the extent of resistance to it (comparative data on the republics' degrees of linguistic Russification are provided in table 3.1) that will be of assistance in interpreting the role of primordial factors in the observed policy variation.

Implications for Theory

The issue of national identity remains far from being satisfactorily investigated through contemporary mainstream IR approaches. Yet, the national identity hypothesis can be useful in understanding issues others than nation foreign economic policy. Below, I briefly outline how various branches of Political Science could benefit from integrating the national identity perspective into their research. While formulated out of the experience of the former Soviet republics, the perspective has wider applications and can be helpful in understanding nation behavior in general.

International Political Economy

In IPE, integration of the national identity perspective can shed some new light on issues of economic security, nation economic viability, and international/ regional economic cooperation.

To begin with, the national identity hypothesis suggests some illuminating ways of looking at economic security dilemmas in world politics. International Relations scholars are quite familiar with the neorealist/neoliberal debate, which views economic security problems primarily in terms of political struggles to acquire absolute and relative gains in the course of states' interactions. States will cooperate, it is assumed, insofar as they continue maximizing their national autonomy and economic benefits. It is wealth and power that figure as the most prominent goals that states pursue in the process of their interactions.[18]

The national identity perspective does not dispute the accomplishments of the "absolute versus relative gains" school in solving some empirical puzzles, but it does imply that economic security cannot always be taken as a static concept, with fixed meanings attached to it. Bringing a crossnational comparative perspective into the analysis, as this study does, immediately suggests that economic security can be viewed by different nations in different, sometimes mutually exclusive ways and that, in at least some cases, such differences are the product of nations' varying cultural perceptions. Our study has demonstrated, for example, that some of the ex-Soviet republics faced similar dilemmas in their economic relations with Russia, but their responses and the very definition of these dilemmas were fundamentally different. What was seen as strategically important to Latvia had relatively low significance in Belarus, and vice versa. The national identity perspective helps us to understand why this has been the case, and suggests that culture-based explanations can further expand our knowledge about nations' economic interactions.

The national identity perspective can also contribute to our knowledge about nation economic viability and competitiveness in the world political economy. Some prominent researchers have already demonstrated that state ability to compete in the world market is not just about economic resources—it has much to do with state institutional capacity, without which adequate international adjustment would be impossible.[19] The national identity perspective reinforces this conclusion and expands the notion of institutions by adding a cultural dimension to it. It suggests, in particular, that culture and identity remain valuable assets in the process of international economic adjustment. However paradoxical it may sound, a strong sense of national Self can allow more flexibility in state adaptation to a rapidly changing international environment.

The study of regional economic cooperation and regionalism can also benefit from integrating a national identity perspective. My study indicates that the process of reshaping post-Communist Eurasia cannot be adequately understood without recognition of the republics' historical pasts and their images of national Selves. In particular, it shows that a development of regional economic ties can be successful and relatively advanced only when appropriate cultural preconditions are in place, and the participants are free from any fear of losing their identity as a result of such a development. Regional economic cooperation can be even more productive when the parties are culturally predisposed toward each other, and are not merely culturally tolerant. A product of history, and religious and linguistic similarity, such compatibility in national cultures can serve as a powerful incentive for building a pattern of regional cooperation. To summarize, making room for cultural variables in the study of the EU, NAFTA, or Association of South East Asian Nations (ASEAN), and integrating these variables in the body of still predominantly economic and/or political explanations of regionalism,[20] can bring some important payoffs to the IPE scholars.

Security Studies

The national identity perspective developed in this study can also enhance our knowledge about security issues in world politics.[21] In particular, it can shed additional light on issues of state sovereignty, nationalism, and military alliances.

The problematic of state sovereignty and autonomy has been receiving considerable attention since the end of the Cold War. With the emergence of the new states in Eurasia, Europe, and elsewhere, and the extension to them of an externally recognized right to exercise final authority over their own affairs,[22] scholars must revisit the issue and ask to what extent (if any) the newly born nations and states are able to exercise the "final authority." The experience of the post-Communist nations suggests, among other things, the difficulty of analyzing state institutional forms without acknowledging the existence of close dialectical relations between sovereignty (the right to exercise final authority) and autonomy (the ability to exercise final authority). Can these nations be called sovereign if anywhere they have a difficult time in handling their internal, let alone external, problems? Can a state still remain sovereign if it is barely able to maintain autonomy over its domestic and external policy decisions? The post-Communist nations face some fundamental economic and political challenges simultaneously, and it remains to be seen whether meeting these challenges will not cost these states their survival as sovereign entities.

Traditional approaches are not fully satisfactory in addressing the sovereignty dilemmas of the newly emerged nations. Legal and realist accounts typically pay little attention to the internal aspects of sovereignty, and interdependence and dependence assessments, while revealing economic factors affecting sovereignty, maintain a similarly low interest in its social and cultural dimensions.[23] The national identity perspective can compensate for this weakness and point to additional cultural factors capable of compromising (or, alternatively, strengthening) the sovereignty of the newly independent states. By focusing on the relationships between a nation's social/cultural characteristics and its political/legal institutions, such a perspective may offer some new ways of studying state institutional forms. For example, it may lead to a somewhat paradoxical conclusion that, with possible exception of the Baltic nations, none of the newly emerged post-Soviet states possesses the identity of a sovereign nation. It may therefore suggest that the institutional forms of the recently emerged nations must be problematized rather than assumed a priori as being sovereign. When applied, the national identity perspective may suggest that it makes more sense to classify the newly independent nations as sovereign, semi-sovereign, and semi-colonial rather than to lump them together in one analytical category.

The national identity perspective can also assist in understanding the nature and intensity of postimperial nationalism. A comparative analysis of Latvian, Ukrainian, and Belarusian policies and societies indicates that the nature and varying intensity of the republics' nationalist feelings had a lot to do with their historically established national Self-images. In its nature, post-Soviet nationalism has been unmistakably anti-Russian, a result of Russia's historical status as the metropole and of the absence of perceived external threats from elsewhere after the Soviet disintegration.[24] Some of the republics had joined the empire voluntarily and benefited from staying in it, but readily took the historical opportunity to secede and (re)establish their national identity. Those with a historically stronger sense of national identity managed to produce nationalist movements that were better organized and able to mobilize the public around a nationalist policy agenda. Conversely, in Belarus or the Central Asian societies, the bona fide nationalists, those that emerged outside the nomenklatura, eventually became marginalized and unable to influence state policies.

Both the nature and intensity of postimperial nationalism were not fully captured by existing perspectives. The systemic perspective pointed out that the rise of nationalism had to do with changing conditions in the international system,[25] but paid relatively little attention to varying domestic perceptions of international change. The supporters of economic explanations[26] tend to miss the fact that nationalism varied not only across more and less advanced republics, but also—and significantly—*within* these groups. Finally, approaches emphasizing nationalist demands for religious and linguistic authenticity[27] underestimate that both religious and linguistic compositions of a country's population are a product of history and, therefore, are hardly independent in their effects on the nature and intensity of nationalism. For example, one cannot assume that a more linguistically or religiously heterogeneous society should necessarily pursue relatively more nationalistic policies; Latvia and Estonia were notoriously different from Ukraine and Kazakhstan in their state policies. The linguistic and religious data then will start making sense only when placed in the relevant sociohistorical context.

Finally, scholars of military alliances/alignments can also benefit from a close study of the cultural characteristics of those nations that choose to participate in a military arrangement in various forms or abstain from it. Our present approach suggests, along with some other recently published studies,[28] that in number of cases, the military alignment's puzzle cannot be adequately solved without addressing the issue of the parties' perceptions of each other. The "balance of threat" way of doing so[29] is insufficient, as it does not fully spell out the sources of the parties' various perceptions of each other. In the realist spirit, the argument assumes nation independent military and security posture and therefore cannot explain why some of the republics, such as Belarus, decide to ally with the ex-metropole, thereby weakening their military status, while others abstained from such an alliance. In at least some cases, the national identity perspective can help to address domestic sources of various security perceptions by suggesting that the ex-imperial republics' varying perceptions of the metropole may be cultural, rather than merely political, in nature.

Comparative Politics

My final illustration of the potential of the national identity hypothesis to advance empirical knowledge concerns some of the issues traditionally addressed by scholars of Comparative Politics. I suggest that application of the national identity perspective can improve our understanding of how states/societies move to changing their economic and political systems and adopt more market- and democracy-based institutions.

Let us first consider the issue of economic transition. Studies devoted to the issue can be briefly summarized as pursuing three lines of reasoning as to why the transition was more successful for some countries than for others. Social scientists underline various structural economic and social factors,[30] politico-institutional conditions,[31] and leaders' personal agendas, qualities, and commitments to economic reform[32] as explanatory variables. In answering questions about economic transitions, as yet much less attention has been paid to cultural factors, not least because of difficulties in finding an appropriate way of measuring and operationalizing them.[33]

Our study suggests a means of doing so by looking at the postimperial states' experience with national independence, as well as at some other indicators. The fact that Latvia turned out to be a fast reformer, Ukraine a slow reformer, and Belarus even tried counter-reform undoubtedly had to do with various factors of economic, political, and psychological natures. Cultural factors, too, played their part: the Baltic states, for example, were well aware of their cultural proximity to Europe and were socially prepared to adopt a shock therapy approach for the sake of their economic development.[34] On the other hand, the Central Asian states (barring Kyrgyzstan) and Belarus proceeded in a slow manner or remained essentially nonmarket economies. A full explanation of why some countries choose to reform rapidly, whereas others moved slowly and still others went with no reform, must not be formulated at the expense of culture-based factors. The challenge is to bring them into the study of economic transition and to attribute them an appropriate place, while neither exaggerating nor underestimating their significance.

The same point can be made about political reform. Integrating cultural perspective into studies of democratization, as Valerie Bunce has argued,[35] may become a more coherent way of capturing the special nature of countries in transition and reducing any ethnocentric bias of the still predominantly Western scholarship on the issue. As with economic reform, one can identify at least three different outcomes of political transition in the post-Communist region. Some countries have moved toward consolidating their now fairly well-established democratic institutions; others, such as Russia, remain an awkward hybrid of democratic and authoritarian elements, with no guarantees that the next move will be toward democracy rather than authoritarian rule.[36] Still others remain predominantly authoritarian, with no promises of adopting even some components of democracy. The fact that Russia, Belarus, and a number of Central Asian nations have so far demonstrated less promise to become democratic than Poland, Czech Republic, Ukraine, and the Baltic republics may have to do with their lack of national independence experience, as well as their generally minor historical familiarity with the institutions composing the Modernity project—sovereign statehood, inclusive citizenship, political democracy, and market economy.

Some Implications for Policy Making

That economic development is an uneven process and assumes multiple paths is old news. What is less well known is how exactly this process unfolds and what are the forces determining the variety of development paths in this increasingly globalized world. This is an area of considerable debate. This study has argued that cultural forces, particularly the strength of national identity, are capable of contributing greatly to shaping foreign economic policies of the newly born nations. In addition to acquiring knowledge about these nations' economic and political characteristics, policymakers will do well to take into account the cultural norms these nations are largely based upon and, therefore, are committed to reproducing in their everyday practices. An informed decision concerning ways of developing economic and political relations with the newly independent states—or providing them with various kinds of external assistance—is impossible if it is rooted in ignorance about these nations' cultural origins. The experience of the post-Soviet nations, as analyzed in this study, suggests two lessons for policymakers within and outside the region:

1. Acknowledging the variety of culture-sensitive paths in human development ought to become the basic assumption and starting point when designing an economic strategy. Our study revealed three different patterns of international economic behavior that emerged after the Soviet disintegration and represented by Baltic states, Ukraine, and Belarus, respectively. In fact, the wide variety of national cultures suggests a variety of nuanced culture-sensitive development strategies, which in no way can be reduced to a fixed number. It is important to be aware that in addition to comparative *economic* advantages, nations may have comparative *cultural* advantages in developing economic relations with one nation/group of nations at the expense of the other. In economic issues, as in every other issue of world politics, policymakers should be aware of the full spectrum of resources at their disposal.

Allowing choices and being sensitive toward nations' cultural origins are therefore something an informed policy decision must start with. No reformer—within or outside of the NIS—must be motivated by some sort of "universal" economic recommendation toward stability and prosperity. What brings stability in one country may bring destabilization in others; what works under some conditions won't work under others, and not merely out of differences in countries' economic characteristics. Culture, too, makes a difference. Latvia's pro-Western strategy, for example, could only have succeeded with the support given it by basic sectors of Latvian nationally oriented population—the outcome would have been different should the memory of the country's inter-war independence and cultural affinity with the West have been weaker. For the same cultural reasons, Belarus, while similar to Latvia in its economic potential, could have not failed to orient itself toward Russia and the CIS rather than countries outside the ex-Soviet area. The course chosen by Alexandr Lukashenka was not inevitable, of course. However, even if leading Belarus nationalist Zyanon Paznyak—by virtue of some peculiar circumstances—had become Belarus's president, he would have almost certainly failed in attempting to accomplish what has been accomplished by Latvia.

By offering a more sophisticated understanding of the former Soviet republics' economic behavior, this study warns against the still common, simplified perception that all the NIS will soon become a part of the "free-market" world, especially those NIS that are strategically located and richly endowed with natural resources. This project indicates that because national identity is involved, the question of "joining" the community of Western developed nations is actually much more complicated than one might think. At the same time, it warns against expectations that all former Soviet republics will return to their traditional trading area sooner or later, that only the political ambitions of their leaders are currently driving them away from establishing some sort of customs union on the territory of the Soviet Union. Again, the issue is more complicated, and some of the NIS, while being relatively weak as economic entities, are still likely to pursue an aggressive policy of restructuring their trade pattern and thereby of "joining" the West. This project suggests that this process is likely to occur in those NIS that possess a relatively strong sense of nationhood and therefore perceive trade with the former metropole as threatening to their national identity.

2. Viewing culture as an opportunity and a constraint in developing economic ties. The previously formulated point leads to the simple conclusion that, under some circumstances, what states can accomplish is limited. Culturally, and not just economically, they are constrained in their time-specific policy design and policy actions. Yet in other circumstances, some states may find themselves in a better position to accomplish their economic goals because of certain cultural advantages.

It would not make sense to ignore that, in the near-term perspective, some countries are closer to others simply by the virtue of their cultural similarity. For Belarus and Russia, for example, the policy challenge is to find a mutually acceptable form of economic union, and not to adopt separate paths of development. The drive toward each other is culturally predetermined, has impressive public support, and must not be overlooked by the countries' politicians. For Latvia and other Baltic nations, the reverse is true: they are culturally closer to Europe and are likely to continue following the path of integration with European economic and political institutions. For Ukraine, a culturally torn country, the challenge is to preserve a balance in its foreign policy vis-à-vis Russia/CIS, on the one hand, and the West, on the other.

On the other hand, it is no less important to identify cultural barriers on the way to far-reaching international economic cooperation among some countries and reduce, when feasible, their possible negative effects by means of economic and political diplomacy. For Russia, for example, this suggests some strategic limits in developing relations with Latvia and other Baltic nations, though it in no way restricts attempts to normalize these relations and avoid further cuts in still significant links to its Baltic neighbors. For the West, the awareness of cultural affinities in world politics should suggest a fair degree of open-mindedness about the strengthening of Belarus-Russia economic and political ties and assisting, when possible, in finding an appropriate form for their unity. Such unity, if accomplished voluntarily and with respect for the two nations' economic and political interests, may assist its participants in adjusting to a more global international environment by making the process of adjustment smother than it might otherwise have been. Armed with such understanding, the West has a number of policy levers to make processes of integration, as well as diversification, in the post-Soviet Eurasia take forms that are most civilized and beneficial for world peace and prosperity.

Notes

1. Valdis Birkavs, "Chetire stolpa" i "chetire semerki" Latviyi, *Nezavisimaia gazeta*, January 16, 1999, 6; *The Jamestown Monitor*, "European Union, Germany Surge Ahead of Russia in Latvia's Trade," October 22, 1998.

2. This finding is now commonplace in constructivist empirical research (Finnemore 1996; Hudson 1996; Katzenstein 1996).

3. See Weber 1958, 280.

4. MFN status subject a countries' exports to tariffs applied exports from Generalized Agreement on Trade and Tariffs (GATT) members; Generalized System of Preferences (GSP) status puts a country's product rates on the same footing as rates applied to imports from selected developing countries (Kaminski 1996, 403-405).

5. Kaminski 1994, 247; Kaminski 1996, 404.

6. Ivars Godmanis, the Latvian Prime Minister, said in October 1991 that "our membership in a Union of any type is excluded." Belarus's leaders, on the other hand, kept pressing for a "renewed" union up until the demise of the USSR (*RFE/RL Daily Report*, "Latvia Will Not Join Soviet Economic Union," October 10, 1991; Mihalisko 1992, 8).

7. Porter and Saivetz 1994; Drezner 1997.

8. For instance, Belarus was the first to turn over its nuclear weapons to Russia; it allowed the presence of Russia's military bases on its territory; and eventually it entered into a military alliance with the ex-metropole (Sanford 1996, 140).

9. As an example of one of the most important statement, see Baldwin 1985.

10. Drezner 1997.

11. *Ibid.*, 97-109.

12. As a result of its willingness to cooperate, Belarus continued to receive Russia's oil and gas at a subsidized rate longer than Latvia and Ukraine and was even forgiven some of its energy debts (Markus 1995d). This, of course, was possible only to a limited degree

given that it was increasingly private companies, such as Gazprom, that were dealing with the republics and seeking a hold in their economies.

13. One possible explanation of such behavior by Russia was its general unwillingness to trade with the cash-stripped republics at the cost of advancing economic ties with the countries of the "Far Abroad."

14. In fact, some sources suggest that even after signing those 1995 agreements, Russia—in violation of the documents—kept practicing trade restrictions (Samodurov 1997, 14; Feofilaktova 1996).

15. The most important statements are Katzenstein 1977; Hall 1986.

16. For a most sophisticated version of the leadership and individual ideas argument applied to the former Soviet states' foreign economic policies, see Darden 2000.

17. Fully 33 percent in Latvia as compared to 13.2 percent of Russians living in Belarus (Chinn and Kaiser 1996, 95, 131).

18. Baldwin 1993.

19. Katzenstein 1985; Ikenberry 1986; Weiss 1998.

20. Mansfield and Milner 1997.

21. Neumann 1992; Katzenstein 1996.

22. This is how sovereignty if often defined (Keohane 1993, 93; Biersteker and Weber 1996, 12).

23. Thomas J. Biersteker and Cynthia Weber's edited volume (1996) made a strong case for the need to rethink traditional approaches to national sovereignty by drawing on material of wide historical and geographical scope.

24. An exception is Armenia, the case addressed in chapter 6.

25. Posen 1993.

26. Snyder and Ballentine 1996; Treisman 1997.

27. Van Evera 1994; Juergensmeyer 1996.

28. Barnett 1996; Risse-Kappen 1996.

29. Walt 1987.

30. Desai 1996; Burawoy 1997; Millar 1998.

31. Brudny 1997; Hellman 1997; Fish 1998.

32. Aslund 1995; Sachs and Pistor 1997.

33. For example, Steven Fish (1998), in his otherwise ambitious and penetrating study, chooses to look at religious tradition as an indicator of societies' cultural preparedness for economic reform, a variable long criticized as reflecting a given scholar's personal ethnocentric biases. For a convincing critique of Fish's treatment of culture, see Kopstein and Reilly 1999.

34. The same, of course, can be said about Poland and some other members of the former Soviet bloc.

35. Bunce 1995. In continuation of this line of reasoning, Philip G. Roeder argues that the degree of completeness of national revolutions has some key consequences for democracy and political stability in the post-Communist world (1999).

36. In fact, a number of scholars argue that a special type of democracy, nonliberal or "delegative democracy," has taken shape in Russia and some other post-Communist nations (O'Donnell 1994; Kubicek 1994; Brudny 1997; Tsygankov 1998).

Bibliography

Abdelal, Rawi. 1999. Economic Nationalism after Empire. Ph.D. diss. Cornell University.

Adalian, Rouben Paul. 1995. Armenia's Foreign Policy. In *The Making of Foreign Policy in Russia and the New States of Eurasia,* edited by Adeed Dawisha and Karen Dawisha. Armonk, New York: M.E. Sharpe, Inc.

Adler, Emmanuel, and Beverly Crawford, eds. 1991. *Progress in Postwar International Relations.* New York: Columbia University Press.

Adler, Emmanuel. 1997. Seizing the Middle Ground: Constructivism in World Politics. *European Journal of International Relations* 3 (3): 319-63.

Alker, Hayward R. 1997. *Rediscoveries and Reformulations.* Cambridge: Cambridge University Press.

Almond, Gabriel A., and G. Bingham Powell, Jr. 1966. *Comparative Politics: A Developmental Approach.* Boston: Little, Brown and Co.

Anderson, Benedict. 1991. *Imagined Communities.* 2nd ed. London: Verso.

Andreev, Vasily. 1997. Nationalist Movements in Belarus. *Prism. A Monthly on the Post-Soviet States E-Mail Bulletin* 3 (January).

Antoniuk, Georgii. 1997. Vneshniie interesi Rossii I Belorussii. *Nezavisimaia Gazeta,* 24 April.

Arel, Dominique. 1995. Ukraine: The Temptation of the Nationalizing State. In *Political Culture and Civil Society in Russia and the New States of Eurasia,* ed. Vladimir Tismaneanu. Armonk, New York: M.E. Sharpe.

Armstrong, John A. 1988. Toward a Framework for Considering Nationalism in Eastern Europe. *Eastern European Politics and Societies* 2 (2): 280-305.

Ashley, Richard K. 1987. The Geopolitics of Geopolitical Space: Toward a Critical Social Theory of International Politics. *Alternatives* 12 (4): 403-34.

Aslund, Anders. 1995. *How Russia Became a Market Economy.* Washington, D.C.: Brookings Institutions Press.

———. 1995. Eurasia Letter: Ukraine's Turnaround. *Foreign Policy* 100 (Fall): 125-43.

Ayoob, Mohammed. 1991. Security Problematic of the Third World. *World Politics* 43
    (January).
———. 1997. Defining Security: A Subaltern Realist Perspective. In *Critical Security
    Studies. Concepts and Cases*, ed. Keith Krause and Michael C. Williams. Minneapo-
    lis: University of Minnesota Press.
Babak, Vladimir. 1995. *Russo-Ukrainian Relations*. Jerusalem: The Hebrew University of
    Jerusalem, Research Paper 77.
Babosov, Yevgenii. 1993. Krutaia lestnitsa krizisa. *Neman* 12: 92-102.
Baldwin, David A. 1985. *Economic Statecraft*. Princeton: Princeton University Press.
———, ed. 1993. *Neorealism and Neoliberalism: The Contemporary Debate*. New York:
    Columbia University Press.
Barkey, Karen. 1997. Thinking About Consequences of Empires. In *After Empire*, ed.
    Karen Barkey and Mark von Hagen. Boulder, Colo.: Westview Press.
Barkey, Karen, and Mark von Hagen, eds. 1997. *After Empire: Multiethnic Societies and
    Nation-Building*. Boulder, Colo.: Westview Press.
Barner-Barry, Carol, and Cynthia A. Hody. 1995. *The Politics of Change: The Transfor-
    mation of the Former Soviet Union*. New York: St. Martin's Press.
Barnett, Michael N. 1996. Identity and Alliances in the Middle East. In *The Culture of
    National Security*, ed. Peter J. Katzenstein. New York: Columbia University Press.
Barrington, Lowell. 1995. The Domestic and International Consequences of Citizenship in
    the Soviet Successor States. *Europe-Asia Studies* 47 (5).
Basarab, John. 1982. *Pereiaslav 1654: A Historiographical Survey*. Edmonton, Ontario:
    CIUS.
Becker, Abraham S. 1996/97. Russia and Economic Integration in the CIS. *Survival* 38
    (4): 117-36.
BELARUS—TO EUROPE! 1997. Documents of the V Congress of the BPF "Adradzennie
    (Renaissance)." 20-21 June.
Berger, Peter J., and Thomas Luckmann. 1966. *The Social Construction of Reality. A
    Treatise in the Sociology of Knowledge*. New York: Doubleday.
Berger, Thomas U. 1996. Norms, Identity, and National Security in Germany and Japan.
    In *The Culture of National Security*, ed. Peter J. Katzenstein. New York: Columbia
    University Press.
Biersteker, Thomas J. 1990. Reducing the Role of the State in the Economy. *International
    Studies Quarterly* 34 (4).
———. 1999. Eroding Boundaries, Contested Terrain. *International Studies Review* 1 (1):
    3-10.
Biersteker, Thomas J., and Cynthia Weber, eds. 1996. *State Sovereignty as a Social Con-
    struct*. Cambridge: Cambridge University Press.
Bilinsky, Yaroslav. 1994. Basic Factors in the Foreign Policy of Ukraine. In *The Legacy of
    History in Russia and the New States of Eurasia*, ed. Frederick Starr. Armonk, New
    York: M.E. Sharpe.
Birkavs, Valdis. 1999. "Chetire stolpa" i "chetire semerki" Latviyi. *Nezavisimaia gazeta*,
    16 January.
Bleiere, Daina. 1997. Integration of the Baltic States in the European Union: The Latvian
    Perspective. In *Small States in a Turbulent Environment*, ed. A. Lejins and Z. Ozo-
    lina. Riga: Latvian Institute of International Affairs.

Bloom, William. 1990. *Personal Identity, National Identity and International Relations.* Cambridge: Cambridge University Press.

Bociurkiw, Bohdan R. 1977. Religious Situation in Soviet Ukraine. In *Ukraine in a Changing World*, ed. Walter Dushnyck. New York: Ukrainian Congress Committee of America.

Boffa, Dzhuzeppe. 1996. *Ot SSSR k Rossii. Istoriia neokonchennogo krizisa, 1964-1994.* Moskva: Mezhdunarodniie otnosheniia.

Bond, Andrew R., and Mathew J. Sagers. 1990. Adoption of Law on Economic Autonomy for the Baltic Republics and the Example of Estonia: A Comment. *Soviet Geography* 31: 1-10.

Boss, Helen, and Peter Havlik. 1994. Slavic (dis)union: Consequences for Russia, Belarus and Ukraine. *Economics of Transition* 2 (2): 233-54.

Bradshaw, Michael. 1993. *The Economic Effects of Soviet Dissolution.* London: The Royal Institute of International Affairs.

Bradshaw, Michael, Philip Hanson, and Denis Shaw. 1994. Economic Restructuring. In *The Baltic States: The National Self-Determination of Estonia, Latvia and Lithuania*, ed. Graham Smith. New York: St. Martin's Press.

Bremmer, Ian, and Ray Taras, eds. 1997. *New States, New Politics: Building the Post-Soviet Nations.* Cambridge: Cambridge University Press.

Breslauer, George, and Philip Tetlock, eds. 1991. *Learning in U.S. and Soviet Foreign Policy.* Boulder, Colo.: Westview Press.

Breton, Albert. 1964. The Economics of Nationalism. *Journal of Political Economy* 72 (4): 376-86.

Bronshtein, Mikhail. 1993. Comment. In *Economic Consequences of Soviet Disintegration*, ed. John Williamson. Washington, D.C.: Institute for International Economics.

Brown, Gordon. 1992. Armenian Nationalism in a Socialist Century. In *Nationalism and the Breakup of an Empire: Russia and Its Periphery*, ed. Miron Rezun. Westport: Praeger.

Brown, Stuart S., and Misha V. Belkindas. 1993. Who's Feeding Whom? An Analysis of Soviet Interrepublic Trade. In *The Former Soviet Union in Transition*, ed. Richard F. Kaufman and John P. Hardt. Armonk, New York: M.E. Sharpe.

Brubaker, Rogers. 1995. National Minorities, Nationalizing States, and External National Homelands in the New Europe. *Deadalus. Journal of the American Academy of Arts and Sciences* 124 (2): 107-32.

———. 1996. *Nationalism Reframed: Nationhood and the National Question in the New Europe.* Cambridge: Cambridge University Press.

Brudny, Yitzhak M. 1997. Neoliberal Economic Reform and the Consolidation of Democracy in Russia. In *The International Dimension of Post-Communist Transition in Russia and the New States of Eurasia*, ed. Karen Dawisha. Armonk, NY: M.E. Sharpe.

Brzezinski, Zbigniew. 1989/1990. Post-Communist Nationalism. *Foreign Affairs* Winter.

———. 1997. *The Grand Chessboard: American Primacy and Its Geostrategic Imperatives.* New York: Basic Books.

Budkin, Viktor et al. 1995. Ukraiina i ES: liberalizatsiia sotrudnichestva. *Politichna Dumka* 6 (2-3): 27-39.

Bunce, Valerie. 1995. Should Transitologists Be Grounded? *Slavic Review* 54.

————. 1997. The Visegrad Group: Regional Cooperation and European Integration in Post-Communist Europe. In *Mitteleuropa: Between Europe and Germany*, ed. Peter J. Katzenstein. Berhahn Books.

Bungs, Dzintra. 1994. Latvia: Transition to Independence Completed. *RFE/RL Research Report* 3, 1, 7 January.

Burant, Stephan R. 1995. Foreign Policy and National Identity: A Comparison of Ukraine and Belarus. *Europe-Asia Studies* 47 (7): 1125-1144.

————. 1997. Ukraiina i Pol'sha: k strategicheskomu partnerstvu. *Politichna Dumka* 3: 104-18.

Burawoy, Michael. 1997. Review Essay: The Soviet Descent into Capitalism. *American Journal of Sociology* 102 (3): 1430-44.

Buzan, Barry. 1991. *People, State and Fear.* New York: Columbia University Press.

Bykowski, Paulyuk. 1997. The "Belarusan Constant." *Prism* 3 (6).

Campbell, David. 1992. *Writing Security: United Sates Foreign Policy and the Politics of Identity.* Minneapolis: University of Minnesota Press.

Cardoso, Fernando Henrique, and Enzo Faletto. 1979. *Dependency and Development in Latin America.* Berkeley: University of California Press.

Casanova, Jose. 1998. Ethno-linguistic and Religious Pluralism and Democratic Construction in Ukraine. In *Post-Soviet Political Order: Conflict and State Building*, ed. Barnett R. Rubin and Jack Snyder. London: Routledge.

Charlton, Sue Ellen M., Jana Everett, and Kathleen Straudt, eds. 1989. *Women, the State, and Development.* New York: State University of New York Press.

Checkel, Jeffrey T. 1993. Ideas, Institutions, and the Gorbachev Foreign Policy Revolution. *World Politics* 45 (2).

————. 1998. The Constructivist Turn in International Relations Theory. *World Politics* 50 (January): 324-48.

Chilton, Patricia. 1995. Mechanics of Change: Social Movements, Transnational Coalitions, and the Transformation Processes in Eastern Europe. In *Bringing Transnational Relations back in*, ed. Thomas Risse-Kappen. Cambridge: Cambridge University Press.

Chinn, Jeff, and Robert Kaiser. 1996. *Russians as the New Minority: Ethnicity and Nationalism in the Soviet Successor States.* Boulder, Colo.: Westview Press.

Clark, Susan. 1994. The Central Asian States: Defining Security Priorities and Developing Military Forces. In *Central Asia and the World*, ed. Michael Mandelbaum. New York: Council on Foreign Relations Press.

Clem, Ralph S. 1996. Belorussians. In *The Nationalities Question in the Soviet Union,* 2nd edition, ed. Graham Smith. New York: Longman Group.

Clemens, Walter C., Jr. 1991. *Baltic Independence and Russian Empire.* New York: St. Martin's Press.

Coleman, James S. 1995. Rights, Rationality, and Nationality. In *Nationalism and Rationality*, ed. Albert Breton, Gianluigi Galeotti, Pierre Salmon, and Ronald Wintrobe. Cambridge: Cambridge University Press.

Connolly, William. 1992. *Identity/Difference.* Ithaca: Cornell University Press.

Connors, Stephen, David G. Gibson, and Mark Rhodes. 1995. Caution and Ambivalence Over Joining NATO. *Transition*, 11 August.

Conquest, Robert, ed. 1986. *The Last Empire: Nationality and the Soviet Future*. Stanford: Hoover Institution Press.

Corbet, Jurgen, and Andreas Gummich. 1990. *The Soviet Union at the Crossoards*. Frankfurt: Deutsche Bank.

Crane, George T. 1998. Economic Nationalism: Bringing the Nation Back. *Millennium* 27 (1): 55-75.

———. 1999. Imagining the Economic Nation: Globalisation in China. *New Political Economy* 4 (2).

D'Anieri, Paul. 1997. Dilemmas of Independence: Autonomy, Prosperity, and Sovereignty in Ukraine's Russia Policy. *Problems of Post-Communism* 44 (1): 16-26.

———. 1999. *Economic Interdependence in Ukrainian-Russian Relations*. Albany: New York: SUNY Press.

Dabrowski, Marek, and Rafal Antczak. 1996. Economic Transition in Russia, Ukraine, and Belarus. In *Economic Transition in Russia and the New States of Eurasia*, ed. Bartlomiej Kaminski. Armonk, New York: M.E. Sharpe.

Dalby, Simon. 1988. Geopolitical Discourse: The Soviet Union As Other. *Alternatives* XIII: 415-42.

Danielyan, Emil. 1998. Armenia's Foreign Policy: Balancing between East and West. *PRISM. E-mail bulleten* 4 (2), 23 January.

Darden, Keith. 2000. Economic Ideas and Institutional Choices among the Post-Soviet States. Paper delivered at the annual meeting of the American Political Science Association.

David, Stephen R. 1991. Explaining Third World Alignments. *World Politics* 43 (1).

Davidenko, E.L. and V.S. Matiushevskii. 1998. *Vneshneekonomicheskaia deiatelnost' respubliki Belarus'*. Minsk: Armita, Menedzhment.

Dawisha, Karen, and Bruce Perrott, eds. 1994. *Russia and the New States of Eurasia*. Cambridge: Cambridge University Press.

———. 1997. *The End of Empire? The Transformation of the USSR in Comparative Perspective*. Armonk, New York: M.E. Sharpe.

———. 1997a. *Democratic changes and authoritarian reactions in Russia, Ukraine, Belarus, and Moldova*. Cambridge: Cambridge University Press.

———. 1997b. *Conflict, cleavage, and change in Central Asia and the Caucasus*. Cambridge: Cambridge University Press.

Declaration of the International Front of Working People in the Latvian SSR. 1990. In *USSR Documents Annual 1989*, ed. J. L. Black. New York: Academic International Press.

Der-Derian, James, and Michael J. Shapiro, eds. 1989. *International/Intertextual Relations. Postmodern Readings of World Politics*. Lexington: Lexington Books.

Dergachev, Aleksandr, ed. 1996. *Ukraiinskaia gosudarstvennost' v XX veke*. Kiev: Politichna Dumka.

Desai, Padma. 1996. Shock Therapy and After: Prospects for Russian Reform. In *Russia and Eastern Europe After Communism: The Search for New Political, Economic, and Security Systems*, ed. Michael Krause and Ronald D. Liebowitz. Boulder, Colo.: Westview Press.

Deutsch, Karl W. 1966. *Nationalism and Social Communication*. Cambridge: MIT Press.

———. 1979. *Tides Among Nations*. New York: The Free Press.

————. 1981. On Nationalism, World Regions and the Nature of the West. In *Mobiliza-tion, Center-periphery Structures and Nation-building*, ed. Per Torsvik. Bergen, Oslo, Tromso: Universitetsforlaget.

Dijkink, Gertjan. 1996. *National Identity and Geopolitical Visions*. London: Routledge.

Diuk, Nadia, and Adrian Karatnycky. 1993. *New National Rising: The Fall of the Soviets and the Challenge of Independence*. New York: John Wiley & Sons, Inc.

Doyle, Michael W. 1986. *Empires*. Ithaca: Cornell University Press.

Drakokhrust, Yury. 1997. Union of Belarus and Russia: Steps Toward Integration—1995-1997. *Belarusian Review* 9, 2 (Summer): 3-6.

Dreifelds, Juris. 1989. Latvian National Rebirth. *Problems of Communism* 4 (4): 77-94.

Drezner, D. 1997. Allies, Adversaries, and Economic Coercion: Russian Foreign Eco-nomic Policy Since 1991. *Security Studies* 6 (3).

Dudwick, Nora. 1997a. Armenia: Paradise Lost? In *New States, New Politics*, ed. Ian Bremmer and Ray Taras. Cambridge: Cambridge University Press.

————. 1997b. Political Transformation in Postcommunist Armenia. In *Conflict, Cleav-age, and Change in Central Asia and the Caucasus*, ed. Karen Dawisha and Bruce Perrott. Cambridge: Cambridge University Press.

Duffield, John S. 1998. *World Power Forsaken: Political Culture, International Institu-tions, and German Security Policy After Unification*. Stanford: Stanford University Press.

Easton, David. 1965. *A Systems Analysis of Political Life*. New York: Wiley & Sons.

EIU, *Economist Intelligence Unit. Quarterly Economic Report*, London.

————. *Country Profiles*, London.

Eichengreen, Barry. 1989. The Political Economy of the Smoot-Hawley Tariff. *Reseach in Economic History* 12 (1): 1-43.

Eisenstadt, S. N. 1963. *The Political Systems of Empires*. New York: Free Press.

————, ed. 1967. *The Decline of Empires*. Englewood Cliffs: Prentice-Hall, Inc.

Elstain, Jean Bethke. 1995. Feminist Themes and International Relations. In *International Theory: Critical Investigations*, ed. James Der Derian. New York: New York Univer-sity Press.

Emerson, Rupert. 1960. *From Empire to Nation: The Rise and Self-assertion of Asian and African Peoples*. Boston: Beacon Press.

Emizet, Kisangani N., and Vicki L. Hesli. 1995. The Disposition to Secede. *Comparative Political Studies* 27 (4): 493-536.

Erikson, Richard E. 1992. Economics. In *After the Soviet Union*, ed. Timothy J. Colton and Robert Legvold. New York: W.W. Norton & Company.

Europe Agreement 1998. www.mfa.gov.lv/mfa/pub/EU/eu020198.htm

European Union Declaration on Belarus. 1997. *Belarusian Review* 9, 2 (Summer): 7-8.

El'anov, A.Ya., and N.A. Ushakova. 1997. Rossiia-Tsentral'naia Aziia: problemi I ten-dentsiyi ekonomicheskogo vzaimodeistviia. *Vostok* (4): 83-111.

Evangelista, Matthew. 1988. *Innovation and the Arms Race*. Ithaca: Cornell University Press.

Evans, Peter B., Dietrich Rueschemeyer, and Theda Skocpol, eds. 1985. *Bringing the State Back In*. Cambridge: Cambridge University Press.

Evans, Peter B., Harold K. Jacobson, and Robert D. Putnam, eds. 1993. *Double-Edged Diplomacy*. Berkeley: University of California Press.

FBIS-SOV. Foreign Broadcast Information Service, Soviet Union. Washington, DC.

Feofilaktova, Anna. 1996. Svet v kontse koridora poka ne viden. *Segodnia,* 28 February.

Finnemore, Martha. 1993. International Organizations as Teachers of Norms. *International Organization* 47 (3): 565-98.

————. 1996. *National Interests in International Society.* Ithaca: Cornell University Press.

Finnemore, Martha and Kathryn Sikkink. 1998. International Norms Dynamics and Political Change. *International Organization* 52 (4): 887-917.

Fish, M. Steven. 1998. The Determinant of Economic Reform in the Post-Communist World. *East European Politics and Societies* 12 (1): 31-78.

Frankel, Jeffrey A., and Miles Kahler, eds. 1993. *Regionalism and Rivalry: Japan and the United States in Pacific Asia.* Chicago: The University of Chicago Press.

Freitag-Wirminghaus, R. 1997. Turkmenistan's Place in Central Asia and the World. In *Security Politics in the Commonwealth of Independent States: The Southern Belt,* edited by Mehdi Mozaffari. London: Macmillan Press/St. Martin's Press.

Fukuyama, Francis. 1995. *Trust: the Social Virtues and the Creation of Prosperity.* New York: Free Press.

Fuller, Elizabeth. 1992. The Transcaucasus: Real Independence Remains Elusive. *RFE/RL Research Report,* 3 January.

————. 1996. Transcaucasus—Doomed to Strategic Partnership. *Transition,* 15 November.

Filipenko, Anton. 1995. Economic Integration in the CIS. In *Ukraine and Integration in the East,* ed. Lena Jonson. Stockholm: The Swedish Institute of International Affairs.

Furman, Dmitrii. 1995. Ukraiina I mi. *Svobodnaia misl'* (1): 69-83.

Furman, Dmitrii, and Oleg Bikhovetz. 1996. Belarusskoie samosoznaniie i belorussikaia politika. *Svobodnaia misl'* (1).

Gaidukov, Leonid, and Liudmila Chekalenko. 1998. SND v ekonomichnomu i politichnomu prostori Ukraiini. *Viche* 3 (72): 33-51.

Le Gall, Francoise. 1994. Ukraine: A Trade and Exchange System Still Seeking Direction. In *Trade in the Newly Independent States,* ed. Constantine Michalopoulos and David G. Tarr. Washington, DC: The World Bank.

Gapova, Elena. 1998. The Nation Between the Dreaming of Its Women. Unpublished manuscript, Minsk.

Garnett, Sherman W. 1997. *Keystone in the Arch. Ukraine in the Emerging Security Environment of Central and Eastern Europe.* Washington, D.C.: Carnegie Endowment for International Peace.

Geertz, Clifford. [1963] 1994. Primordial and Civil Ties. In *Nationalism,* ed. John Hutchinson and Anthony D. Smith. Oxford: Oxford University Press.

————. 1973. *The Interpretation of Cultures.* New York: Basic Books.

George, Alexander L. 1982. Case Studies and Theory Development. Paper presented to the Second Annual Symposium on Information Processing in Organizations, Carnegie-Mellon University.

Gellner, Ernest. 1983. *Nations and Nationalism.* Ithaca: Cornell University Press.

Geremek, Bronislav. 1998. Osnovniie napravleniia vneshnei politiki Pol'shi. *Politichna Dumka* (1): 64-78.

Gerner, Kristian, and Stefan Hedlund. 1993. *The Baltic States and the End of the Soviet Empire.* London: Routledge.

Gerschenkron, Alexander. 1962. *Economic Backwardness in Historical Perspective.* Cambridge: Harvard University Press.

Giddens, Anthony. 1985. *The Nation-State and Violence.* Berkeley: University of California Press.

Girnius, Saulius. 1994. Relations between the Baltic States and Russia. *RFE/RL Research Report* 3 (33), 26 August.

Gleason, Gregory. 1990. *Federalism and Nationalism: The Struggle for Republican Rights in the USSR.* Boulder, Colo.: Westview Press.

Glivakovski, A.K. 1992. *Samostiinaia Ukraiina: istoki predatel'stva.* Moskva: National'no-Respublikanskaia partiia Rossii.

Goff, Patricia. 2000. Invisible Borders: Economic Liberalization and National Identity. *International Studies Quarterly* 44 (4): 533-62.

Goldstein, Judith, and Robert O. Keohane, eds. 1993. *Ideas and Foreign Policy: Beliefs, Institutions, and Political Change.* Ithaca: Cornell University Press.

Goldstein, Judith. 1993. *Ideas, Interests, and American Trade Policy.* Ithaca: Cornell University Press.

Gonchar, Nikolai. 1995. From Respectful Dialogue to Agreement. In *Russia and Eurasia Documents Annual 1994.* New York: Academic International Press.

Gourevich, Peter. 1986. *Politics in Hard Times.* Ithaca: Cornell University Press.

Gowa, Joanne. 1994. *Trade and Alliances.* Princeton: Princeton University Press.

Gowa, Joanne, and Edward D. Mansfield. 1993. Power Politics and International Trade. *American Political Science Review* 87.

Grieco, Joseph M. 1990. *Cooperation among Nations: Europe, America and Non-Tariff Barriers to Trade.* Ithaca: Cornell University Press.

Grinkevich, Oleksandr, and Valerii Kuz'menko. 1998. Ukraiina I Rosiia: Shche odin krok u virnomu napriami. *Politika i chas* (3): 7-17.

Gurr, Ted Robert, and Barbara Harff. 1994. *Ethnic Conflict in World Politics.* Boulder, Colo.: Westview Press.

Guthier, Steven L. 1977. The Belorussians: National Identification and Assimilation, 1897-1970. *Soviet Studies* 29 (1): 37-61 and (2): 270-83.

Haas, Ernst B. 1997. *Nationalism, Liberalism, and Progress.* Vol. 1. *The Rise and Decline of Nationalism.* Ithaca: Cornell University Press.

Haggard, Stephan, and Robert R. Kaufman. 1995. *The Political Economy of Democratic Transitions.* Princeton: Princeton University Press.

Hall, Peter A. 1986. *Governing the Economy: The Politics of State Intervention in Britain and France.* Oxford: Oxford University Press.

———, ed. 1989. *The Political Power of Economic Ideas.* Princeton: Princeton University Press.

Hanson, Philip. 1990. An Economic Deal between Russia and the Baltic Republics? *Report on the USSR* 2, 26 January.

Havrylyshyn, Oleh. 1997. Ukraine: Looking East, Looking West. *The Harriman Review* 10 (3): 19-23.

Hellman, Joel S. 1997. Constitutions and Economic Reform in the Post-Communist Transitions. In *The Rule of Law and Economic Reform in Russia*, ed. Jeffrey D. Sachs and Katarina Pistor. Boulder, Colo.: Westview Press.

Herman, Robert G. 1996. Identity, Norms, and National Security: The Soviet Foreign Policy Revolution and the End of the Cold War. In *The Culture of National Security*, ed. Peter J. Katzenstein. New York: Columbia University Press.

Hewett, Edward A. 1976. A Gravity Model of CMEA Trade. In *Quantitative and Analytical Studies in East-West Economic Relations*, ed. Josef C. Brada. Bloomington: Indiana University Press.

Hiden, John, and Patrick Salmon. 1994. *The Baltic Nations and Europe.* Revised edition. London and New York: Longman.

Hirschman, A. 1969. *National Power and the Structure of Foreign Trade.* Berkeley: California University Press.

Holdar, Sven. 1995. Torn Between East and West: The Regional Factor in Ukrainian Politics. *Post-Soviet Geography* 36 (2).

Hollis, Martin, and Steve Smith. 1991. *Explaining and Understanding in International Relations.* Oxford: Clarendon Press.

Holsti, Kal J. 1986. Politics in Command: Foreign Trade as National Security Policy. *International Organization* 40.

Hope, Nicholas. 1994. Interwar Statehood: Symbol and Reality. In *The Baltic States: The National Self-Determination of Estonia, Latvia and Lithuania*, ed. Graham Smith. New York: St. Martin's Press.

Hopf, Ted. 1998. The Promise of Constructivism in International Relations Theory. *International Security* 23 (1): 171-200.

Hovannisian, Richard G. 1994. Historical Memory and Foreign Relations: The Armenian Perspective. In *The Legacy of History in Russia and the New States of Eurasia*, ed. S. Federick Starr. Armonk: M.E. Sharpe.

Hudson, Valerie, ed. 1996. *Culture and Foreign Policy.* Boulder, Colo.: Lynne Rynner.

Hunter, Shireen T. 1996. *Central Asia since independence.* Washington, D.C.: The Center for Strategic and International Studies.

Huntington, Samuel P. 1968. *Political Order in Changing Societies.* New Haven: Yale University Press.

———. 1996. *The Clash of Civilizations and the Remaking of World Order.* New York: Simon & Schuster.

Huntington, Samuel P., and Jorge I. Dominguez. 1975. Political Development. In *Handbook of Political Science.* Vol. 3. *Macropolitical Theory*, ed. Fred I. Greenstein and Nelson W. Polsby. Addison-Wesley Publishing Company.

Ikenberry, G. John. 1986. The Irony of State Strength: Comparative Responses to the Oil Shocks in the 1970s. *International Organization* 40: 105-37.

IMF, *Economic Review, Ukraine.* September 1993. Washington, D.C.: International Monetary Fund.

IMF, *Economic Review, Ukraine 1994.* 1995. Washington, D.C.: International Monetary Fund.

IMF, *Republic of Latvia—Recent Economic Development.* 1996. Washington, D.C.: International Monetary Fund Staff Country Report No. 96/143.

IMF, *Ukraine—Recent Economic Development*. October 1997. Washington, D.C.: International Monetary Fund Staff Country Report No. 97/109.

IMF, *Republic of Belarus: Recent Economic Development*. August 1998. Washington, D.C.: International Monetary Fund Staff Country Report No. 98/108.

IMF, *Direction of Trade Statistics Yearbook 1998*. 1999. Washington, D.C.: International Monetary Fund.

Islam, Shaficul. 1994. Capitalism on the Silk Route? In *Central Asia and the World*, ed. Michael Mandelbaum. New York: Council on Foreign Relations Press.

Johnson, Harry G. 1965. A Theoretical Model of Economic Nationalism in New and Developing States. *Political Science Quarterly* 80 (2): 165-85.

————, ed. 1967. *Economic Nationalism in Old and New States*. Chicago: University of Chicago Press.

Jonston, Lena. 1995. Introduction. In *Ukraine and Integration in the East*, ed. Lena Jonson. Stockholm: The Swedish Institute of International Affairs.

Juergensmeyer, Mark. 1996. The Worldwide Rise of Religious Nationalism. *Journal of International Affairs* 50 (1): 1-20.

Jung, Monika. 1995. Looking Both Ways. *Transition* 1 (6), 28 April.

Kaiser, Robert J. 1994. *The Geography of Nationalism in Russia and the USSR*. Princeton: Princeton University Press.

Kaminski, Bartolomiej. 1994. Trade Performance and Access to OECD Markets. In *Trade in the Newly Independent States*, ed. Constantine Michalopoulos and David G. Tarr. Washington, D.C.: The World Bank.

————. 1996. Factors Affecting Trade Reorientation of the Newly Independent States. In *Economic transition in Russia and the new states of Eurasia*, ed. Bartolomiej Kaminski. Armonk, New York: M.E. Sharpe.

Karklins, Rasma. 1994. *Ethnopolitics and Transition to Democracy: The Collapse of the USSR and Latvia*. Washington, D.C.: The John Hopkins University Press.

Karmanov, Yuras'. 1996. Opublikovan proiekt konstitutsii. *Nezavisimaia Gazeta*, 3 September.

Katzenstein, Peter J., ed. 1978. *Between Power and Plenty: Foreign Economic Policies of Advanced Industrial States*. Wisconsin: The University of Wisconsin Press.

————. 1984. *Corporatism and Change*. Ithaca: Cornell University Press.

————, ed. 1996a. *The Culture of National Security: Norms and Identity in World Politics*. Ithaca: Columbia University Press.

————. 1996b. *Cultural Norms and National Security: Police and Military in Postwar Japan*. Ithaca: Cornell University Press.

Katzenstein, Peter J. et al., eds. 1999. *Exploration and Contestation in the Study of World Politics*. Cambridge: The MIT Press.

Keohane, Robert O. 1993. Sovereignty, Interdependence, and International Institutions. In *Ideas and Ideals: Essays on Politics in Honor of Stanley Hoffmann*, ed. Linda B. Miller and Michael Joseph Smith. Boulder, Colo.: Westview Press.

Keohane, Robert O., and Helen V. Milner, eds. 1996. *Internationalization and Domestic Politics*. Cambridge: Cambridge University Press.

Kliachko, Tatiana, and Valerii Solovei. 1995. Neozhydanniie lyki Yegora Gaidara. *Novoie vremia* 11 (12).

Klotz, Audie. 1995. *Norms in International Relations: The Struggle Against Apartheid.* Ithaca: Cornell University Press.

Knopf, Jeffrey W. 1998. The Importance of International Learning. Paper presented at the annual meeting of the International Studies Association, Minneapolis, Minnesota, March 17-21.

Knorr, Klaus. 1975. *The Power of Nations.* New York: Basic Books.

Kohut, Zenon E. 1994. History as a Battleground: Russian-Ukrainian Relations and Historical Consciousness in Contemporary Ukraine. In *The Legacy of History in Russia and the New States of Eurasia*, ed. Frederick Starr. Armonk: M.E. Sharpe

Kopstein, Jeffrey S., and David A. Reilly. 1999. Explaining the Why of the Why: A Comment on Fish's Determinants of Economic Reform in the Post-Communist World. *East European Politics and Societies* 13 (3): 613-624.

Kotikov, Aleksandr. 1996. Belorusiia—Rossiia. Model postsovetskoi integratsii. *Nezavisimaia Gazeta*, 21 March.

Kowert, Paul, and Jeffrey Legro. 1996. Norms, Identity, and Their Limits. In *The Culture of National Security*, ed. Peter J. Katzenstein. New York: Columbia University Press.

Kozhokin, Yevgeny. 1996/97. Belarus" Russia's Access Route to Europe. *Belarusian Review* 8 (4): 14.

Krasner, Stephen D. 1976. State Power and the Structure International Trade. *World Politics* 28 (3): 317-47.

———. 1978. *Defending the National Interests: Raw Materials Investment and US Foreign Policy.* Princeton: Princeton University Press.

Krasts, Guntar. 1998. Latvia's Strategy—Economic Reforms and Integration into the EC. *Politichna Dumka* (1): 28-39.

Krause, Keith, and Michael C. Williams, eds. 1997. *Critical Security Studies: Concepts and Cases.* Minneapolis: University of Minnesota Press.

Kravchuk, Leonid. 1992. *Ie taka derzhava—Ukraiina.* Kiev: Globus.

Krickus, Richard J. 1993. Latvia's "Russian Question. *RFE/RL Research Report* 2 (18), 30 April.

Krivogorsky, Victoria, and John W. Eichenseher. 1996. Some Financial and Trade Development in the Former Soviet States. *Russian and East European Finance and Trade* 32 (5): 16-38.

Kubicek, Paul. 1994. Delegative Democracy in Russia and Ukraine. *Communist and Post-Communist Studies* 27 (4): 423-41.

Kulinich, Nikolai A. 1995. Ukraine in the New Geopolitical Environment. In *The Making of Foreign Policy in Russia and the New States of Eurasia,* ed. Adeed Dawisha and Karen Dawisha. Armonk, New York: M.E. Sharpe.

Kutsai, Tamara. 1995. "Piatna" na svobodnoi torgovle. *Biznes* 26, 11 July.

Kuzio, Taras. 1994. Ukraine and Its "Near Abroad." *Politichna Dumka* (3): 198-207.

Kuznetsov, I. 1998. *"Baltiyskii koridor" i ekonomika Rossiyi.* Moskva: MGIMO.

Laikov, Mikhaiil. 1999. Gosudarstvo—dorogoie udovol'stviie. *Sodruzhestvo HG* (1): 1, 3.

Lainela, Seija, and Pekka Sutela. 1997. Institutional Choice in Transition Economies: The Baltic Monetary Reform. In *The Challenge of Globalization and Institution Building*, ed. Randall W. Kindley and David F. Good. Boulder, Colo.: Westview Press.

Laitin, David D. 1991. The National Uprising in the Soviet Union. *World Politics* 44 (1).

Laitin, David D. 1998. *Identity in Formation.* Ithaca: Cornell University Press.

Lake, David A. 1988. *Power, Protection, and Free Trade: International Sources of U.S. Commercial Strategy, 1887-1939*. Ithaca: Cornell University Press.

Lapid, Yosef, and Friedrich Kratochwil, eds. 1996. *The Return of Culture and Identity and IR Theory*. Boulder, Colo.: Lynne Rienner Publishers.

Lapidus, Gail W. 1984. Ethnonationalism and Political Stability: The Soviet Case. *World Politics* 36 (4): 555-81.

Lapychak, Chrystyna. 1995. Back on Track. *Transition* 1 (3), 15 March.

Lieven, Anatol. 1993. *The Baltic Revolution: Estonia, Latvia, Lithuania and the Path to Independence*. New Haven: Yale University Press.

Lekant, Andrei. 1992. Karbovanets s vozu—Gaidaru legche. *Nezavisimaia gazeta*, 14 November.

Levi, Margaret, and Michael Hechter. 1985. A Rational Choice Approach to the Rise and Decline of Ethnoregional Political Parties. In *New Nationalisms of the Developed West: Toward Explanation*, ed. Edward A. Tiryakian and Ronald Rogowski. Boston: Allen & Unwin.

Lipset, Seymour Martin. 1960. *Political Man: The Social Bases of Politics*. Garden City: Doubleday.

Lofgren, Joan. 1998. A Different Kind of Union. *Transitions* (November): 46-52.

Lukashenka, Aleksandr. 1997a. Shapka Monomakha ostanetsia v Rossii. *Nezavisimaia Gazeta*, 29 May.

———. 1997b. Soiuz ot Bresta do Vladivostoka. *Zavtra* (19), May.

———. 1998. "Soiuz dvukh"—ne zastivsheie poniatiie. *Nezavisimaia Gazeta*, 8 May.

Luzan, Anatolii, and Sergei Luzan. 1998. Ukraiina I Rossiia: faktori otchuzhdeniia i sblizheniia. *Viche* 6 (75): 96-110.

MacArthur, Alan. 1997. Current Trade Policies and Proposals for Reform. In *Ukraine: Accelerating the Transition to Market*, ed. Peter K. Cornelius and Patrick Lenain. Washington, D.C.: IMF.

Mackenzie, W.J.M. 1978. *Political Identity*. England: Penguin Books.

Maillet, Lynda. 1995. New States Initiate New Currencies. *Transition* 1 (9), June 9.

Maisenia, Anatol'. 1996. Belorusskaia anomalia. *Nezavisimaia Gazeta*, 18 June.

Malashenko, Alexei. 1998. Turning Away from Russia. In *Commonwealth and Independence in Post-Soviet Eurasia*, ed. Bruno Coppieters, Alexei Zverev, and Dmitri Trenin. London: Frank Cass.

Mansfield, Edward D., and Helen V. Milner, eds. 1997. *The Political Economy of Regionalism*. NY: Columbia University Press.

Maravall, J. M. 1997. *Regimes, Politics, and Markets: Democratization and Economic Change in Southern and Eastern Europe*. Oxford: Oxford University Press.

Mares, David R. 1985. Explaining Choice of Development Strategies. *International Organization* 37 (Fall).

March, James G., and Johan P. Olsen. 1989. *Rediscovering Institutions: The Organizational Basis of Politics*. New York: Free Press.

Markus, Ustina. 1995a. Still Coming to Terms with Independence. *Transition* 1, 15 February.

———. 1995b. Lukashenka's Victory. *Transition* 1, 11 August.

———. 1995c. Missed Opportunities in Foreign Policy. *Transition* 1, 25 August.

———. 1995d. Heading Off An Energy Disaster. *Transition* 1, 14 April: 10-13.

———. 1995e. Business as Usual With Lukashenka. *Transition* 1, 26 May.

———. 1995f(d). To Counterbalance Russian Power, China Leans Toward Ukraine. *Transition* 1, 22 September.

———. 1997. Russia and Belarus: Elusive Integration. *Problems of Post-Communism* 44 (5): 55-61

Marples, David R. 1993. "After the Putsch": Prospects for Independent Ukraine. *Nationalities Papers* 21 (2): 35-46.

———. 1995. Lukashenka Removes the "Last Oppositionist." *Belarusian Review* 7 (3): 8-9.

———. 1995a. Belarus: The Politics of the Presidency. *Belarusian Review* 7 (2): 9-11.

———. 1996. *Belarus: From Soviet Rule to Nuclear Catastrophe.* New York: St. Martin's Press.

———. 1996b. Belarus: The Black Sheep of Eastern Europe? *Belarusian Review* 8 (3): 2-4.

———. 1998. Ukraine and Belarus in the Post-Soviet Era: A Comparative Study. *Belarusian Review* 10 (1): 13-16.

Martyniuk, Jaroslaw. 1993. The Demographics of Party Support in Ukraine. *RFE/RL Research Report* 2 (48), 3 December.

Mastanduno, Michael, David A. Lake, and John G. Ikenberry. 1989. Toward a Realist Theory of State Action. *International Studies Quarterly* 33 (4).

McAdam, Doug, John D. McCarthy, and Mayer N. Zald, eds. 1996. *Comparative Perspectives on Social Movements.* Cambridge: Cambridge University Press.

McNamara, Kathleen R. 1998. *The Currency of Ideas: Monetary Politics in the Economic Union.* Ithaca: Cornell University Press.

Mead, George H. 1934 [1974]. *Mind, Self and Society: From the Standpoint of a Social Behaviorist.* Chicago: The University of Chicago Press.

Melnyk, Z. Lew. 1977. The Economic Price of Being a Soviet Republic: The Case of Ukraine. In *Ukraine in a Changing World*, ed. Walter Dushnyck. New York: Ukrainian Congress Committee of America.

Menon, Rajan. 1998. After Empire: Russia and the Southern "Near Abroad." In *The New Russian Foreign Policy*, ed. Michael Mandelbaum. New York: The Council on Foreign Relations.

Mesbahi, Mohiaddin, ed. 1994. *Central Asia and the Caucasus after the Soviet Union.* Gainesville: University Press of Florida.

Mhitaryan, Natalia. 1996. Turkish-Ukrainian Relations. *Eurasian Studies* 3 (2): 2-13.

Michalopoulos, Constantine and David Tarr. 1994. Summary and Overview of Developments Since Independence. In *Trade in the New Independent States*, ed. Constantine Michalopoulos and David Tarr. Washington, D.C.: The World Bank.

———. 1996. *Trade Performance and Policy in the Newly Independent States.* Washington, D.C.: The World Bank.

Mihalisko, Kathleen J. 1991. The Popular Movement in Belorussia and Baltic Influences. In *Toward Independence: The Baltic Popular Movements*, ed. Jan Arveds Trapans. Boulder, Colo.: Westview Press.

———. 1992. Belarus. *RFE/RL Research Report* 1, 14 February.

———. 1994. The Belarusian National Dilemma. *Demokratizatsiya. The Journal of Post-Soviet Democratization* 2 (1): 108-119.

————. 1995. Yeltsin Outlines Strategy for a Renewed Superpower. *Prism* 1 (21).

————. 1997. Belarus: Retreat to Authoritarianism. In *Democratic Changes and Authoritarian Reactions in Russia, Ukraine, Belarus, and Moldova*, ed. Karen Dawisha and Bruce Parrott. Cambridge: Cambridge University Press.

Migdal, Joel S. 1974. Internal Structures and External Behavior. *International Affairs* (May).

————. 1997. Studying the State. In *Comparative Politics: Rationality, Culture, and Structure*, ed. Mark Irving Lichbach and Alan S. Zuckerman. Cambridge: Cambridge University Press.

Millar, James. 1998. Empire Envy and Other Obstacles to Economic Reform in Russia. *Problems of Post-Communism* 45 (3): 58-64.

Mills, Wright. 1956. *The Power Elite*. New York: Oxford University Press.

Milner, Helen V. 1988. *Resisting Protectionism: Global Industries and the Politics of International Trade*. Princeton: Princeton University Press.

————. 1992. International Theories of Cooperation among Nations: Strengths and Weaknesses. *World Politics* 44 (3): 466-96.

————. 1997. *Interests, Institutions, and Information: Domestic Politics and International Relations*. Princeton: Princeton University Press.

Milner, Helen V., and David Yoffie. 1989. Between Free Trade and Protectionism. *International Organization* 43 (2): 239-72.

Misiunas, Romuald J., and Rein Taagepera. 1993. *The Baltic States: Years of Dependence, 1940-1990*. Expanded and updated edition. Berkeley: University of California Press.

Misiunas, Romuald J. 1994. National Identity and Foreign Policy in the Baltic States. In *The Legacy of History in Russia and the New States of Eurasia*, ed. Frederick Starr. Armonk, New York: M.E. Sharpe.

Moyiseiev, Ye.G. 1997. *Mezhdunarodno-pravoviie osnovi sotrudnichestva stran SNG*. Moskva: Yurist.

Mols, Mangred. 1996. Regional Integration and the International System. In *Cooperation or Rivalry? Regional Integration in the Americas and the Pacific Rim*, ed. Shoji Nishijima and Peter H. Smith. Boulder, Colo.: Westview Press.

Morrison, John. 1993. Pereyaslav and After: The Russian-Ukrainian relationship. *International Affairs* 69 (4): 677-703.

Motyl, Alexander. 1992a. The Modernity of Nationalism. *Journal of International Affairs* 45 (2): 307-324.

Motyl, Alexander J. 1992b. From Imperial Decay to Imperial Collapse: The Fall of the Soviet Empire in Comparative Perspective. In *Nationalism and Empire: The Hapsburg Empire and the Soviet Union*, ed. R. L. Rudolph and D. F. Good. New York: St. Martin's Press.

Motyl, Alexander, and Bohdan Krawchenko. 1997. Ukraine: From Empire to Statehood. In *New States, New Politics: Building the Post-Soviet Nations*, ed. Ian Bremmer and Ray Taras. Cambridge: Cambridge University Press.

Moore, Barrington, Jr. 1965. *Social Origins of Dictatorship and Democracy*. Boston: Beacon Press.

Muiznieks, Nils R. 1995. The Influence of the Baltic Popular Movements on the Process of Soviet Disintegration. *Europe-Asia Studies* 47 (1): 3-25.

Muiznieks, Nils R. 1997. Latvia: Restoring a State, Rebuilding a Nation. In *New States, New Politics. Building the Post-Soviet Nations,* ed. Ian Bremmer and Ray Taras. Cambridge: Cambridge University Press.

Nahaylo, Bohdan. 1992a. *The New Ukraine.* London: Royal Institute of International Affairs.

Neufeld, Mark. 1993. Interpretation and the "Science" of International Relations. *Review of International Studies* 19: 39-61.

Neumann, Iver B. 1992. Identity and Security. *Journal of Peace Research* 29 (2).

———. 1996. *Russia and the Idea of Europe: A Study in Identity and International Relations.* London and New York: Routledge.

———. 1997. Self and Other in International Relations. *European Journal of International Relations* 2 (3): 139-74.

Nissman, David. 1995. Turkmenistan Seeks to Exploit Both Gas and Geography. *PRISM: A Biweekly on the Post-Soviet States.* 1 (10), 7 July.

Niyazov, Saparmurat. 1995. We Fully Trust Russia. *International Affairs,* Moscow (10): 41-43.

———. 1998. Aktivnaia sotsial'naia politika za schet rezervov gosudarstva. *Nezavisimaia gazeta,* 27 October.

Nørgaard, Ole et al. 1996. *The Baltic States after Independence.* Cheltenham, UK: Edward Elgar.

Nordlinger, Eric A. 1981. *On the Autonomy of the Democratic State.* Cambridge: Cambridge University Press.

Nyberg, Peter. 1993. Comment. In *Economic Consequences of Soviet Disintegration,* ed. John Williamson. Washington, D.C.: Institute for International Economics.

Nye, Joseph. 1987. Nuclear Learning. *International Organization* (3).

Ochs, Michael. 1997. Turkmenistan: The Quest for Stability and Control. In *Conflict, Cleavage, and Change in Central Asia and the Caucasus,* ed. Karen Dawisha and Bruce Perrott. Cambridge: Cambridge University Press.

Odell, John S. 1982. U.S. *International Monetary Policy: Markets, Power, and Ideas as Sources of Change.* Princeton: Princeton University Press.

———. 1988. From London to Bretton Woods: Sources of Change in Bargaining Strategies and Outcomes. *Journal of Public Policy* 8 (3-4): 287-316.

O'Donnell, Guillermo A. 1978. Corporatism and the Question of the State. In *Authoritarianism and Corporatism in Latin America,* ed. J.M. Malloy. Pittsburgh: University of Pittsburgh Press.

———. 1988. *Bureaucratic Authoritarianism: Argentina, 1966-1973 in Comparative Perspective.* Berkeley: University of California Press.

———. 1994. Delegative Democracy. *Journal of Democracy* 5 (1): 55-68.

O'Halloran, Sharyn. 1994. *Politics, Process, and American Trade Policy.* Ann Arbor: University of Michigan Press.

Olson, Mancur. 1993. Dictatorship, Democracy, and Development. *American Political Science Review* 87 (3): 567-76.

OMRI Daily Report, Open Media Research Institute, Prague.

Ozolina, Zaneta. 1998. Latvia. In *Bordering Russia: Theory and Prospects for Europe's Baltic Rim,* ed. Hans Mouritzen. Aldershot: Ashgate.

Palii, Oleksandr. 1997. Shcho nam robiti z Rossieiu? *Pidtekst* 44 (66): 30-35.

Pannier, Bruce and Peter Rutland. 1996. Central Asia's Uneasy Partnership With Russia. *Transition* 3, 15 November.

Parrott, Bruce. 1997. Analyzing the Transformation of the Soviet Union in Comparative Perspective. In *The End of Empire?* ed. Karen Dawisha and Bruce Parrott. Armonk, New York: M.E. Sharpe.

Parsons, Talcott. 1963. On the Concept of Political Power. *Proceedings of the American Philosophical Society* 107.

Paznyak, Zenon. 1989. Belorussiia: Vandeia? "Ochakov"? Zimnii? *Sovetskaia molodezh'*, 20 April.

Paznyak, Vyacheslau E. 1995. Belarus's Foreign Policy Priorities and the Decision-Making Process. In *The Making of Foreign Policy in Russia and the New States of Eurasia,* ed. Adeed Dawisha and Karen Dawisha. Armonk, New York: M.E. Sharpe.

Penikis, Andrejs. 1996. The Third Awakening Begins. *The Journal of Baltic Studies* 27 (4): 261-76.

Peterson, Susan. 1996. *Crisis Bargaining and the State.* Ann Arbor: University of Michigan Press.

Pikhovshek, Viacheslav. 1998. Samii strategicheskii partner. *Zerkalo nedeli* 27(196), 4 July.

Plakans, Andrejs. 1997. Democratization and Political Participation in Postcommunist Societies. In *The Consolidation of Democracy in East-Central Europe*, ed. Karen Dawisha and Bruce Parrott. Cambridge: Cambridge University Press.

Plan to Achieve Latvian Independence. 1990. *Latvian Information Bulletin* 1-90, January.

Plushch, Ivan. 1993. *Hto mi I kudi idemo.* Kiev: "Ukraiina."

Pogrebinsky, Mikhail. 1993. The Experience of Overcoming Reforms. *New Times* (50): 9-11.

Porter, Michael. 1990. The Competitive Advantages of Nations. *Harvard Business Review* 90 (2): 73-92.

Porter, B., and C. Saivetz. 1994. The Once and Future Empire: Russia and the "Near Abroad." *Washington Quarterly* 17 (3): 75-90.

Posen, Barry. 1993. The Security Dilemma and Ethnic Conflict. *Survival* 35: 27-47.

Poznanski, Kazimierz Z., ed. 1992. *Constructing Capitalism.* Boulder, Colo.: Westview Press.

Prazauskas, Algimantas. 1994. The Influence of Ethnicity on the Foreign Policies of the Western Littoral States. In *National Identity and Ethnicity in the New States of Eurasia,* ed. Roman Szporluk. Armonk, New York: M.E. Sharpe.

Prestowitz, Clyde V. 1992. Beyond Laissez Faire. In *International Political Economy: Perspectives on Global Power and Wealth.* 3rd edition, ed. Jeffrey Frieden and David A. Lake. New York: St. Martin's Press.

Price, Richard. 1994. Interpretation and the Disciplinary Orthodoxy in International Relations. *Review of International Studies* 20: 201-204.

Price, Richard, and Nina Tannenwald. 1996. Norms and Deterrence: The Nuclear and Chemical Weapons Taboos. In *The Culture of National Security*, ed. Peter J. Katzenstein. New York: Columbia University Press.

Prizel, Ilya. 1997. Ukraine between Proto-democracy and "Soft" Authoritarianism. In *Democratic Changes and Authoritarian Reactions in Russia, Ukraine, Belarus, and*

Moldova, ed. Karen Dawisha and Bruce Parrott. Cambridge: Cambridge University Press.

Prizel, Ilya. 1998. *National Identity and Foreign Policy: Nationalism and Leadership in Poland, Russia, and Ukraine*. Cambridge: Cambridge University Press.

Pro liberalizatsiiu zovnishnoekomichnoi diial'nosti. 1993. Decree # 54-93. Ukraine's Cabinet of Ministers, 20 May.

Pro perelik tovariv, schodo eksportu yakihk vstanovluietstia rezhim litsenzuvannia I kvotuvannia na 1992 rik. 1992. Decree # 2332-XII. Ukraine's Verkhovna Rada, 12 May.

Pro poriadok provedeniia barternikh (tovaroobminnikh) operatsii v galuzi zovnishnoekonomichnoi diiatelnosti. 1992. Decree # 6-92. Ukraine's Cabinet of Ministers, 9 December.

Przeworski, Adam. 1991. *Democracy and the Market: Political and Economic Reforms in Eastern Europe and Latin America*. Cambridge: Cambridge University Press.

Putnam, Robert D. 1976. *The Comparative Study of Political Elites*. Englewood Cliffs: Prentice-Hall, Inc.

Rakowstone-Harmstone, Teresa. 1974. The Dialectic of Nationalism in the USSR. *Problems of Communism*, 23 (3): 1-22.

Rezun, Miron. 1992. The Muslim Borderlands: Islam and Nationalism in Transition. In *Nationalism and the Breakup of an Empire: Russia and Its Periphery*, ed. Miron Rezun. Westport: Praeger.

RFE/RL Daily Report. Radio Free Europe / Radio Liberty, Munich.

Richardson, David J. 1990. The Political Economy of Strategic Trade Policy. *International Organization*, 44 (1): 107-35.

Risse-Kappen, Thomas. 1991. Public Opinion, Domestic Structures, and Foreign Policy. *World Politics* 41 (3).

———, ed. 1995. *Bringing Transnational Relations back in*. Cambridge: Cambridge University Press.

———. 1996. Collective Identity in a Democratic Community: The Case of NATO. In *The Culture of National Security*, ed. Peter J. Katzenstein. New York: Columbia University Press.

Robison, R. 1988. Authoritarian States, Capital-Owning Classes, and the Politics of Newly Industrialized Countries. *World Politics* 38 (4).

Roeder, Philip G. 1991. Soviet Federalism and Ethnic Mobilization. *World Politics* 43 (2): 196-232.

———. 1999. The Revolution of 1989: Postcommunism and the Social Sciences. *Slavic Review* 58 (4): 743-56.

Rogowski, Ronald. 1985. Causes and Varieties of Nationalism. In *New Nationalisms of the Developed West*, ed. Edward A. Tiryakian and Ronald Rogowski. Allen & Unwin.

———. 1989. *Commerce and Coalitions: How Trade Affects Domestic Political Alignments*. Princeton: Princeton University Press.

Rosecrance, Richard, and Arthur A. Stein, eds. 1993. *The Domestic Bases of Grand Strategy*. Ithaca: Cornell University Press.

Ross, Marc Howard. 1997. Culture and Identity in Comparative Political Analysis. In *Comparative Politics: Rationality, Culture, and Structure*, ed. Mark Irving Lichbach and Alan S. Zuckerman. Cambridge: Cambridge University Press.

Rossiisko-Ukraiinskiie otnosheniia, 1990-1997. Sbornik dokumentov. 1998. Moskva: Ministerstvo Inostrannikh Del, MGIMO.

Rossiia I Pribaltika. 1997. *Nezavisimaia gazeta,* 28 October.

Rosiia, iaku mi. 1997. Kiev: Ukraine Center for Independent Political Research.

Rossiia-Ukraina-Vishegradskaia gruppa: partnerstvo ili sopernichestvo? 1997. *Mirovaia ekonomika i mezhdunarodniie otnosheniia* (10): 95-109.

Rotar', Igor. 1995. Will Natural Gas Save Turkmenistan? *PRISM: A Biweekly on the Post-Soviet States* 1, (19), 8 September.

Rozanov, Anatolii. 1998. Vneshnaia politika Belorussii: predstavleniia i real'nosti. *Pro et Contra* 3 (2): 68-80.

Rudnytsky, Ivan L. 1987. Pereiaslav: History and Myth, in his *Essays in Modern Ukrainian History.* Edmonton, Ont.: CIUS.

Ruggie, John Gerard. 1982. International Regimes, Transactions and Change. *International Organization* 36 (2): 379-415.

————. 1998. *Constructing the World Polity.* London: Routledge.

Rumer, Eugene B. 1994. Will Ukraine Return to Russia? *Foreign Policy* 96 (3): 129-81.

Rustow, Dankwart A. 1997. The Habsburg and Ottoman Empires and Their Aftermaths. In *The End of Empire?* ed. Karen Dawisha and Bruce Parrott. Armonk, New York: M.E. Sharpe.

Sachs, Jeffrey D., and Katharina Pistor. 1997. Introduction: Progress, Pitfalls, Scenarios, and Lost Opportunities. In *The Rule of Law and Economic Reform in Russia,* ed. Jeffrey D. Sachs and Katarina Pistor. Boulder, Colo.: Westview Press.

Samodurov, Oleksandr. 1997. Torgovii rezhim ne zminivsia. *Politika I chas* (9): 12-16.

Samorodni, Oleg. 1993. Black Sea—Baltic Commonwealth: The Emergence and Transformation of an Idea. In *New Actors on the International Arena,* ed. Pertti Joenniemi and Peter Vares. Helsinki: Tampere Peace Research Institute.

Sanford, George. 1996. Belarus on the Road to Nationhood. *Survival* 38 (1): 131-53.

Schattschneider, E.E. 1935. *Politics, Pressures and the Tariff.* Englewood Cliffs: Prentice-Hall.

Schroeder, Gertrude E. 1986. Social and Economic Aspects of the Nationality Problem. In *The Last Empire: Nationality and the Soviet Future,* ed. Robert Conquest. Stanford: Hoover Institution Press.

————. 1992. On the Economic Viability of New Nation-States. *Journal of International Affairs* 45 (2).

————. 1996. Economic Transformation in the Post-Soviet Republics. In *Economic Transition in Russia and the New States of Eurasia,* ed. Bartlomiej Kaminski. Armonk, New York: M.E. Sharpe.

Sekarev, Aleksei. 1997. O konkurentosposobnisti Ukraiini na rossiiskom rinke. In *Ryvok v rynochnuyu ekonomiku. Reformi v Ukrayine: vzgliad iznutri,* ed. Luts Hoffmann and Aksel Zyndenberg. Kiev: UANNP "Feniks."

Senn, Alfred Erich. 1997. Lithuania: Rights and Responsibilities of Independence. In *New States, New Politics: Building the Post-Soviet Nations,* ed. Ian Bremmer and Ray Taras. Cambridge: Cambridge University Press.

Sergeiev, Nikolai and Aleksandr Fadeiev. 1998. Anatomiia soiuza Rossii i Belorussii. *Sodruzhestvo NG* (8): 12-13.

Sergounin, Alexander. 1998. The Russia Dimension. In *Bordering Russia. Theory and Prospects for Europe's Baltic Rim*, ed. Hans Mouritzen. Aldershot: Ashgate.

Seton-Watson, Hugh. 1977. *Nations and States: An Inquiry into the Origins of Nations and the Politics of Nationalism*. Boulder, Colo.: Westview Press.

Shen, Raphael. 1994. *Restructuring the Baltic Economies: Disengaging Fifty Years of Integration with the USSR*. Westport: Praeger.

Shishkov, Yu.V., ed. 1997. *Blizhneie i dal'neie zarubezhie v geoekonomicheskoi strategii Rossii*. Moskva: IMEMO.

Shteinbuka, Inna. 1993. An Economic Survey of the Baltic Republics. In *Economic Consequences of Soviet Disintegration*, ed. John Williamson. Washington, D.C.: Institute for International Economics.

Shtromas, Aleksandras. 1994. The Baltic States as Soviet Republics. In *The Baltic States: The National Self-Determination of Estonia, Latvia and Lithuania*, ed. Graham Smith. New York: St. Martin's Press.

Shulman, Stephen. 2000. National Sources of International Economic Integration. *International Studies Quarterly* 44 (3): 365-90.

Shushkevich, Stanislav. 1997. Nado li obustraivat' Rossiiu po obraztsu Belarusi? *Izvestia*, 27 February.

Sidenko, Volodymyr. 1997. Proriv u Yevropu—yakim chinom? *Politika i chas* (11): 18-27.

Silva, Eduardo. 1993. Capitalist Coalitions, the State, and Neoliberal Economic Restructuring: Chile, 1973-1988. *World Politics* 45 (4).

Simmons, Beth A. 1996. *Who Adjusts? Domestic Sources of Foreign Economic Policy During the Interwar Years*. Princeton: Princeton University Press.

Skocpol, Theda. 1979. *States and Social Revolutions*. Cambridge: Cambridge University Press.

Slay, Ban. 1991. On the Economics of Interrepublican Trade. *RFE/RL Research Institute* 3 (48), 29 November.

Smith, Anthony D. 1986. *The Ethnic Origins of Nations*. Oxford: Blackwell.

———. 1993. *National Identity*. Reno: University of Nevada Press.

Smith, Graham, ed. 1996. Latvia and Latvians. In *The Nationalities Question in the Post-Soviet States*, ed. Graham Smith. London: Longman.

Slezkine, Yuri. 1996. The USSR as a Communal Apartment. In *Becoming National: A Reader*, ed. Geoff Eley and Ronald Grigor Suny. Oxford: Oxford University Press.

Smolansky, Oles M. 1995a. Ukraine's Quest for Independence: The Fuel Factor. *Europe-Asia Studies* 47 (1): 67-90.

———. 1995b. Ukrainian-Turkish Relations. *Ukrainian Quarterly* LI (1).

Snyder, Jack L. 1989. International Leverage on Soviet Domestic Change. *World Politics* 42 (4).

———. 1993. Nationalism and the Crisis of the Post-Soviet State. *Survival* 35 (2).

Snyder, Jack and Karen Ballentine. 1996. Nationalism and the Marketplace of Ideas. *International Security* 21 (2): 5-40.

Solchanyk, Roman. 1990. Ukraine, Belorussia, and Moldavia. In *The Nationalities Factor in Soviet Politics and Society*, ed. Lubomyr Hajda and Mark Beissinger. Boulder, Colo.: Westview Press.

————. 1992. Ukraine, The (Former) Center, Russia, and "Russia." *Studies in Comparative Communism* 25 (1): 31-45.

————. 1993. Russia, Ukraine, and the Imperial Legacy. *Post-Soviet Affairs* 9 (4): 337-65.

————. 1995. Ukraine: The Politics of Reform. *Problems of Post-Communism* 42 (6): 46-51.

Sorsa, Piritta. 1994. Latvia: Trade Issues in Transition. In *Trade in the New Independent States*, ed. Constantine Michalopoulos and David Tarr. Washington, D.C.: The World Bank.

Stalin, Joseph. [1905] 1994. The Nation. In *Nationalism*, ed. John Hutchinson and Anthony D. Smith. Oxford: Oxford University Press.

Stallings, Barbara, ed. 1995. *Global Change, Regional Response.* Cambridge: Cambridge University Press.

Strange, David. 1996. Contested Sovereignty: The Social Construction of Colonial Imperialism. In *State Sovereignty as Social Construct*, ed. Thomas J. Biersteker and Cynthia Weber. Cambridge: Cambridge University Press.

Subtelny, Orest. 1995. The Ukrainian-Russian Nexus. In *Political Culture and Civil Society in Russia and the New States of Eurasia*, ed. Vladimir Tismaneanu. Armonk, New York: M.E. Sharpe.

Suny, Ronald G. 1993. *The Revenge of the Past: Nationalism, Revolution, and the Collapse of the Soviet Union.* Stanford: Stanford University Press.

Szporluk, Roman. 1979. West Ukraine and West Belorussia: Historical Tradition, Social Communication and Linguistic Assimilation. *Soviet Studies* 31 (1): 76-98.

————. 1989. Dilemmas of Russian Nationalism. *Problems of Communism* 38 (4): 15-35.

————. 1992. The National Question. In *After the Soviet Union. From Empire to Nations*, ed. Timothy J. Colton and Robert Legvold. New York: Norton & Company.

Tamir, Yael. 1995. The Enigma of Nationalism. *World Politics* 47 (2).

Tarasiuk, Borys. 1998. Ukraiina i mir. *Sodruzhestvo NG* (10): 1, 11.

Taylor, Charles. 1977. Interpretation in the Social Sciences. In *Understanding and Social Inquiry*, ed. Fred R. Dallmayr and Thomas A. McCarthy. South Bend: Notre Dame Press.

Taylor, Peter. 1989. *Political Geography. World-Economy, Nation-State and Locality.* England: Longman Scientific & Technical.

Tedstrom, John. 1989. USSR Draft Program on Republican Economic Self-Management: An Analysis. *Report on the USSR* 1 (16), 21 April.

Tickner, Ann J. 1992. *Gender in International Relations: Feminist Perspectives on Achieving Global Security.* New York: Columbia University Press.

Todorov, Tzvetan. 1984. *The Conquest of America: The Question of the Other.* New York: Harper & Row.

Torbakov, Igor. 1996. Historiography and Modern Nation-Building. *Transition*, 6 September.

Trade Policy and the Transition Process. 1996. Paris: Organization For Economic Cooperation and Development.

Trade Policy Reform in the Countries of the Former Soviet Union. 1994. Washington, D.C.: International Monetary Fund.

Trapans, Andris. 1991. Moscow, Economics, and the Baltic Republics. In *Toward Independence*, ed. Jan Arveds Trapans. Boulder, Colo.: Westview Press.

Treisman, Daniel S. 1997. Russia's "Ethnic Revival." The Separatist Activism of Regional Leaders in a Postcommunist Order. *World Politics* 49 (1): 212-49.

Trends in Developing Economies. 1995. Washington, D.C.: The World Bank.

Trofimov, Dmitri. 1994. *Tsentral'naia Aziya: problemi etno-kohfessional'nogo razvitiya.* Moscow: MGIMO / Center for International Studies.

Tsegolnikov, Leonid. 1994. Belorussiia: doroga v nikuda. *Segonia*, 29 April.

Tsygankov, Andrei P. 1998. Manifestations of Delegative Democracy in Russian Local Politics. *Communist and Post-Communist Studies* 31 (4): 329-44.

———. 2000a. Defining State Interests After Empire: National Identity, Domestic Structures, and Foreign Trade Policies of Latvia and Belarus. *Review of International Political Economy* 7 (1): 101-37.

———. 2000b. Trade Dependence, National Autonomy, and the Policy Dilemmas in the Relations of the Western Newly Independent States and Russia. *Soviet and Post-Soviet Review* 25 (3): 223-43.

Turevich, Art. 1995. In Belarus, All Indicators Are Down! On the Eve of Elections. *Belarusian Review* 7 (1): 10-11.

———. 1996. What's in Belarus-Russia Treaty. *Belarusian Review* 8 (1): 7-8.

———. 1998. Belarus's "Economic Miracle" Unraveling. *Belarusian Review* 10 (1): 12-13.

Tyson, Laura. 1992. *Who's Bashing Whom? Trade Conflict in High Technology Industries.* Washington, D.C.: The Institute of International Economics.

Ukraine, Russia, Germany: New Realities. Round table discussion. 1994. *Politichna Dumka* (2): 167-74.

Ulmanis, Guntis. 1998. Nedoveriye mezhdu Moskvoi i Rigoi ischeznet. *Nezavisimaia gazeta*, 29 December.

Vakar, Nicolas P. 1956. *Belorussia: The Making of a Nation.* Cambridge: Harvard University Press.

Van Evera, Stephen. 1994. Hypotheses on Nationalism and War. *International Security* 18 (4): 26-33.

———. 1997. *Guide to Methods for Students of Political Science.* Ithaca: Cornell University Press.

Van Selm, Bert. 1997. *The Economics of Soviet Break-Up.* London: Routledge.

Vares, Peeter. 1995. Dimensions and Orientations in the Foreign and Security Policies of the Baltic States. In *The Making of Foreign Policy in Russia and the New States of Eurasia,* ed. Adeed Dawisha and Karen Dawisha. Armonk, New York: M.E. Sharpe.

Varfolomeyev, Oleg. 1998. Ukraine's "European dream." *Prism* 15 (2), 24 July.

Vavilov, Andrey and Oleg Vjugin. 1993. Trade Patterns After Integration Into the World Economy. In *Economic Consequences of Soviet Disintegration,* ed. John Williamson. Washington, D.C.: Institute for International Economics.

Viner, Jacob. 1950. *The Customs Union Issue.* New York: Carnegie Endowment for International Peace.

Violation of Human Rights in Belarus. 1997. *Belarusian Review* 9 (2): 3-6.

Walker, R. B. J. 1988. Genealogy, Geopolitics and Political Community. *Alternatives* 13 (1): 84-88.

Wallerstein, Immanuel. 1974. *The Modern World System: Capitalist Agriculture and the Origins of the European World Economy in the Sixteen Century*. New York: Academic Press.

Walt, Stephen M. 1987. *The Origins of Alliances*. Ithaca: Cornell University Press.

Watson, Robin A. 1994. Interrepublic Trade in the Former Soviet Union: Structure and Implications. *Post-Soviet Geography* 35 (7).

Webber, Mark. 1996. *The International Politics of Russia and the Successor States*. Manchester: Manchester University Press.

———. 1997. *CIS Integration Trends: Russia and the Former Soviet South*. London: The Royal Institute of International Affairs.

Weber, Max. 1958. Social Psychology of the World's Religions. In *From Max Weber*, ed. H. H. Gerth and Wright Mills. Oxford: Oxford University Press.

———. 1977. "Objectivity" in Social Science and Social Policy. In *Understanding and Social Inquiry*, ed. Fred R. Dallmayr and Thomas A. McCarthy. Notre Dame, London: University of Notre Dame Press.

———. 1978. *Economy and Society*. Berkeley: University of California Press.

Weick, Karl E. 1995. *Sensemaking in Organizations*. Thousand Oaks: SAGE Publications.

Weiss, Linda. 1998. *The Myth of the Powerless State*. Ithaca: Cornell University Press.

Weiver, Ole, Ulla Holm, and Henrik Larsen. 1997. *The Struggle for "Europe."* London: Routledge.

Wendt, Alexander. 1992. Anarchy Is What States Make of It: The Social Construction of Power Politics. *International Organization* 46 (2): 391-425.

———. 1999. *Social Theory of International Politics*. Cambridge: Cambridge University Press.

Whitlock, Erik. 1993. Ukrainian-Russian Trade: The Economics of Dependency. *RFE/RL Research Report* 2 (43), 29 October.

Wiarda, Howard J. 1997. *Corporatism and Comparative Politics: The Other Great "Ism."* Armonk, New York: M.E. Sharpe.

Williams, David. 1999. Constructing the Economic Space: The World Bank and the Making of Homo Oeconomicus. *Millennium*. 28 (1).

Williamson, P.J. 1985. *Varieties of Corporatism: A Conceptual Discussion*. Cambridge: Cambridge University Press.

Williamson, John, and Oleh Havrylyshyn. 1991. *From Soviet Disunion to Eastern Economic Community?* Washington, D.C.: Institute for International Economics.

Wilson, Andrew. 1993. The Growing Challenge to Kiev from the Donbass. *RFE/RL Research Report* 2 (33), 20 August.

———. 1998. *Ukrainian Nationalism in the 1990s: A Minority Faith*. Cambridge: Cambridge University Press.

Wintrobe, Ronald. 1995. Some Economics of Ethnic Capital Formation and Conflict. In *Nationalism and Rationality*, ed. Albert Breton et al. Cambridge: Cambridge University Press.

Woods, Ngaire. 1995. Economic Ideas and International Relations: Beyond Rational Neglect. *International Studies Quarterly* 39: 161-80.

World Bank, *Trends in Developing Economies*. 1995. Washington, D.C.: The World Bank.

World Bank, *Belarus: Prices, Markets, and Enterprise Reform.* 1996. Washington, D.C.: The World Bank.

Wyzan, Michael L., ed. 1995. *First Steps Toward Economic Independence: New States of the Postcommunist World.* Westport: Praeger.

Yanevsky, Danylo. 1995. New Government Program Strikes a Discordant Nore. *Transition* 1, 15 December.

Yarbrough, Beth, and Robert Yarbrough. 1987. Cooperation and Liberalization of International Trade. *International Organization* 41 (1): 1-26.

Yee, Albert S. 1996. The Causal Effects of Ideas on Policies. *International Organization* 50 (1): 69-108.

Zagorskii, Andrei, ed. 1997. *SNG: tsifri, fakti, personalii.* Minsk: International Institute of Political Studies.

Zaprudnik, Jan. 1989. Belorussian Reawakening. *Problems of Communism* 4 (5).

———. 1993. *Belarus: At a Crossroads in History.* Boulder, Colo: Westview Press.

———. 1994. Development of Belarusian National Identity and Its Influence on Belarus's Foreign Policy Orientation. In *National Identity and Ethnicity in the New States of Eurasia,* ed. Roman Szporluk. Armonk, New York: M.E. Sharpe.

Zaprudnik, Jan, and Helen Fedor. 1995. Belarus. In *Belarus and Moldova: Country Studies,* edited by Helen Fedor. Washington, D.C.: Library of Congress.

Zaprudnik, Jan and Michael Urban. 1997. Belarus: From Statehood to Empire? In *New States, New Politics: Building the Post-Soviet Nations,* ed. Ian Bremmer and Ray Taras. Cambridge: Cambridge University Press.

Zhang, B. 1994. Corporatism, Totaliarianism, and Transition to Democracy. *Comparative Political Studies* 27 (1).

Zviglyanich, Volodymyr. 1996. The State and Economic Reform in Ukraine: Ideas, Models, Solutions. *The Ukrainian Quarterly* LII (2-3): 122-46.

Index